Caught in the Middle

By the same author

Global Squeeze: The Coming Crisis for First-World Nations

Caught in the Middle

America's Heartland
in the Age of Globalism

Richard C. Longworth

BLOOMSBURY

NEW YORK · BERLIN · LONDON

Map on pp viii–ix by Steve Layton

Published by Bloomsbury USA, New York

All papers used by Bloomsbury USA are natural, recyclable products made from wood grown in well-managed forests. The manufacturing processes conform to the environmental regulations of the country of origin.

LIBRARY OF CONGRESS CATALOGING-IN-PUBLICATION DATA HAS BEEN APPLIED FOR.

ISBN-10 1-59691-413-0
ISBN-13 978-1-59691-413-1

First U.S. Edition 2008

5 7 9 10 8 6 4

Typeset by Westchester Book Group
Printed in the United States of America by Quebecor World Fairfield

To Barbara
and to Peter and Susan

Contents

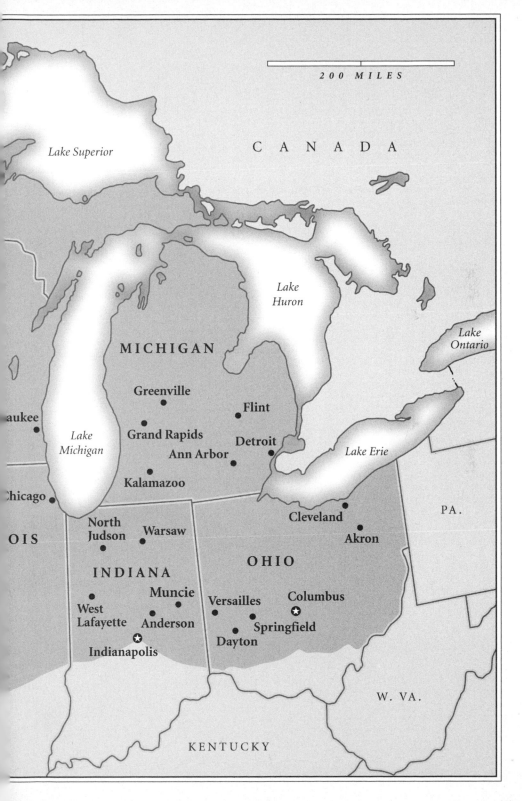

200 MILES

Lake Superior

CANADA

Lake Huron

Lake Ontario

MICHIGAN

Greenville

Flint

aukee

Lake Michigan

Grand Rapids

Detroit

Ann Arbor

Lake Erie

Kalamazoo

Chicago

PA.

Cleveland

North Judson

Warsaw

Akron

OIS

OHIO

INDIANA

Muncie

Versailles

Columbus

West Lafayette

Anderson

Springfield

Dayton

Indianapolis

W. VA.

KENTUCKY

Prologue

I grew up in a small town in central Iowa, a safe and secure place, confident in its isolation. This was lonesome-whistle territory, where passing trains announced another world out there. In time, some of us got on those trains and went to seek that world; we knew it wasn't going to come to us.

Not too much happened in my town, a county seat called Boone. But there was a bustle in the mid-1960s when a British newspaper proclaimed it the typical American small town, geographically and socially, and sent a reporter to write about it. He interviewed one local elder who pronounced, "We are pretty well self-sufficient. We don't need the world."

Even then, this was a blinkered attitude. After all, somebody out there bought the corn and hogs we raised. But it was true that distant events—in Europe, China, Latin America—did not dictate our daily lives. Businesses were locally owned. Jobs were secure and lasted for life. Everybody looked like everybody else, and immigration amounted to a few Greek restaurant owners, such as Danny Canakes, and their families. If a store closed, it was because the owner retired, not because a Wal-Mart opened out on the highway.

For the most part, this sense of stability and self-sufficiency stretched across the vast middle of America, the heartland region called the Midwest. Things were more complicated in the great cities, such as Chicago or Detroit, but even they pumped out their steel and cars with no thought that events and trends thousands of miles away, across oceans and continents, would turn their lives upside down.

By the 1970s, the Rust Belt era and the rural debt crisis shattered this smug certainty. But few saw these as global events. When industries left the Midwest, they went to the Sun Belt, seldom to Mexico, certainly not to China. When farms failed, it was because they took on too much debt, not because Brazil had started to grow soybeans.

Then, about a decade ago, globalization arrived and changed the Midwest forever. Traditional family farms vanished. Steel mills closed and auto factories shrank. "Downsizing" and "outsourcing" enriched our vocabularies and frightened our workforce. Some big cities, such as Chicago, coped. Others, like Detroit, rotted. Small industrial cities fought to stay alive. "Rural" became a synonym for "poor." Immigrants, mostly Mexicans but Africans and Asians, too, moved into towns and regions that were all European, and northern European at that. Self-sufficient little places, such as my hometown, became bedroom suburbs if they were lucky enough to lie within commuting distance of bigger cities. Those beyond this range, or too far from the interstate, shriveled.

I left Boone for a life mostly spent in other regions and other countries. Out in this world, I learned that, when economies change, everything else changes, too. How we earn our living determines how we live and who we are. This is true for people, and it's true for towns, and regions, and countries. The Midwest does two big things for a living—farming and heavy industry—and globalization has turned both upside down. In many ways, Boone—and the Midwest—look as they always have. But their character has changed totally.

Once Boone was a farm and railroad center. Mostly, it existed as a market town that served farm families, each tilling its 160 acres of rich Iowa earth, and as a stop for the passenger trains heading west from Chicago to Denver and Los Angeles. Competition was local: Ames, thirteen miles to the east, loomed as the great rival, especially in high school football. Des Moines, forty miles to the south, was the metropolis: trips there, for shopping or basketball tournaments or the state fair, represented forays into the outside world.

Ted Kooser, until recently the poet laureate of the United States, grew up in Ames. "I had a friend in Ames who got a job in Boone," Ted told me, "and we never saw him again."

These days, Boone appears little changed. Its population, about twelve thousand, has barely budged for a half century. Giant oaks still shade the Victorian and Georgian houses on the south side of town and the working-class homes on the north side. There's a beautiful big swimming pool down in McHose Park. Nearby, the softball diamond looks little changed from the days when I cut my journalistic teeth there, covering sports for the local daily, the *News-Republican.*

But there's a difference. The town, once self-sufficient, now is a place where workers in Ames and Des Moines come home at night. About twenty-two hundred people, a quarter of its workforce, commute out each day. In the morning, all the traffic on U.S. 30 is one-way east, toward Ames and the interstate to Des Moines. In the evening, the traffic flows back west, carrying people who like life in a small town but who earn their livings somewhere else. Freight trains still go through, but the passenger trains are long gone. So are the 160-acre farms and the people who worked them: an era of farm consolidation has left a barony of big farms, run by a handful of families, the survivors of the great Midwestern agricultural shakeout, too few to even begin to support a market town.

Story Street is still the main drag, but it's a sorry place now, with closed stores and inessential commerce, such as gift shops. The big employers are out on the highway, and they're all global. There's a company that makes plasma out of cattle blood; it has thirty other plants or joint ventures, many in the United States but also in Denmark, Argentina, Brazil, Spain, and Britain. There's a Japanese-owned firm that produces antibodies for testing kits. There's a dental-supply company headquartered in Minneapolis. There's a genetics company owned by South Africans that does high-tech applications of seed corn. And there's a vast building with four hundred workers, mostly women with high school degrees, who handle subscriptions for some of the world's most sophisticated publications: if you want to subscribe to the *New Yorker* or *Gourmet*, you have to send a letter to Boone, Iowa.

I went to see Bob Fisher, an old friend whose family ran a

first-rate shoe store for two generations. There's not enough business on Story Street today to support a shoe store. Bob, now retired, oversees the local economic development agency, working to create a new economy utterly different from the one that he—and I—knew when we grew up. "Yes, globalization has sunk in," Bob told me. "When France says it's not going to import American blood plasma, Boone, Iowa, gets shut down."

This book is about change. It's about the transformation of a place, the American Midwest, that always symbolized stability and rootedness. The Midwest is geared to permanence, and it isn't handling this transformation very well.

Some cities, like Chicago, or college towns, like Madison, Wisconsin, thrive in this new world. Others, like my hometown, struggle to find their place; many are failing. Change has come to Boone and the rest of the Midwest and forced a redefinition of their place in the world. In the age of globalism, do many of the Midwest's towns and cities, and their people, have a future? For that matter, does the Midwest have a future?

To find out, I got behind the wheel and took to the interstates and back roads of the Midwest. I spent eleven thousand miles on the road, driving around this new Middle West. I found dying farm villages and crumbling old factory towns, which may not survive. I found once great cities that have become empty shells, and I found displaced farmers and workers, adrift in communities consumed by denial and bitterness and a real political anger. I found inadequate schools and a political system that seems almost designed to fail.

I found people left behind by a new economy for which nothing prepared them.

This book is a report from the front line of America's new economy.

CHAPTER 1

Caught in the Middle

The Midwest is the bellwether of America, the spearpoint of the American economy.

It was the frontier when the first pioneers moved west, across the Alleghenies. The mills of Chicago and the factories of Detroit powered America's industrial revolution. Here commerce boomed and labor wars first raged. The great reformers—Debs and Dewey, Bryan and La Follette, Jane Addams and Betty Friedan—sprang from Midwestern soil. The Great Depression began on Midwestern farms, ten years before the Crash. When the nation recovered in the 1940s, the Midwest recovered first, and most spectacularly. When American industry declined twenty years later, the decline started in the Rust Belt of the Midwest, along with the textile towns of New England. Midwestern steel mills, Midwestern auto factories, and Midwestern television makers felt the first sting of foreign competition, especially from Japan, as world markets began to open, long before globalization appeared.

Chicago invented the skyscraper. Henry Ford invented modern manufacturing. Midwestern unions invented the weekend.

What happens to America happens first to the Midwest.

It's happening again. When Americans think about the Midwest, they think about stability, the rhythmic turn of the seasons, the unchanging solidity of towns and cities where everyone knows everyone else, a land of deep roots. Now, for better or for worse, this Midwest has changed. If no part of America is immune to globalization, its impact is felt most here in the heartland, in the great fecund plain that spawned the American dream and nurtured its values. No part of the Midwest, neither Ohio nor Iowa, Michigan nor Missouri, escapes. The problems are similar or the same in each state. The issues facing each state—farming, industry, immigration, rural decline, education—vary in degree, if at all.

Globalization unites and divides. It cements ties across borders while weakening old ties at home. It celebrates the transnational at the expense of old loyalties. It brings people together from around the globe while stirring new xenophobia. It destroys old industries and economies and creates new ones—not always in the same places. It makes some people richer and other people poorer, and this gap is growing.

And like any huge economic revolution, globalization has the power to remake societies—not just their economies but their politics, the shape of their towns and cities, the way their people think and live. The industrial revolution did this. In fact, the entire Midwest is the result of the technology—railroads, harvesters, the telegraph—that powered the industrial era: this era and its machines created the Midwest's cities, formed its farm economy, shaped its universities. The global era is powered by technology as well, and it, too, is transforming the Midwest.

To grasp what is happening, we need to understand how globalization works. At its base, globalization means a revolution in communications—specifically, communications satellites and the Internet. This ease of communication has created a global money market—you can buy dollars or euros or yen for the same price in Chicago or Frankfurt or Singapore. This means that investors can borrow anywhere and invest anywhere. This means that big corporations are no longer cooped up within national boundaries or limited to a few "multinational" operations, such as factories overseas. Instead, these firms have turned themselves into global corporations, viewing the world as one big market and treating frontiers as though they don't exist. These corporations, which are the driving force of globalization, can put their design, manufacturing, marketing, and almost everything else anywhere they want, so long as it makes economic sense. They can set up business where taxes are low and regulations lax: the biggest corporations, such

as Wal-Mart or Exxon/Mobil or Toyota, are richer and more powerful than many of the countries where they do business. It also
means that it's cheap to ship things, and virtually free to ship ideas
and services. In turn, this creates more trade: why buy one of something in Ohio when you can buy three from China for the same
price? The digital-age communications, then, enable a relative handful of executives in the headquarters back home to control their
empire with the click of a computer key.

Mostly, globalization makes it possible to hire workers almost
anywhere in the world. This means that the corporations can put
operations anyplace where workers are skilled but wages are low.

This all adds up to the one big fact of globalization: companies
and workers who used to compete with the next town or the next
state now compete with China, India, Ghana, Poland, Costa Rica,
or anywhere else that global technology—which is to say, communications and shipping technology—makes investment possible
and profitable.

The impact of this is being felt across the Midwest and especially in its old manufacturing towns. Galesburg, Illinois, the
home of Carl Sandburg, is a town of thirty-three thousand that
had a place in the industrial era but may not have one in the global
age. In 2000, the Galesburg area provided 35,000 jobs. Then its
Maytag refrigerator plant moved to Mexico, killing 1,600 jobs.
The Australian owners of Butler, which had built steel buildings in
Galesburg for seventy-five years, closed the plant, firing another
270 workers. A rubber-hose plant, an industrial-screens factory, a
plant making landfill liners—all are gone. A local pottery works is
down to a skeleton staff. Altogether, the Galesburg area has lost
about 7,000 jobs in seven years. The town is too far from Chicago
or St. Louis to live off the economies of those cities. Its workforce,
basically hardworking high school graduates without the skills or
education that the new economy demands, may be unemployable.

Galesburg, like much of the Midwest, is reeling before forces
that it doesn't understand.

But really, what's so new? Trade has been growing since Marco
Polo went to China. Distances shrank with every new invention,

from the steamship to the telegraph. Multinational corporations have made things in other countries for decades. In a recent speech, Ben Bernanke, the new chairman of the Federal Reserve Bank, said, yes, a lot of this is new, for three reasons.

First, he said, change has shifted into top gear. The Web and the browser, which make all this possible, are younger than today's high school seniors. China and India have become the two biggest new players in the global economy: China decided to join that economy only thirty years ago, and India's rise dates back barely a decade. There's always been trade, foreign investment, flows of money, and they have always changed the way we live. But now the flows are global and the change is coming faster and faster. Globalization today is about where the industrial revolution was in 1790, twenty years after James Watt invented the steam engine. It took two more centuries for Watt's revolution to run its course. We're just at the beginning of ours.

Second, Bernanke says, globalization erases the dividing line between the First World and the Third. Once, poor countries and colonies shipped raw materials to the rich countries, which made the goods. Now both processes go both ways.

Geopolitics had a lot to do with it. The collapse of Communism, less than twenty years ago, added 2 billion new workers to the global economy. But these workers came from countries such as China, Russia, and Eastern Europe, plus India, that were poor and added little to the world's supply of money. In other words, you now have 3.5 billion workers competing for the same pot of money, more or less, that was formerly shared by 1.5 billion workers. These 2 billion new workers are willing to work cheap. So the 1.5 billion First World workers will have to work cheap, too. No wonder Third World wages are low and First World wages are going down.

Third, production—of goods and ideas—is fragmented as never before. Once, an auto factory in Detroit produced most of a car, perhaps buying some parts from another factory next door. The boss worked upstairs over the factory. So did the designers, salesmen, and bookkeepers. Later, the company opened some factories in places like Europe, but kept everything else in Detroit. Now, as

Bernanke says, an American chip producer does research in California, production in Texas, Germany, and Japan, and final processing and testing in Thailand, Singapore, Malaysia, and China, then sells its product all over the world. If it were cheaper and better to do the research in China and the testing in Texas, that's how the producer would do it. And that's what a lot of Midwestern companies, including the auto suppliers that used to sell to that car factory in Detroit, have done.

Globalization transforms the way that even traditional businesses operate. In my hometown, I talked with Stan Redeker, who owns one of the biggest furniture stores in central Iowa. Redeker's has been a fixture in Boone since Stan's father started the store in 1930. Stan and his wife, Maxine, both eighty, still go in regularly, but their son runs the store now, with help from his children: it's a four-generation business.

Stan always bought a few accessories, such as lamps or vases, overseas. But the so-called case goods—bedroom and dining-room furniture, sofas, entertainment centers—were American-made, mostly top-of-the-line brands such as Ethan Allen and Thomasville. "Then, five years ago, everything changed dramatically," he recalls. Chinese factories started licensing and producing top American brands, using the latest technology, achieving high quality and low prices.

"We get three forty-eight-foot containers a week from China now," he says. "In major wood furniture, seventy-five percent of what we sell is Chinese. Maxine and I went over there for two weeks last year. We went through a case goods plant that employs seventy-five hundred people and a leather goods plant that employs four thousand. They house their people in dorms. I watched Thomasville coming out of a chute. Then some Ethan Allen started coming out of the same chute. At the Chinese ports, there were thousands and thousands of containers stacked up. Unbelievable. They're put on ships that handle four thousand containers, and then on a railcar to Omaha or Kansas City. They're put on a truck to our back door. They're sealed in China, opened in Boone.

"You name the company, they're over there. Thomasville used

to have fourteen plants in North Carolina. They have one now and probably are having trouble keeping that going."

Only big furniture makers can survive this competition. At the other end, only big stores like Redeker's, which buy enough stock to fill a container, can stay in business. "When I started, every little town around here—Ogden, Jewell, Stratford—had a family furniture store. Jefferson and Perry had three. They're all gone now.

"The thing that scares everybody is that the Chinese might come over here and open their own stores. They're making the stuff, and they have the financial capability to do this."

It's like that in every arena. Only big companies can spread production and administration across a dozen countries. Only big stores can afford to deal with these companies. Only big farmers can deliver food to the specifications of the big corporations that dominate agribusiness. Only big cities offer the business services and intellectual pizzazz to compete in global services and global ideas. This is what is happening to small companies, mom-and-pop stores, family farms, and small towns. The implications are endless. Midwest farms and factories compete daily with farms and factories in China and Brazil. So do their workers. This means that jobs that used to be done here are moving overseas, mostly to places where workers can't follow. All the signs indicate that it's just beginning.

I drove to Freeport, Minnesota, a little town north of Minneapolis, best known as the place where Garrison Keillor lived when he began to write his Lake Wobegon stories. Keillor modeled much of Lake Wobegon on Freeport, including Ralph's Pretty Good Grocery, the Sidetrack Tap, and the Chatterbox Café: the town epitomized the safe, isolated Midwest of yesteryear. But globalization has come to Lake Wobegon. Freeport's small industry competes with factories in China. Factory farming, Mexican immigration, big-box retailing—the area has them all. "Globalization?" said Paul Hetland, Freeport city clerk. "It's here. You bet. We think about it, all the time."

We've had outsourcing before, of course. The Midwest became the Rust Belt when all those manufacturing jobs went south, to nonunion towns in Dixie, or were driven under by Japanese competition. That's what happened to the steel industry in Chicago and the auto industry in Flint: these industries collapsed two or three decades ago, before anyone had ever heard of globalization.

The Japanese invasion struck the Midwest first, wiping out the region's television industry, revolutionizing its steelmaking, shattering the dominance of its Big Three automakers, destroying its machine tool companies. What's happening now is different. The Japanese were good at what they did, with the aim of achieving dominance for Japanese firms, while keeping their own markets firmly closed. Globalization, by contrast, is based on open markets, not closed ones, and it's American firms, not Chinese or Indian ones, that lead the charge. Now Midwestern workers see their jobs move to Mexico first, then to China. Many of the cities we will visit in this book, from Dayton in Ohio to Newton in Iowa, are reeling from this second wave of outsourcing.

Most of this earlier outsourcing dealt with manufacturing and factory workers. For people who make economic policy or write editorials, this blue-collar outsourcing happened to uneducated people whom they don't know and was a regrettable price to pay for free trade and an open market. The newest wave is different. It's white-collar outsourcing, with jobs mostly going to India, not China, and it can hit anyone whose job isn't absolutely nailed down. The old globalization dealt with money, goods, and factory jobs; the new globalization deals with all this, and with service jobs, too. The color of your collar, the years of your education, and the size of your paycheck have less to do with this than the kind of job you have. Suddenly, for those policy-makers and editorial writers, it's personal.

Basically, any job that does not require face-to-face contact with a customer can be outsourced. Defense attorneys who must appear in a Wisconsin court cannot be in India, but real estate lawyers searching titles can. An Indiana X-ray technician has to be in the same room with the patient; the doctors who read the X-rays can be anywhere. Barbers in Columbus, taxi drivers in Chicago, and kindergarten teachers in Des Moines are outsource-proof. Stockbrokers and tax accountants aren't. All this is happening now. Already, more than half a million American tax returns are being prepared in India each year: all it takes is a smart Indian accountant who understands American tax law.

Nandan Nilekani, cofounder of the Indian IT company Infosys (and the man who gave Thomas L. Friedman the idea that "the world is flat"), told the *Financial Times* newspaper that we haven't seen anything yet. "Anything that can be sent over a wire can be outsourced, anything fungible is up for grabs, any tradable service anywhere in the world," Nilekani said. "Fifty percent of global GDP is services, and a lot of that is tradable."

Most of the Midwest remains in denial. Other regions of the world, from New England to India, know they are in global competition and are off and running. This truth is just beginning to dawn on much of the Midwest. Heavy manufacturing isn't just in a slump: it's going. The family farm has been replaced by the factory farm. Schools that were good enough to train workers for assembly-line jobs aren't good enough anymore.

Globalization poses a conundrum that will bedevil the Midwest—and America—for the rest of this century. If globalization has a moral justification, it lies in its ability to raise the Third World to the level of economic decency that has enriched the lives of First Worlders, especially Americans.

But this is the question: must this be done on the backs of American workers? Can globalization work for both Chinese peasants and the factory workers of Indiana? Can we raise living standards in India without lowering them in Michigan or Iowa?

So far, globalization has destroyed more in the Midwest than it has created. But there are success stories. Globalization, like any economic trend, is impersonal. It can do great harm and great good, often at the same time. What it does depends on how it is shaped and guided.

Twenty years ago, Chicago epitomized the Rust Belt. Today it is a global city, reborn and revitalized. On a smaller scale, other Midwestern cities such as Minneapolis and Omaha find a global niche. Kansas City, sitting astride the trade route from Mexico, feels reenergized by the North American Free Trade Agreement, or NAFTA.

St. Louis has put all its bets on bioscience. Some Midwestern industries—medical instruments, for instance—boom. Some small Midwestern cities thrive: Warsaw, Indiana, is a world center for the manufacturing of implantable joints. Even the clapped-out iron mines of northern Minnesota still produce, thanks to investment from China.

But challenges and problems outweigh the boons. Even potentially positive forces, such as immigration, sit uneasily on a region that distrusts change.

Tom Friedman, the author and *New York Times* columnist, has written that a globalized world is a flat world. What he means is that global communications have brought previously remote places, like India, into real-time competition with the United States. Thus, there really is a level global playing field, and anyone anywhere with enough broadband capacity can compete on an equal basis with anyone else in the world.

But Friedman's "flat world" metaphor misses a crucial point. This new world isn't really flat. Instead, it's made up of peaks and valleys. On the peaks stand the global cities, global universities, global research centers, hubs of global wealth and creativity. Chicago and Minneapolis are such global cities. Madison and Ann Arbor, arks of creativity, share this rarefied atmosphere. Other peaks rise in such places as Shanghai, Guangzhou, Bangalore, and Chennai. The West no longer dominates the world. In that sense, Friedman is right.

But that doesn't mean that everyone, in America or India, shares this level playing field. From their mountaintops, the happy residents of the peaks—the global citizens—talk to each other and carry on the business of globalization. Far below, down in the valleys, live the rest of mankind, globalization's have-nots, all but shut out of this conversation. They live in Calcutta's slums and on China's farms—and in much of the Midwest, in inner cities and remote rural villages. For these people, globalization is at best a rumor, at worst a threat.

The changes are felt everywhere—in farming, which has always defined the Midwest; in manufacturing, which has put bread on its tables; in education, long a source of pride but now a vital concern; in immigration, which made the region and is now remaking it; in politics, where its greatest divisions lie—as well as its great hopes. In later chapters, this book will deal with each area and introduce the people who are leading the changes, or coping with the effects.

Larry Summers, the former Harvard president and treasury secretary, summed up the pressures in an article a week before the 2006 elections: "The vast global middle is not sharing the benefits of the current period of economic growth. As the great corporate engines of efficiency succeed by using cutting-edge technology with low-cost labor, middle-class workers and their employers—whether they live in the American Midwest, the Ruhr Valley, Latin America or Eastern Europe—are left out." But it's no comfort to Midwesterners to know that Europeans and Latin Americans share their pain, because this pain isn't going to stop. As Summers said, globalization is going to grow, and "the economic logic of free, globalized, technologically sophisticated capitalism may well be to shift more wealth to the very richest and some of the very poorest of the world, while squeezing people in the middle."

The Midwest can thrive only if it meets its global challenges on a regional basis. Globalization's impact in the heartland is different from its impact on the West Coast, say, or the South, or New England. If the problems are regional, then the thinking should be regional, to find regional solutions. But this regional thinking and regional leadership are nowhere in sight.

Both Midwestern politics and Midwestern thinking are fragmented, based on states, not the region. As a result, the Midwest is coping with a twenty-first-century problem with a nineteenth-century political and social structure. In my travels, I was astounded to find so many "experts" in these states who had no idea what was going on next door, across the state line.

All over the world, in Asia and in Europe, regions are coming together to meet the challenges of globalization. As globalization weakens the reach of national governments, regions with common histories and problems find common cause. The Midwest also is a region with its own particular history, economics, demographics, and politics. There's no reason why it can't find its own way to cope with the world.

But first it must find its voice.

Big cities, smaller industrial cities, corporations, universities—all face common problems but wouldn't dream of working together to solve them. It is time for them to talk together, perhaps at a think tank funded by the Midwest's foundations.

In the Midwest, nostalgia comes easily. All Midwesterners lament the passing of a golden era that, even if it never shone as brightly as we remember it, remains vivid in our minds. But nostalgia is the flip side of denial. The Midwest's collective myth and memory keep it from dealing with the problems at hand.

The Italian philosopher Antonio Gramsci described the crisis of an era when "the old is dying and the new cannot be born." The Midwestern crisis is just the opposite. The future is already here, but the past refuses to die. The good news is that globalization is new and can be shaped. The bad news is that the Midwest is already behind.

The American future does not lie in Alabama or Las Vegas. It lies where it has always lain, in the heartland, in the battered bellwether in the very middle of the country. So far, the Midwest is failing the global challenge. This book intends to ask how the Midwest—and America—can win that battle.

CHAPTER 2

The Midwest and the Globe

Thinking about the Midwest is hard, because no one can say just what it is. When I grew up in Iowa, we looked at Ohio and saw the effete East. Some Ohioans see Iowa as part of the Great Plains. Friends who do business in China say it's hard to sell the Midwest there, because the Chinese think it's in Arizona. One book argues that the Midwest's real pastoral heart lies in Kansas; not surprisingly, the author was a professor at the University of Kansas.

The Midwest presents a blurry landscape, a squishy concept, an area with no real boundaries. It doesn't begin or end so much as it oozes into the East on one end and the Great Plains on the other. In the north, it looks like Canada. In the south, it sounds like Arkansas.

To talk about the Midwest, we must decide what it is. This book argues that the Midwest exists as a coherent region, a single unit, with a common history, people, economy, politics, needs— and a common global challenge. This true Midwest embraces the vast American midsection of America from east-central Ohio to the eastern fringe of the Great Plains, just west of the Missouri River. This definition cuts across states, including all of some and only parts of others. State lines, drawn arbitrarily in the nineteenth century, have little to do with twenty-first-century reality. The states themselves are no longer political or social units but hives of warring interests, split by the forces of globalization and the modern world. If the Midwest has common problems, state boundaries, being irrelevant to the problems, are irrelevant to the solutions. Rooted in the past, they are roadblocks to the future.

The Midwest then includes all of Michigan, Iowa, Minnesota, and Wisconsin. It includes the northern two thirds of Ohio and Illinois and the northern halves of Indiana and Missouri. On its western fringe, the Midwest crosses the Missouri River, but not by much. Both Kansas Cities and Lawrence, Kansas, are Midwestern. So are Omaha and Lincoln, in Nebraska (although some people there say they truly belong to the Great Plains). This area (as shown in the map on pages viii and ix) contains about fifty-six million people, or roughly 20 percent of all Americans.

And there it ends. The southern third of Ohio and Illinois and the southern half of Indiana are Southern, closer to Mississippi than to Minnesota. The northern half of Missouri is mostly Midwestern, but the southern half, south of the Missouri River, is Ozarks, in economy and character. In the west, the rest of Kansas, Nebraska, and the Dakotas belong to the Great Plains.

My Midwest hangs together for two reasons. One is its economy, which stands on two legs, agriculture and manufacturing. The Midwest is a thousand-mile swath across the middle of America that depends on farming and heavy industry for its livelihood. The other reason is its people—their character and, especially, where they came from. The Midwest was formed by a great wave of nineteenth-century immigration from northern Europe and the eastern United States and retains that character to this day. If the early explorers were French, the Midwestern ethos is German, Scandinavian, Dutch, and English.

This definition consigns to the South that which is truly Southern, in heritage and attitudes. In southern Indiana and Illinois, the Ku Klux Klan flourished until the middle of the twentieth century. It also recognizes that the Great Plains is a separate region, drying out, depopulating, beset by problems that have more to do with geography and climate than with globalization. Some scholars see the region around the Great Lakes as the true Midwest, but any definition that includes upper New York State, Ontario, and Quebec is simply too unwieldy.

There is more to the Midwestern economy today than farms and factories, and later newcomers—largely black or Hispanic—have altered and enriched its people. But these two traits—economy and demography—give the Midwest its basic character and enable its people to talk together, a kin with a common cause.

This Midwest is a region, not just a collection of states. When we talk about the Midwest in this book, we'll be talking about the core region that shares this economy and this kinship, because it is this community that will shape the Midwestern future.

Naturally, differences exist between the Midwestern states, even if they are less than the natives claim. Minnesota has colder weather and better schools than Missouri. Michigan and Indiana build cars and car parts, Iowa and Illinois specialize in farm machinery. Central Ohio is more crowded and more religious than central Iowa. Michigan has more heavy industry than Minnesota and, hence, more industrial problems.

Attitudes differ, too. Michigan and Iowa talk about globalization all the time; Indiana seems barely aware it exists.

But in months of traveling across the Midwest, I found more similarities than differences. This region shares a character, a politics, and a set of common problems arising from common causes. First, though, this Midwest shares a history.

The first settlers in the Midwest arrived in the late eighteenth and early nineteenth centuries, and they came up from the South, from Appalachia, from Virginia, Kentucky, Tennessee, and the piedmont of the Carolinas. They crossed the Ohio River into southern Ohio or rode the river into southern Indiana and Illinois. These early pioneers were true frontiersmen, tough, independent, scornful of government, "with an emphasized loyalty to clan, a hierarchical sense of the social orders, relative indifference or skepticism toward education and a fatalistic outlook," as an Illinois historian, Cullom Davis, put it. They sank cultural roots where they settled, and their part of the world—the southern tier of southern Ohio, Indiana, and Illinois—remains Southern in outlook to this day, more fundamentalist, patriotic, nationalistic, than the lands to the north. Their landscape is rolling, wooded, and harshly beautiful. Their economy rests on small farms, far from the great spreads and industrial towns farther north, and their accents are closer to the drawl of Alabama than the flat vowels heard farther north.

The settlers who gave the Midwest its true character came later, toward the middle of the nineteenth century, and they could not have been more different in origin and outlook. They moved straight west, from New York and New England, or directly from northern Europe—Scandinavians, Germans, English, and other nationalities. These people, according to Davis, "were much more modern in orientation, stressing individualism and ambition, faith in social progress and education, and civic egalitarianism." These later immigrants both built the Midwest and gave it the reputation it has never lost, as a balanced society, hardworking, religious, stolid, and dull.

Other nationalities, especially Poles and other Slavs, flooded cities like Detroit and Chicago. Later, in the twentieth century, came two more waves of immigration, the great black movement from the South and, still later, the arrival of millions from Mexico. The newcomers modified the Midwestern character, especially in the cities, but never replaced it.

This Midwest also shares a common political history, stemming from two big national decisions. The first was the Northwest Ordinance, passed by the Continental Congress in 1787, which set up the Northwest Territory. This territory stretched from the Ohio River to the Canadian border and included the land that later became Ohio, Indiana, Illinois, Michigan, Wisconsin, and part of Minnesota. The second decision, in 1803, was the Louisiana Purchase, stretching from New Orleans to Canada; this vast swath later became many states, including Missouri, Iowa, and the rest of Minnesota.

The Northwest Ordinance, enacted 220 years ago, before most of the Midwest was even settled, decreed state boundaries that bedevil the region's thinking to this day. The Ordinance said the territory would eventually become at least three and possibly five states, as soon as it was settled. It laid out the north-south boundaries, which are pretty much where the Ohio-Indiana and Indiana-Illinois state lines exist today. The existence of Michigan and Wisconsin, and the lines between them and their neighbors to the south, grew out of political horse-trading. The final result makes as much sense today as the arbitrary frontiers that colonialist governors drew in Africa and Iraq and cause almost as much trouble.

This Midwest shares a common economy, agricultural and industrial. It's the breadbasket. The Midwest produces 85 percent of the nation's corn and soybeans, 70 percent of its hogs, 45 percent of its eggs, 33 percent of its milk. Iowa and Illinois have more corn, Indiana and Ohio produce more cows and eggs. Take farming away from the Midwest and you've stolen not only its economy but its identity.

It's also the foundry. Like farming, industry spreads fairly evenly across the Midwest. The five American states that depend most heavily on manufacturing for their income are all Midwestern—Indiana, Wisconsin, Michigan, Ohio, and (yes!) Iowa.

This Midwest shares a common focus. Midwesterners see Chicago as the metropolis, the city that defines and dominates the region. Any region needs a capital, as Barcelona is the capital of Catalonia. In southern Illinois and Indiana, they look to Memphis, a Southern city. Once into the Plains, they look to Denver. In the Midwest, it's Chicago.

And this Midwest shares a common culture and a common reputation, which it goes to some effort to live down. The middle of the country gets low marks for exotica, which is unfair. Its flat landscape seems to excite some urge to the bizarre, from the pathologies of Bonnie and Clyde, to the rise and fall of utopian communities, to the pastoral purity of the Amish. A traveler through the Midwest runs often into strange and isolated little towns like Fairfield, Iowa, which has thrived ever since the Maharishi Mahesh Yogi came to town and set up his university there. Or Nauvoo, the Illinois town where Mormons have returned in droves to reclaim the community that once expelled them to Utah. Or another Iowa town, Postville, split between its native Germans and Norwegians, an influx of ultraorthodox Hasidic Jews who came there to open a kosher packinghouse, and the hundreds of Mexicans who work there.

But the fact is that the Midwest lacks a vivid identity, and most of its people seem to like it that way. Historian Andrew R. L. Cayton calls it "the anti-region." If there's a Midwestern bumper sticker, it would read, "It's no big deal." Cayton wrote, "The premium in the Midwest is on politeness, on the vague and unthreatening universal rather than on the unfamiliar and dangerous particular." It is a region with no regional feel.

The Midwest is often called the Heartland or the Homeland or Middle America, but these concepts rise mostly from the politics of the moment. They imply a solid, down-home area filled with practical but parochial folks, mostly rural, friendly and dull, and inclined to vote conservative. The Midwest has plenty of this, but so does every other region.

Everybody knows what the South is: it has a vivid common history defined by the Civil War and a clear boundary drawn by Charles Mason and Jeremiah Dixon. New England is a geographic and historical unit: the very words *New England* conjure up a certain scenery, architecture, manners.

The Midwest enjoys no such clarity. Almost no institutions study it or speak for it as a region. Books about the South could fill a library. There are many books about Midwestern places, from Chicago to the bridges of Madison County. But books about the region itself—its history, politics, economics, character—fit on a very short shelf.

Instead, Midwesterners flaunt Midwestern "values" and argue among themselves over which state exemplifies these values. In a book called *Heartland,* an Indiana historian named James Madison asked scholars from each state to describe their state's history and character. Each scholar, writing about his or her own state, proclaimed it the repository of true Midwestern values.

"Missouri is the most American state," said the Missourian. The others chimed in. "Michigan is first of all Midwestern," said the scholar from Michigan. North Dakota "is the most Midwestern state." "Iowa is indeed the middle land, lying at the center of the Midwest and therefore at the center of the nation." What's more, "If the Middle West is the nation's heartland, then perhaps Iowa is the heart itself, pulsating quietly, slowly and evenly." It's hard to top that, but Ohio tries, by being both "the gateway to the Midwest" and "the epitome of Midwestern distinctiveness." It was a relief to come to the wry chapter on Nebraska and to read that the state's qualities of "determination, friendliness, generosity, stoicism and daring," the ability of its people to be "audacious, honest, creative, imaginative, frugal, practical and so on," make sense only if these virtues are found only in Nebraska and nowhere else. Perhaps, the author suggests, good folk also live in Iowa, Kansas, even in Missouri.

Midwesterners do like to boast, in their quiet way, about "the bucolic and pastoral stability of the region, its traditional moral values and its down-to-earth veneration of family and hard work," as Madison put it. He quoted a magazine called *Midwest Living* to the effect that Midwesterners value "the land we live on. Clean air. Wide open spaces. Genuine friendships. Our family-oriented values."

Part of this is an aw-shucks act put on for outlanders. In reality, from John Dillinger to Charles Manson to Charles Starkweather, the Midwest has produced its share of psychopaths. More recently, watchers of the Enron scandal noted that virtually all the top players grew up on Midwestern farms or in small towns such as Tyrone, Missouri, or Aurora, Illinois, or Broken Bow, Nebraska. But part of it is a genuine appreciation of those values. And part amounts to a compensation for a small-town way of life that even boosters concede can be pretty boring.

These small-town values always were overrated. In life and in literature, the Midwest has too often been a place to leave. The small towns of Iowa post signs commemorating famous natives— the Donna Reed Theater in Denison, John Wayne Drive in Winterset, Mamie Eisenhower Avenue in Boone—but all these sons and daughters had to go away to get famous. The Midwest's great writers—Ernest Hemingway, F. Scott Fitzgerald, Sherwood Anderson, Sinclair Lewis—mostly left to write novels about heroes and heroines who themselves fled the "dark fields of the republic," as Fitzgerald put it, for more expansive places. Glenway Wescott, the Wisconsin-born novelist, called the Midwest "a state of mind of people born where they do not like to live." These days, if any writer defines the Midwest today, it's Garrison Keillor. But his Lake Wobegon, too, describes a Midwest that no longer exists, any more than the South of *Gone with the Wind* exists.

The stereotype of the narrow, bigoted, unworldly bumpkin, the image of the Midwesterner passed down by Lewis and other authors, clashes with reality. Across the Midwest, I found residents of once all-white towns dealing with maturity and sophistication with waves of Hispanic immigrants. Virtually every city of any size has its opera, symphony, ballet, art museum. And Midwesterners, especially in rural areas, also know they live far from the action and go to a great deal of trouble to stay in touch. If half the Midwest listens to Rush Limbaugh, the other half listens to NPR. As I drove through the Midwest, my car radio never passed out of range of Limbaugh and his brothers in bile, nor of first-rate classical-music stations, often broadcasting from local colleges and universities.

The Midwest is neither solidly conservative, like the South, nor as progressive as the cities of the seaboards. Rather, it's both. Midwestern factory workers may be baffled by the global forces that steal their jobs. But Midwestern farmers and small-town businesspeople have been dealing globally for years. If you want a smart discussion on global currency fluctuations, just go talk to a farmer who depends on exports for a living.

In other words, Midwesterners are tolerant, narrow-minded, cultured, crass, sophisticated, and naïve in pretty much the same measure as other Americans. What makes them unique, though, is their isolation, especially from each other. Rural villages, immigrant towns, factory cities, all battle the problems of globalization in isolation from each other, unaware that other people in neighboring states are fighting the same battle. By nature, Midwesterners can be aloof and uncooperative. That nature is hurting them now.

This nature springs from the region's sense of security, of distance from the evils of the outside world. Those of us who left the Midwest wanted glitter, excitement, the crush of cities. Those who stayed wanted something else—safety, or belongingness. Gopher Prairie was, as Sinclair Lewis wrote, "merely safe." Ginny, the heroine of Jane Smiley's novel *A Thousand Acres*, felt that "our farm and our lives seemed secure and good."

To see into the region's heart, I needed a poet. So I went to Nebraska, to meet Ted Kooser, and we talked one morning in a coffee shop in Lincoln, near the rural acreage where he lives. After an

Iowa boyhood, Kooser became an insurance executive in Omaha. But his real life belongs to poetry. He has published ten collections of poems, plus two small books of prose that may be the most evocative writing anywhere on Midwestern life. In 2004–5 he served two terms as America's poet laureate. Wonderfully intelligent, wryly funny, Ted Kooser would have shone in any society. Why did he stay in the Midwest? I asked.

"I think it was because I felt safe here," he said. "Most people here, you got a job, never asked for a raise. If you're digging a ditch, you don't ask why. I had enough of that in me. I got a steady paycheck. It was so much safer to stay where I was.

"My friend Margie Rine, her mother is elderly, lives in Seward. She's on an electric cart. On a Sunday morning, when she was in her garden, she got dumped. She had to wait forty minutes until the neighbors came home from church and found her. Margie said, 'Ma, what did you do for forty minutes?' and she said, 'I weeded the strawberries.' That's very Midwestern.

"We've got tractor pulls here. No amount of Islamic terrorism can ever touch this part of America."

As Kooser suggested, the Midwest shares a communal myth, part Grant Wood, part Booth Tarkington, part Meredith Willson.

The Midwest lives on this historical myth, Ted Kooser told me. It's a memory of a time that never really existed and is all the more powerful for that, like Garrison Keillor's Lake Wobegon. It's a past that keeps the Midwest from coping with its present.

Ted said, "This resistance to change is a big force. Our past is a fiction. It's all stories. It may be that the collective past in an area like this is so uniform—so tied into the Depression and the golden Ike years—that it makes us resistant. If you have a common collective past that you keep vivifying, that affects how we deal with change." And now change is here, and that sense of safety is vanishing.

"In 1905," Ted said, "leather-harness makers could retool for cars. Now nobody can retool that fast. You're teaching computer codes that are going to be obsolete. If you're a Californian, you resort to crystals or I Ching. If you're a Midwesterner, it's Bud Light."

A communal myth or idealized history is no help in a time of transformative change. Every hundred years or so, an economic revolution comes along and changes everything. This means that all of us—societies as well as people—must reinvent ourselves. But as the Chicago-born sociologist Richard Sennett says, this is easier said than done.

"Instability can be an opportunity," Sennett wrote about globalization, "if you have real wealth to invest, or are young and unattached, or an immigrant exploring cracks in the labor force. If you are dutiful but not brilliant at work, if you have children and a mortgage, if you are worried about old-age hardship, then instability does not equal opportunity."

"Dutiful but not brilliant," aging and insecure—that sums up much of the Midwest. Faced with globalization, the region seems in denial. As Ted Kooser says, we don't handle change, let alone revolutions, very well.

CHAPTER 3

From Rust to Bust

It wasn't always this way. The Midwest reigned as the Silicon Valley of the industrial era. Innovation flew from fertile imaginations and invented a new economy. Companies that began with a lonely tinkerer in a garage grew into mighty corporations. Young men sowed ideas like seed on the Midwestern soil and reaped riches. From around the world—from Poland and Lithuania, from New England and Appalachia—men and women poured into the Midwest to work and to found a civilization. In 1900, the United States held only fourteen factories, each employing more than six thousand workers: three were in the Midwest, all in Chicago. Fifteen years later, dozens of Midwestern factories were that big, including six auto plants in Detroit alone. Half of everything made in America was made in the Midwest.

It must have been an exhilarating time. In Dearborn and Detroit, Henry Ford and Ransom Olds launched the age of the automobile. The Dodge brothers, John and Horace, set up their auto plant in Hamtramck. In Flint, J. H. Whiting and William Durant created General Motors. Studebaker began in South Bend, Nash in Kenosha. The auto plants needed parts, and a vast swath of the upper Midwest became Auto Alley. In Akron, three firms—Goodyear, Firestone, and B. F. Goodrich—became the biggest tiremakers in the nation. In Canton, the sons of Henry Timken turned his invention of a roller bearing into an empire of auto axles. In Indiana, Judge Elbert Gary founded the steelmaking capital of the nation and named it after himself. More steel poured from Chicago and

Youngstown. In Milwaukee, Allis-Chalmers made turbines. In Racine, J. I. Case made tractors.

Midwestern might was based, as we know, on easy access to iron and coal, on money, on railroad transport, on new methods of mass production. But mostly it rested on ideas, on the minds and imaginations of a generation of entrepreneurs, dreamers, and doers, unafraid to risk all on a roll of the industrial dice. As in Silicon Valley now, Midwestern innovation created a new world.

Where did it all go? A century later, the industrial Midwest amounts to a wasteland of empty factories, corroding cities, and crumbling neighborhoods. Some cities found new ways to earn a living, but nowhere is heavy manufacturing part of the solution. For the Midwest, mass production was a one-shot infusion, producing a boom that lasted one season and is now gone.

In many ways, the Midwest is the victim of its own success. These were company towns, totally dependent on one big corporation. Their founders had one really good idea, and that idea sustained their corporations for decades, eliminating the need for more good ideas. For workers, the factories provided a living—in time, a good living—so there was no need to go elsewhere, look elsewhere, imagine anything different, for themselves or their children. For the cities, the corporations were a constant, steady source of jobs, taxes, and leadership, so no mayor or city manager needed to seek new investment.

Why change? It worked.

"Just imagine," says George Erickcek, a Michigan economist, "just imagine that you're the mayor of Flint in 1923. There's a knock on the door. It's the devil and he says, 'Mr. Mayor, I'll give you sixty years of prosperity.' 'Okay,' you say, 'what comes after that?' and the devil says, 'You don't want to know.' " The Midwest took the devil's deal. Sixty years? Not bad. And after that, we're all dead.

Or if not dead, then dozing. I drove into Dayton, Ohio, on a recent Monday in May. The first building on Third Street as I entered downtown was the Montgomery County Building. Next door stood the Coroner-Crime Laboratory. Most of the other buildings also were government buildings—police, city administration, a courthouse, a small college. Downtown held one decent hotel, a Doubletree, not much for a city of 165,000. I saw a little commerce—a few clothing stores, discount stores, pawnshops. Nor much traffic. Parking is easy to find. The city looked neat, not shabby, but dull, with little life.

Not to knock government, nor to glorify traffic jams. But a healthy downtown needs more than government buildings, and real cities are busy places, filled with commerce and people and traffic. Downtowns aren't supposed to be quiet.

Dayton helped create the twentieth century, and that century returned the favor. Now Dayton, like many of the Midwest's major manufacturing cities, is struggling with the twenty-first century, and with globalization. The city has a rich past. No one knows yet if it has a future.

Dayton, of course, is where manned flight began. In a Dayton bicycle shop, Orville and Wilbur Wright designed the first airplane. But that was only the start. Dayton has more patents per capita than any other American city. The cash register was invented here and so were microfiche and the bar code; if we live in a world of fast-moving commerce and carefully stored data, Dayton can take some credit. People in Dayton invented the parking meter, the movie projector, the parachute, the gas mask, and the pop-top can. The stepladder was born in Dayton. So was the food that astronauts eat in space.

Most important for Dayton was the arrival in 1904—one year after the Wright brothers made their maiden flight at Kitty Hawk—of a young Ohio State graduate named Charles Kettering. Kettering came to Dayton to work for the National Cash Register Company, but he spent most of this time trying to develop an electric ignition for automobiles. By 1909 he was ready to go. With his NCR boss Edward Deeds, he formed a company to make ignitions. They called it Dayton Engineering Laboratories Company, or Delco for short. By 1913 it already employed fifteen hundred people in Dayton.

Delphi, the successor to Delco, remains the nation's largest auto-parts supplier. But Delphi has gone global. It employs 185,000 persons now, but only 50,000 of them in the United States. Its biggest customer is General Motors, which is shedding sales, workers, and money. In 2005, Delphi declared bankruptcy—or rather, its American branch did: non-U.S. subsidiaries were not part of the filing. The purpose of the bankruptcy filing was to enable Delphi to cut costs by closing American plants, laying off American workers, getting rid of pension and health obligations to its American retirees, and shifting most production overseas.

The filing succeeded. General Motors and Delphi, working with the emasculated United Auto Workers, agreed to a deal to buy out 47,600 workers altogether. Of these, 12,600 worked at Delphi. The bulk will come from the Midwest: about 70 percent of Delphi's total U.S. employment is in the Midwest, mostly in Ohio, Michigan, and Indiana. Senior workers who kept their jobs agreed to accept wage cuts, from $28 per hour to $14 to $18.50 per hour, in exchange for a "buy-down" payment of $105,000 spread over three years.

These are big, abstract figures. In Dayton, it gets personal. In Dayton, Delphi is still the big employer, and basically, it's leaving town. Delphi has five big plants in Dayton and its region and employs fifty-seven hundred workers. It plans to close four of the five plants. It may end up with two hundred workers in Dayton. What Charles Kettering began in the early twentieth century is dying in the early twenty-first century.

Not that anyone should be surprised. Delphi employed thirty thousand workers in the Dayton region in the midseventies and twenty thousand in the mideighties. Those jobs have been disappearing for years. Some went early to the Sun Belt. Others left for Mexico. Some just went, lost to automation. Now they're going to China and other Third World countries.

Dayton, like almost all major manufacturing centers in the Midwest, fought this trend. It held on to its shrinking industries, supporting them at all costs. It assumed that things would stabilize, that a tide would flow back in. The big mills and factories might shed jobs, but they remained the biggest employers in town. Besides, they had always been there. They were what Dayton was all about. They were all there was. Having lived off them for a century, nobody could imagine life without them.

"It's been death by a thousand cuts," Joe Tuss, the county economic development director, told me when I went to his office. "In the Dayton region, we've been blessed and cursed. We've hung on to the core manufacturing jobs, both as a percentage of jobs and as part of our total output, for a much longer time than most places. We worked very hard to provide tax incentives. We worked with the auto sector, and all this let them continue to operate facilities long after they were shutting down elsewhere. We allowed a large workforce to make a good union wage.

"But now the economic forces are catching up with us. Now we are seeing that in a big way. The Delphi bankruptcy is our tipping point. We have to try to reinvent ourselves—but this work to preserve our base, it all took time and energy away from reinventing ourselves."

Tuss described a transformation of the very world in which Dayton has lived: "We're going through a global macroeconomic change that, at our local level, we can do very little about."

Dayton can't be compared to true basket cases, such as Gary or Flint or Benton Harbor, Michigan, or East St. Louis, Illinois. These cities died in the Rust Belt era and may never revive. But there are many Midwestern cities like Dayton—Akron and Toledo in Ohio, Grand Rapids in Michigan, Waterloo in Iowa, Rockford in Illinois—that once buzzed and hummed with industry and are now smaller, sadder, down but not completely out, trying to figure out what to do next.

John Austin sees the problem clearly. Not many Midwesterners do. In traveling the Midwest, I found many persons talking about globalization, but few with the breadth to see it in the regional framework, or to understand why it is hitting the Midwest so hard.

Austin is a University of Michigan scholar and state school-board official who has studied the Midwestern economic crisis. Austin finds a culprit in the Midwestern mentality—the sort of complacency that enabled the region to forget its roots in innovation and settle for a slow, steady decline as a way of life. Faced with change, Midwesterners tend to stick with what works,

Austin says. But they can also be "anti-intellectual, nativist and in-sular." Worst, they can be smug.

As their economy crumbled, "a culture of expectation and enti-tlement grew around the success of the mass production economy and the prosperous middle class life it afforded," Austin wrote. "A sense that this relative prosperity would always endure, that the region could reap good wages without education and continuing innovation, stilled the dynamic of entrepreneurialism and eco-nomic churn that built the region."

Both business and unions are to blame, he said. "As industrial unions gained co-equal status and organization to the increasingly large and paternalistic big businesses, both became change and risk averse, seeking protection of what they had, versus innovation and creation of the new."

It's a deep-seated malaise, Austin said, a social nostalgia wide-spread across Midwesterners who are "not fully aware of new de-mands of the global knowledge economy."

Perhaps Midwesterners have a hard time grasping what's hap-pening because it's been going on so long, and because what they had seemed so good. In the years after the war, the labor battles of the first half of the twentieth century ended in an accommodation between big unions and big business. Corporations and unions ne-gotiated contracts that provided high wages, good pensions, solid health-care plans, and good working conditions, in exchange for the unions' agreement not to strike. The result was an era of labor peace and the creation of what may have been the crowning glory of the American economy—the birth of an industrial middle class, men and women who worked in factories, at blast furnaces and as-sembly lines, but who owned their own homes, drove good cars, took vacations, educated their kids, and, in general, lived at a level never before achieved by a blue-collar population.

Some of this was an out-and-out mistake. The provision of health insurance through individual union-corporation contracts prevented the establishment of a national health program and, in the long run, saddled the corporations with ruinous health respon-sibilities for their employees and retirees. Even Walter Reuther, the labor leader who helped negotiate these deals, saw the flaw but could not persuade corporations, with their hatred of government programs, to see sense.

But mostly, it is hard to blame the men who made these deals. Companies bought labor peace and thrived. Workers achieved an unprecedented level of economic decency. When Midwesterners now look back on this era with nostalgia, they have something to be nostalgic about.

This era rested on a set of temporary circumstances. Mostly, it could exist only inside a closed economy, without competition from outside. The Midwest had this huge industry all to itself. No Japan, no Sun Belt, no Mexico, could do it better—or do it at all. The Midwesterners who made the cars, steel, machine tools, and auto parts could run their economy any way they wanted.

The decline of the Midwest's industrial base began in the 1970s and 1980s, possibly earlier: manufacturing employment peaked in the late 1970s and has been going down ever since. Globalization only seems to be finishing off what the earlier crisis spared.

Thirty years after World War II, a revitalized Japan entered the American economy with a wave of imports and investment that stunned Americans. Some of this Japanese success was based on savage price-cutting, subsidies, and the ability of its companies to compete abroad because they were protected by tariff walls at home. But the Japanese also were good. They put out high-quality products at low prices. They had imaginative design and efficient management.

Several other things happened at the same time. Third World countries such as Brazil began producing high-quality steel and other basic products and exporting them to the United States. Mexico began attracting American companies to move their mass operations and basic assembly processes south of the border, where cheap labor awaited. The invention of air-conditioning turned the American South into a plausible place to live and work, and companies began moving to the Sun Belt.

The first wave of competition hit the Midwest particularly hard. Partly, the Japanese turned out to be good at precisely the industries that underpinned the Midwest economy—autos, television sets, machine tools. Partly, some major Midwestern industries, like the integrated steel mills, produced basic, uncomplicated products that Third Worlders like the Brazilians could make just as well and a lot cheaper. Partly, Midwestern companies that were heavily unionized—and that included most of them—proved vulnerable to the nonunion lures of the Sun Belt.

Some competition for the Big Three auto companies came from imports. More came from "transplants"—that is, foreign companies like Toyota or Honda that set up factories in the United States. For the most part, these factories settled not in the Midwest but in the border states or Deep South, places with weak or nonexistent unions. Some of these transplants bought their auto parts from companies that also located in the South; others imported parts. Either way, the Midwest lost out.

The transplants have another built-in advantage that dates to the postwar glory days of Midwestern manufacturing. Ford and General Motors calculate that their health and pension costs for retirees add about $1,300 to the cost of every car and truck they make. Most of the transplants have been in the United States for only twenty years or so—not long enough to have any retirees. Someday they will, and that advantage will disappear. The question is, will Ford and General Motors disappear first?

Some Midwestern industries simply vanished in this era: TV manufacturing went away and never came back. But many industries, like auto parts, and many cities, like Dayton, fought back with severe cost cuts, automation, downsizing, and layoffs. In many cases, overall production stayed up: Gary, Indiana, produces more steel now than it ever did, but with one tenth the workforce. Their communities paid a stiff price. Gary basically is a slum, subsisting on taxes from casinos. More fortunate cities saw populations decline, schools decay, opportunity flee, but they survived. Diminished though they were, they still employed enough people in the remaining industries to maintain the façade of their old industrial selves.

And then came globalization, for which there was little defense. Some workers, such as bioscientists, have special skills; some industries, such as medical instruments, own a competitive edge;

some cities, such as Madison or Ann Arbor, provide unbeatable access to expertise. These workers, industries, and cities can compete in a global market. But much of the Midwest simply can't compete. Midwestern high school dropouts performing repetitive work on an assembly line for high wages cannot compete with Chinese high school graduates doing the same work for low wages. Midwestern factories making basic auto parts or refrigerators cannot compete with factories in China or other Third World countries. Midwestern cities that depend on these workers and these industries cannot compete in a world in which China and India are investing heavily in research, technology, and, especially, education.

In the Rust Belt era, American firms, especially car companies, had positions to defend and led the losing fight against the Japanese invasion. Now, these companies have gone global themselves. General Motors makes cars and trucks in thirty-three countries and is part of a worldwide auto glut that is driving down prices everywhere. Delphi manufactures in thirty-four countries. No longer do foreign firms threaten American jobs. Now it's American firms that have taken jobs overseas, in a desperate attempt to meet the global competitive challenge from overseas. These companies, like Delphi, will stay in business. They just won't stay in business in Dayton.

In this debate, there are two schools of thought. One side wants to keep what's left of the Midwest's heavy industry and use it as the base of a revived economy. The other side says the region should let this industry die, sooner rather than later, and get on with the economy of the future.

The biggest heavy industry of all is the auto industry, which dominates Michigan, Ohio, and Indiana and spreads its influence throughout the Midwest. When Midwesterners talk about industry, they often mean cars. The future of the auto industry is where this battle will be fought.

On one side is Patrick Barkey, at Ball State University in Muncie, Indiana. Barkey sees the auto industry as the millstone of the past, not an anchor for the future. "In a very short span of time, perhaps as little as two or three years, the era of the highly paid automobile-industry production will come to an end," Barkey has written. When I went to his office, he told me, "We're in an economy in transition. Globalization profoundly affects the environment. The Midwest is one of the last undiversified places in the United States. That's why globalization is hitting so hard here.

"Production isn't doomed. There are still plenty of things for us to produce. But mass production with low skills—that's doomed."

Barkey's right. The Midwest still makes lots of things. In the past twenty years, manufacturing output in the Midwest soared by 50 percent or more. But the number of jobs in manufacturing fell by about 20 percent in the major industrial states. This means fewer people are making more things. It also means that heavy industry can no longer support the Midwest and its people: there just aren't enough jobs there.

On the other side are a number of Midwestern economic planners, especially inside state governments, who remain rooted in the industrial past.

"We are the center of the global auto universe," a Michigan state economic-development official named Mike Shore told me, "and we are looking to hold on to what we have as long as we can." The state government, driven by this attitude, recently passed a $600-million-per-year tax cut for manufacturers. It will have no effect at all. In the previous three years, Michigan lost 163,000 manufacturing jobs. It has 700,000 manufacturing jobs left, and many of those will go, too, tax cut or no tax cut.

These state officials know perfectly well that globalization will swallow their traditional industries. But they're stuck. Workers vote, and a voter who has just lost his job will be an angry voter. When a plant is threatened, the local legislators hear about it constantly—from workers worried about their jobs, from cities worried about tax money. When an old factory closes, governors get blamed. When a new factory opens, governors get to cut ribbons. Every time a factory dies, its workers go from a private payroll to the public dole; in every Midwestern state, unemployment pay and retraining costs take money away from programs, such as education, that might offer some advantage in the new economy.

And so the pressure builds to subsidize the old industries, to do anything to keep them from moving away. Every state and every town tries. Most lose, and the time and money they spend trying to keep twentieth-century jobs prevent them from creating twenty-first-century jobs.

If state governments seem determined to hold on to old jobs and old industries, attitudes outside governments vary from state to state. Indiana, for instance, is a glum, depressed place, more Southern than Midwestern, resigned to a slow and steady decline and seemingly not very upset by it. In Indiana, they say, "Good enough is good enough." There's a hope that the good days will come back. But if they don't, that's okay, because the state will cope somehow. Good ideas that involve sharp change don't stand much of a chance. As one fed up Indiana official told me, "When an idea has some potential, people say that's pretty risky. Our jobs are going down but total output is going up, and that's okay. We're getting poorer and poorer in comparison to other states, but in absolute terms, we're growing. Not much but a little, and a lot of people in Indiana feel that's good enough. Change is risky, they say, so let's stick with what we've got."

Go north into Michigan and the attitude changes entirely. Not that Michigan doesn't have problems. It's the car capital of the world, the home of Ford and General Motors, and for that reason alone it's been hit harder than anywhere else. Perhaps it took this pain to get the state's attention. Its state government, as we've seen, is in denial. But if there's any place where scholars and planners have accepted the cold reality of globalization and are thinking hard about it, it's Michigan.

"Michigan's problem is that the big, unionized auto industry is no longer competitive," Donald Grimes at the University of Michigan said. "It's a price-cost squeeze. The price of cars has actually declined since 1995. So if labor costs are going up and the price of the car is going down, the industry is in this squeeze.

"Before, companies had a monopoly power over prices. It can't do this anymore. This has been going on for some time, and globalization is the culmination of this process."

The next steps, toward a knowledge economy, have already been taken—and they're based on what the state has done in the past. Michigan isn't going to make cars anymore, but it still knows more about cars than any other place in the world. New investment is going into the southeastern part of the state for auto research, design programs, marketing ideas. The idea is to make this area the global center for automotive ideas and innovation—even if the actual manufacturing will take place thousands of miles away.

Ann Arbor is the engine of this activity, not Detroit. It's fueled by the brainpower at the University of Michigan, not the brawn of the old Polish and African-American neighborhoods. The jobs pay well but there are fewer of them. No one knows how big this new economy will be, or how many people it will support.

At Dundee, south of Ann Arbor, two new engine plants are being built by the Global Engine Manufacturing Alliance, a joint project by DaimlerChrysler of Germany and the United States, Mitsubishi of Japan, and Hyundai of Korea. Nominally competitors, these companies are betting they can save $100 million per year to develop an engine together, instead of working separately. The two plants will produce 840,000 engines per year with only 562 workers. The state expects total employment to be eight hundred—about one third the number of jobs in a typical old-time engine plant. But the average wage is about $30 per hour. The plant is unionized, just like the old auto plants, but the rules have changed. For instance, there is one job classification, meaning that anyone can do anything: the old union rules that kept anyone but an electrician from changing a lightbulb are out.

"Southeast Michigan has talent and engineers and universities and designers, and they all know about cars," Grimes told me. "That's where we want to be."

It's the future, Grimes says. "On both sides of the political aisle, all that anybody talks about is how to save the auto industry. Granholm is smart," he said, referring to the governor, Jennifer Granholm, "but she's fighting an uphill fight. You're fighting against a very real loss that people face. These guys are going to lose their jobs or take a substantial pay cut."

It's more than that. Rural areas that had small manufacturing plants will shrink economically. Small farmers who subsidized their farms with factory jobs may have to sell out. Third-generation factory workers without the basic education for retraining will never again hold a good job. Cities like Flint and Saginaw will become rusted relics.

But "there's no option," says Grimes. "I'm saying, sorry, but this is the way the world goes, and that generates a lot of bitterness."

It's easy to say that the labor unions dug their own grave by winning high wages and restrictive work rules. But the fact is that these unions—especially the UAW—helped build the glory years of the American industrial era. Millions of workers shared the riches of that era. Unions underpinned an epoch of economic decency and political stability. Along with the public schools, they created the American dream. The Midwest was the crucible in which labor power was forged, where the great battles were fought and the great victories won. Midwestern history is unthinkable without the unions.

But their time has passed. The only unions that are growing are in the service sector, those that sign up housekeepers, hospital orderlies, or line cooks in hospitals and hotels. These are jobs that can't be outsourced. They also are jobs at the bottom of the pay scale; the people who hold them are often women and Hispanic.

The contrast with the dying old industrial unions—mostly white, mostly men, mostly middle class in pay scale and benefits, mostly vulnerable to outsourcing—could not be greater. Most of these union locals will simply close, as UAW locals are closing around the Midwest now. Others have been reduced to managing decline. The UAW collaborated with GM and Delphi in negotiating the forty-seven thousand buyouts. That means that the union will soon have forty-seven thousand fewer members. Another thirty-eight thousand Ford workers have taken buyouts. The UAW once had 1.5 million members; now it's 580,000, and falling. Before, the UAW fought legendary union battles, led strikes and factory sit-downs, and used its clout to win a new life for its workers. Now, it has no clout. No strike could possibly succeed.

The UAW isn't dead yet, but it's most useful in persuading its members to do what companies want; the deal at Dundee is an example. So is Peoria, Illinois, where Caterpillar, the giant earthmoving-equipment maker, is hiring workers—but on a two-tier scale that has always been anathema to unions. Older, less-skilled workers still earn more than $20 per hour, but new hires in the same job grades make barely half that, about $12.50 per hour. The upside is that workers get hired. The downside is that they will never have the middle-class life their fathers enjoyed.

Back in Dayton, I went to see Wes Wells, the regional director for the AFL-CIO in the Dayton/Miami Valley area of southwestern Ohio. Wells is a blunt, angry old union man, proud of the past and scared of the future. Once, running the AFL-CIO in the Dayton region must have been a good job. Now Wells sits in his office on the east side of Dayton, out near the Wright-Patterson air base, and tries to ease the pain. The industrial era is ending, in Dayton as elsewhere in the Midwest, and with it the unions' golden age.

In Dayton, Wes Wells knows that the economy that framed his life is going. "We've got fifty-seven hundred workers in the Valley at Delphi [the biggest employer]," Wells said. "Several years ago it was upward of twenty thousand. Dayton has lost twenty-six thousand jobs since 2000—about twenty-one thousand in manufacturing." Maybe some of the remaining jobs will survive. Most won't.

Wells, like all union leaders, rejects the idea that unions played a role in their own decline, that this decline is a result of the wages and workers' rights that unions won. Instead, he blames corporate mismanagement and corporate greed—an easy target because there's so much of it around.

"Let me tell you something," he said. "When you look at the golden parachutes of Delphi executives, Delphi is in this spot because of one thing—mismanagement."

Another favorite culprit is trade and especially NAFTA. China may be the biggest competitive challenge to Midwestern industry right now, but most workers and their union leaders cannot look beyond NAFTA and Mexico. Their solution is simple—controls or barriers to trade. Economists, government officials, and editorial writers roll their eyes at this solution, but they are kidding themselves if they ignore the real pain that trade inflicts on much of the Midwest and the potential here for a political backlash: we saw the first signs in the 2006 congressional elections. Economists cite figures showing the dependence of Midwestern industry and farming on exports, and this is true enough. But while trade can bring broad benefits to a society, it can cause sharp pain locally. Every imported car or car part means one less car or car part made in Dayton or Detroit, and one less worker with a job. The same worker can buy imported goods cheaper at his local Wal-Mart, but this doesn't soothe him if he has no income. In the old industrial cities, there soon will be workers with nothing left but their votes.

"How in hell do you compete with China?" Wes Wells asked me. "How do you compete with Mexico? The only thing I fault Clinton for is NAFTA. NAFTA is not about bringing Mexico's standard of living up to our level, but in taking our standard down to Mexico's level. The only alternative I see is by legislative action. We have to have an administration that understands the plight of the manufacturing base in this country and can put in a fair-trade policy, which is an equal-trade policy."

Then Wells said something that really startled me. He told me that Lyndon LaRouche, the conspiracy theorist and perennial presidential candidate, is gaining converts among the distressed workers of Dayton. "Some of our people are going to his meetings. Some of the materials he puts out make some sense."

Globalization is made to order for demagogues and conspiracy theorists. By its nature, it exposes the vulnerable to distant and mysterious forces. It enriches a new class of global citizens, but undermines a way of life for middle-class workers who can't understand what is happening to them and don't feel they deserve it. This is not the way life was supposed to be, and they seek someone to blame.

This backlash is not inevitable but it is likely unless the cities and regions where these workers live can find new ways to earn their living and support their people. Today's workers may be a lost generation, and their children face an uncertain future. In cities like Dayton, the logical forecast is for more decline and more economic misery.

Well, maybe so. But after listening to a litany of gloom about Dayton's present and future, I came away with an odd sense that, if any place is likely to reinvent itself and make it in a globalizing world, it might be Dayton. It's not just because there's more to Dayton and its economy than Delphi and cars. Many of the town's other business, unlike Delphi, belong in the twenty-first century. There's a vigorous community college named Sinclair and two good universities, the University of Dayton and Wright State, both committed to the community. It also has a good and courageous newspaper, the *Daily News*, that is forcing the city to look hard at itself.

Most important, everyone I met in Dayton seemed to be asking the right questions. Perhaps the Delphi bankruptcy has really been a wake-up call. Throughout Ohio and Indiana especially, there is a terrific sense of denial about globalization and what it's doing. Both civic leaders and scholars insist that these states will keep on earning their livings the same old way. Dayton, at least, understands what is happening to it, and why. It grasps that the industrial era is gone and globalization is here.

Perhaps disaster concentrates the mind. Much of the industrial Midwest is hanging on and so can keep kidding itself. But it should look to Chicago: nothing happened there until the city lost virtually all of its heavy industry—the steel mills, canning plants, stockyards, metalworking industries—and had to reinvent itself. Twenty-five years later, Dayton faces that challenge.

Chicago had strengths—its universities, hospitals, big consulting firms, especially its commodities markets—and it built on those to reinvent itself. In many ways it built on its past, on its expertise in farm markets and heavy industry, to create the new industries of the future. Dayton and many other cities have hidden strengths, some of them tied to their traditional industries, some entirely separate. If they can give up the old, they have a chance to thrive on the new.

Until 1970, National Cash Register still employed twenty thousand people in Dayton, most of them in manufacturing. Now NCR does no manufacturing in Dayton at all. But the company now specializes in data warehousing and solutions to information-systems problems. This is harder to understand than auto parts and employs fewer people, but it provides something that the twenty-first century needs.

Reynolds and Reynolds, a major seller of business forms to auto dealers, now leads the market for information solutions for these dealers. A similar company, Standard Register, has moved from business forms for hospitals to management solutions for hospitals. LexisNexis, the computer archive, is headquartered in suburban Miamisburg. Alien Technologies runs its RFID solutions center in Dayton. RFID stands for Radio Frequency Identification and is used by companies to track supply chains and logistics: someday it will replace bar codes.

Dayton has a National Composites Center, which researches lightweight materials. Not far away, the University of Dayton has a research institute that also studies composite materials. These materials may make the next generation of auto parts—a natural spin-off for a town that made its living on auto parts. They may not be made in Dayton, but they'll be developed there; as in Ann Arbor, it's a case of fewer high-tech jobs replacing many low-tech jobs.

Wright State University is next to Wright-Patterson Air Force Base. The university has a good medical school. The air force is moving its aerospace medical research and training to the base. Civic leaders in Dayton see jobs in space-age medicine moving into the gap left by Delphi.

Most of the rest of Ohio, which looks down its nose at Dayton, doesn't think the city has a chance. Ned Hill, the state's leading urban economist, calls Dayton "a hospice for Delphi," scoffs that the air base's only mission "is to blow things up," and argues that "it's not research that drives economies—it's products."

Perhaps he's right. Dayton isn't there yet. It isn't even close to there. But the tired old city, against the odds, is taking three venerable institutions—auto parts, financial data, and the air force base—and seeing if they add up to a fingerhold on the global future.

CHAPTER 4

Unplugged

The old manufacturing towns of the Midwest bear their age and history with a weathered grace. Many are small places, some fewer than ten thousand people, some as many as sixty thousand or so, and they're all about 150 years old, born in the first years of the machine age. Their problems show in the closed shops on Main Street, where gift stores and Medicaid clinics have replaced the groceries and two-story department stores of old, in the pot-holes and broken curbs and surface shabbiness. The old factories, dead or dying, stand on the edge of town, near the railroad tracks. Out on the highway is a strip of Wal-Mart and Denny's businesses that have sucked the life and commerce out of downtown.

These were once well-to-do towns. Each has its neighborhood of old Victorian and Edwardian houses, sheltered by giant oaks, a whisper of better days. The millowners built these houses; they are home now to doctors or lawyers or émigrés from the city, seeking a mansion for $200,000. On the other side of town, often literally on the other side of the tracks, are the small clapboard houses where the workers live, still tidy but scuffed, many with an old stove or a rusted car in the front yard.

In these quiet neighborhoods, beyond the mills and the parking lots, the old towns look as if nothing has changed, although everything has.

This description fits Newton and Ottumwa in Iowa, Galesburg and Decatur in Illinois, Springfield and Lima in Ohio, Anderson and Muncie in Indiana, Greenville in Michigan. There are more, many more. Some will survive and may even find another way to make their living. Most will not. Take away these manufacturing towns and you carve out the core of the Midwestern economy.

For most Americans, the words *Middle West* conjure up images of cornfields and bucolic towns. That never was true. As the historians Brian Page and Richard Walker wrote, "The Midwest has been characterized by vigorous urbanization throughout its history. Southern Wisconsin and Michigan, eastern Iowa and Minnesota, northern Illinois and Indiana, and virtually all of Ohio are characterized by dense city systems."

This is the manufacturing heartland of America, and much of the manufacturing took place in the small towns and cities that radiated out from metropolitan centers such as Chicago or Detroit. The industrial era needed a lot of these cities. The global era doesn't. As John Austin wrote, "The restructuring of the economy towards knowledge creation and talent agglomeration means current dislocations of people and places." In plain words, which Austin spelled out for me, an economic pattern created these smaller cities. The new pattern is different. Globalization concentrates everything, and it's concentrating the new workforce—the educated knowledge workers, the creative people, the idea-mongers—in cities. You don't need to scatter the production of ideas across the countryside, as we scattered the production of goods. You need to bring ideas together in one place and let them bounce off each other.

In truth, the best and the brightest have always gone to cities. Skilled and hardworking people with some secondary education could lead a middle-class life back in the old hometown, working in the local factories. That's what's gone now, and it dooms these towns, just as surely as it has doomed the old rusting mill down by the tracks.

"Many of them are just going to die," Austin told me. "It's hard to say that to them, but it's true."

Oddly enough, many of these small and medium-size manufacturing cities survived the Rust Belt collapse better than the big cities did. Chicago hit bottom in 1980. Milwaukee and Dayton are still shedding industry: their reinvention is yet to come. Others, such as Detroit, may never recover.

The smaller places fought back. They retooled to meet the Japanese challenge. They sought foreign investment. A combination of cheap land, tax breaks, smart farm-town workers, and a fierce work ethic often did the trick. Investors arrived and much of the Midwest rode out the crisis.

No one knew that, just over the horizon, a bigger challenge loomed. That challenge is globalization. It is precisely the towns and cities that bought another twenty or thirty years for their economies that are now being hit by outsourcing and by low-wage competition from China and other Third World countries.

"We ran that horse too long," one Indiana economist told me.

Not that these old towns will vanish, like the rural ghost towns of the Great Plains. They'll keep their schools and hospitals, their government offices, their gas stations and Wal-Marts. Some will be cheap places to live for people who work an hour's drive away. But they had a heyday as real centers of industry, as real civilizations, the spark plugs that made the Midwest run, and that day is gone.

Muncie and Anderson lie only fourteen miles from each other in east-central Indiana, not far from Ohio. Between them, they are exemplars of the old manufacturing economy and what happened to it.

Muncie once had a General Motors transmission plant employing more than three thousand workers. It closed in 2006. So did New Venture Gear, which had twenty-five hundred jobs in 2005, but was down to four hundred jobs a year later when it, too, closed. The town's Borg-Warner auto parts maker has been downsizing for years. There's an abandoned wire-and-steel plant. Mostly, Muncie had the Ball Corporation, founded in 1887 when the five Ball brothers, who had invented a home-canning jar, arrived to be close to recently discovered fields of natural gas, which was critical to glassmaking.

For a century, the Balls dominated the town. The company expanded into aluminum cans and then into satellites. Ball philanthropies made good things happen, including Ball State University, now the town's leading employer. (The second biggest is Ball

Memorial Hospital.) Although never beautiful, Muncie was a solid, thriving place, exuding such an air of Midwestern normality that sociologists Robert and Helen Lynd picked it for their classic study of an American "Middletown."

The Balls built Muncie. They also broke ground on its grave. Much of the industrial decline has taken place in the past decade, but the corporation's decision in 1998 to move its headquarters to Boulder, Colorado, "created the biggest sucking sound you ever heard," according to Roy Budd, director of the local economic-development commission. The corporation wanted to be closer to the Air Force, its biggest customer, and its departure robbed the town of the institution that had formed its character.

Many Midwestern towns grew up around one locally owned factory, and the owners provided not only jobs but leadership. The Balls' Muncie is a prime example. Like the Maytags in Newton, the Balls played a seignorial role, lavishing their wealth on parks and playhouses, financing schools and other good works. Families like these ruled their towns, certainly, and demanded homage, but their philanthropy gave these towns both institutions and character. Over the years, though, the older generations died off, and the children, less bound to a small and gray factory town, fled to New York or California. Often the company went public (as the Ball Corporation did in 1972). In time, no family members remain: there is one elderly Ball left in Muncie. Nothing personal, neither family nor local ownership, ties the company to its town. It makes business sense to move the factory and then the headquarters to somewhere else—the manufacturing to Mexico or China, the headquarters to wherever the current CEO wants to live. And so it goes, leaving a hole where a town's heart used to be.

That's part of what happened to Muncie. The rest is the decline of Auto Alley, which stretched from Flint and Detroit in Michigan through Toledo and Dayton in Ohio and embraced the dense cluster of auto-dependent towns in Indiana, such as Muncie, Anderson, Kokomo and Marion.

In the seventies and eighties, Muncie and Anderson and the other auto cities courted investment from abroad, set up industrial parks, gave companies tax breaks to move in or stay. For a while, it worked. And now, they're paying the price. They didn't really recover: they just went into remission. Japan proved to be only a symptom of a more serious disease. Factories and towns that survived the Japanese invasion built up no antibodies against globalization. Had the old parts plants collapsed in the 1980s, Muncie would have been forced to face its future, reeducate its workforce, seek out new twenty-first-century industries. Instead, it hung on, growing weaker every year, until globalization came along and finished the job.

"Things stabilized in the nineties," Kevin Smith, the mayor of Anderson, told me. "Things began to settle down. It looked like a cyclical downturn." These auto towns had always had their ups and down, a few years of layoffs followed by a few more years of boom. That's what the eighties and nineties looked like. When the century turned and globalization hit, "People here just thought GM was mad at us and they'd come back. There was a denial that the auto industry was in a real state of change. Now people do understand."

Muncie once defined Midwestern private capitalism. Today, its biggest employers are all public institutions—Ball State, the big hospital, the school system. Borg-Warner is still there, the fourth-biggest employer, but no one will be surprised if it closes in a year or two. This, too, is part of a Midwestern pattern. In town after town, privately owned factories employing thousands of people close, leaving government, hospitals, and schools to supply jobs. Increasingly, in many towns, Wal-Mart has become the biggest private employer.

In Muncie, as jobs go, so do people. One third of the town, about thirty thousand people, have died or gone away and haven't been replaced. There are sixty thousand left now, and nearly one fifth of them live below the poverty level. Banks report a wave of property foreclosures.

After a while, a town forgets how to earn its living, just as an unemployed worker loses the skills that made him employable. I talked with an analyst who has studied these towns, including Anderson and Muncie, and he had a bleak assessment:

"There's a malaise here. A defeatist attitude. People have been so beat down by layoffs, they've lost the will. Maybe it's the Indiana attitude. I've never been anywhere that is so risk-adverse. A lot of parents just don't value education, and they've passed that on to their kids. There's a lack of leadership. Indiana people seem to be content to be mediocre people living in mediocre cities."

The fighting spirit isn't entirely gone from these old Indiana towns. They compete fiercely in basketball, and they deeply resent anything good that happens to any other town. This happened recently when Muncie had a stroke of luck. It landed a debt-management center for the Sallie Mae Corp., the big private lender. The center will provide seven hundred jobs. Granted, the pay is only $9 per hour, less than half what the old manufacturing wages in town were. But as Patrick Barkey, the Ball State professor, said, it was a boon not only for Muncie but for the region, which will supply many of those seven hundred workers.

"The trouble was, Anderson had also been trying to get this center," Barkey recalled. Many of the workers will come from Anderson, only fourteen miles away, "but when it went to Muncie, Anderson was livid. That's ridiculous."

Anderson has one thing going for it that Muncie doesn't. It is only forty-eight miles up I-69 from Indianapolis, fourteen miles closer than Muncie, and so is a plausible bedroom suburb for workers there looking for low-cost housing. Smith, the town's go-getting mayor, has been to Israel and Japan seeking investment.

But Anderson once was a GM company town, and the company is gone. In the late 1970s, Anderson had seventy thousand people and GM employed 22,000 of them—a dependence on one employer matched only by Flint, Michigan. By early 2007, that was down to 2,600 persons employed at two plants—Guide, which made headlights for GM, and Delphi, which was in bankruptcy. Then Guide closed, killing 1,325 jobs.

Anderson's total population is down from seventy thousand to fifty-eight thousand and is not falling off so much as dying off. Ten thousand residents are GM retirees, living on pensions and medical benefits, both of which GM is trying to cap or cut back. Thousands of others are surviving spouses of GM workers. The two big hospitals are major employers and will stay that way so long as the aging GM veterans stay alive. Someday, the GM retirees will be gone and so will about 20 percent of the care provided by these two hospitals.

Newton is an Iowa version of Muncie, a quintessential company town. Fred Maytag founded the Maytag Company in Newton in 1893. In a town of 15,000 the company employed 3,800 people in its downtown headquarters and in the sprawling home-appliance factory on the northeast side. Every year, Newton crowned the Maytag Queen in the Maytag Bowl at Maytag Park. Kids swam in Maytag Pool, went to schools run from offices in the old Maytag home, got Maytag scholarships if they went to college, or went to work for Maytag if they didn't. There's even a Maytag Dairy Farms making Maytag blue cheese. If there hadn't been Maytag, there wouldn't have been Newton.

Now there isn't a Maytag anymore. The family moved away long ago. After years of rumors, Whirlpool Corporation bought the Maytag brand, moved its headquarters to Benton Harbor, Michigan, and announced it would close the plant in late 2007. In the competitive global appliances market, the old plant out on North Nineteenth Street was an albatross. In a world of corporate consolidation, Whirlpool didn't need two headquarters.

Without Maytag, will Newton survive?

The mayor, Chaz Allen, is relentlessly upbeat. Newton will diversify, he says. The town has two wineries. It has a bid in for a biofuels plant. Its workers can commute to jobs with John Deere near Des Moines, or the window factories in Pella, or the Fisher Controls operation in Marshalltown. Mostly, the town counts on a new auto racetrack south of town to attract tourists, stimulate hotels and restaurants, and, with luck, create a thousand new jobs.

In her office off the town square, Kim Didier, the director of the Newton Development Corporation, talks about diversification, and the tourists who will drive up from Kansas City to see the auto races, and the companies she wants to recruit to fill the two million square feet of empty space that Maytag will leave behind. The state has offered $10 million to bribe companies to move to Newton, but what Newton really needs, she says, is money for a training center or an arts center or, especially, a mental health center, because there's a lot of depression going around just now.

Didier knows that Kalamazoo, Michigan, ignited a boom with a program to finance a four-year college education for any local high school graduate. Newton is pushing a similar program, called Newton Promise, which would spend up to $2 million per year—part privately financed, part from state and city funds—to send high school graduates to any Iowa public university or community college.

Maybe this will work, maybe it won't. But the fact is that Newton is losing more than three thousand well-paying jobs at Maytag and may gain one thousand worse-paying jobs at that racetrack. Newton's first task now is to come to terms with its new place in a new world.

"People here felt that the Maytag family always took care of them and always would do," Doug Frazer, the academic adviser at the local community college, told me. The community college will carry the burden of retraining laid-off workers, but, as Frazer said, "People come to us at age forty, for a change of direction—and they've never had to change direction in their life. People are shocked. There's a sense of betrayal. They're in denial."

Mostly, people are angry. There is anger at NAFTA, at corporations, and, more personally, at Maytag and its last CEO, an out-of-towner named Ralph Hake who spent four years in Newton, drove the factory into weakness, according to the locals, and then left town with a $10 million payoff.

Mike Blouin, the former state economic-development director, was heavily involved in enticing Maytag to stay in Newton. The state offered to build a new factory, to retrain workers, to lavish tax and energy incentives. All the incentives—bribes, really—came to $95 million. Maytag kept Iowa dangling, then cut the string and closed.

"That company decided ten years ago it was going to rape and pillage," Blouin says now. "They stopped R and D. They stopped advertising products that were made here. They planned to sell all along. The Maytag board just raped and pillaged that community."

When Newton looks at globalization, this is what it sees, and it doesn't like it.

I spent a morning with Ted Johnson, the president of the UAW local at Maytag. There was a sign on his office wall: Maytag—100 Years of Dependability. No irony intended. He was forty-four but wore a full gray beard and looked older. He was hurting, personally and for his people. He's a thoughtful man and knows that, even if a new factory opened tomorrow, it would never be the same.

Here's what Ted Johnson told me:

"My wife and I both got twenty years in at Maytag. I was a fork-truck driver for ten years there. She's a processing specialist. We could have retired at fifty-four, another ten years from now. We've got two kids still at home. I tell them about getting their education. I can't emphasize it enough. But the other side of it is, you can't afford to send them to college. We've got a small business— a tanning salon and a twenty-four-hour fitness center—but it makes about enough to pay the help.

"This factory will be empty. That [Maytag] factory in Galesburg is still empty. Nobody's coming. There's no incentive for anybody to start a factory operation in this county, because of globalization. We've got these terrific trade agreements. They open up the whole world to Third World countries with American incentives. They put impoverished workers to work, keep them impoverished, then sell the stuff back to the United States for almost the same price as if they're made here. Our government doesn't even want us to have a decent standard of living.

"What's changed? You know, you used to have CEOs that were veterans, who had fought, who had a love of their country. Now corporate America is determined only to give us the minimum. They're not lining us up and shooting at us. But they keep chipping away and chipping away at our lives."

By the time I talked with Johnson, the final layoffs had begun. Where were people going?

"Oh, they're scattered all over. Some moved. A few went to school. They're getting training assistance, with up to 104 weeks of unemployment pay. That's $380 per week, minus taxes. At the plant, they were getting $720 per week, before overtime. Can you keep up your standard of living on that? No. How long can you float before you sink? Not long. There are a lot of divorces, a lot of houses repossessed.

"These are working people here, and working people always wait until the end to ask for help, and then they find it's not there.

"You know, the Maytag workforce used to be the best of the best. But it was hard. Our line pace was 4.5 miles per hour, the fastest in the nation. There were a lot of injuries. Carpal tunnel. Shoulders are shot. Truthfully, older workers don't want to go back into the factory. A lot of people at Maytag, they had two-year degrees, but they couldn't find work in their fields. They would have found it if it had been there. Do you think they laid awake nights in their teens, dreaming about driving ten thousand screws a day?

"I don't want to move away. But I never went through anything like this. I'm older, too, you know. I had back surgery and shoulder surgery. I'm not what I was."

I had never thought about it this way. Not many desk workers with a sit-down job do. At age forty-four, Ted Johnson was wearing out, and he can't afford to wear out. After twenty years, workers don't mind leaving the factory and getting another job with less physical punishment. But they also have mortgages, families, children that they desperately hope will get an education and a better life. The old jobs in factories such as Maytag paid these bills. The new jobs at the racetrack won't.

There has to be a better way of living and working than in the heavy manufacturing that has supported the Midwest and its people for a century. Where is it, and will it support a town and a civilization like Newton? The information economy, with its knowledge jobs, is supposed to be the future. This future hasn't arrived yet.

Michigan's Austin, in a draft paper on the Midwest for the Brookings Institution, talked at length about the culture and mind-set of these old industrial towns and why they and their industries have such a hard time coming to terms.

What we have, Austin said, is "a pattern of development that supported a large number of populous cities scattered through the region that the current economic forces of [concentration] can't sustain." This pattern has saddled the Midwest with "legacy costs," he said—not only the heavy pension and health costs that are crippling the big companies, but a legacy of old houses, decrepit downtowns, aging infrastructure, and out-of-date governments.

A century after the Balls and Maytags invented these towns, "what was once the most dynamic innovative economy in the country is now a change-averse economic culture—low entrepreneurship and sticky attitudes of entitlement and belief that 'things should stay as they were.'" It was a "paternalistic" culture, with a few wealthy companies at the top and a mass of comfortable workers at the bottom. Periodic layoffs were part of this world, but no downturn lasted forever. Education wasn't necessary to work the lines that would provide a life's work; today's parents have a hard time seeing why their children need the education that no one needed before.

This adds up to low ambition and low innovation. Neither ambition nor innovation has been needed for a century. Now they are crucial, and no one knows where to find them.

In this bleak industrial landscape, not all hope is gone. Some towns remain successful because old families and old corporations stick with them, identifying with their communities and their people. Pella, Iowa, sparkles behind the backing of two major corporations, a window maker and a farm-equipment manufacturer. Columbus, Indiana, is an amazing mecca of fine architecture because of the vision and support of its biggest employer, Cummins Inc., which makes diesel engines, and its late chairman, J. Irwin Miller. About sixty years ago, Cummins offered to pay the architect's fee on any building, public or private, if the owner picked an architect from Miller's list. That list included Eero and Eliel Saarinen, I. M. Pei, César Pelli, and other international superstars. The result, in a town of forty thousand people, is a veritable living museum of sixty dazzling buildings, including six National Historic Landmarks.

Kalamazoo, Michigan, was reeling after plant closings by major employers such as General Motors and Upjohn Corp. Like Newton, it faced a Rust Belt future. Then the school system announced the Kalamazoo Promise, the program that Newton hopes to copy:

anonymous local donors offered to pay full tuition to any Michigan public college or university for all graduates of the local high school. The donors remain officially anonymous, although they appear to be led by the Stryker family, founders of a medical-devices manufacturer that has stuck with the city. The first result of the Kalamazoo Promise has been a housing boom, as parents who had moved out of a crumbling town decided to return to get their children into local schools. The housing boom seems likely to lead to new stores and other economic activity. Newton, as we saw, wants to copy this program, although it would mix private and public funds.

I found hope in two other towns. One was Warsaw, Indiana, which can claim to be the orthopedics capital of the world. The other was Greenville, Michigan, an example of old-style manufacturing that seems to be reviving through new-style manufacturing.

Greenville certainly looked like one of globalization's casualties on the day that I drove there to attend what most people felt was the town's economic funeral. Until that day, Greenville had been home to the world's largest refrigerator plant. A local man named Gibson first made wooden iceboxes there more than a century ago. Under its last owner, Electrolux, the Swedish giant, the plant's 2,781 workers turned out Frigidaires, Kelvinators, Kenmores, White-Westinghouses—some of the world's best-known brands. Now it was closing. From now on, those brands would be made at an Electrolux plant across the Mexican border in Juárez.

For Greenville, Electrolux was only the latest blow. Country Roads, which made auto seats, is closed: a sign outside the vacant factory reads Out of Job Will Work for Community Relief. The local plant of Tower Automotive, another global corporation founded in Greenville, already was down from 450 to 235 workers. Just one week before the Electrolux plant closed, Tower also announced it would shut down at year's end. Federal Mogul, a stamping plant down to two hundred workers, had filed for bankruptcy. Greenville, a town of eight thousand people, had lost more than three thousand jobs, virtually overnight. The biggest employers left were the hospital, the prison, and Wal-Mart.

Greenville not only looks like so many other Midwestern man-ufacturing towns. What happened to it echoed the news from sim-ilar towns across the region.

Once, the Electrolux factory on South Charles Street was owned and run by people who lived in Greenville and worked upstairs over the shop. At the end, it was part of a global empire, headquar-tered in Sweden but answerable to global markets. In 2003 the Electrolux CEO, Hans Straberg, told financial analysts that he could save $81 million per year by moving the Greenville opera-tions to Mexico. Unions in Greenville, especially the United Auto Workers, offered $32 million in annual wage concessions, with some workers agreeing to take a one-third wage cut. The town agreed to build Electrolux a brand-new factory. The town and the state promised a twenty-year tax holiday. Altogether, Greenville and its people came up with a package of $74.3 million in annual savings—on top of $8.7 million that Michigan had already given Electrolux for infrastructure and job training in the previous twelve years.

Nobody in Greenville thinks Electrolux was bargaining in good faith. "They said they didn't want to leave and all Greenville had to do was come close" is the verdict of George Bosanic, the energetic city manager whose job is to save the town. "When we did come close, the company balked. They intended all the while to leave."

Whatever the company's intentions were, the $74.3 million wasn't enough. Electrolux pulled the plug and the plant closed. More than two thousand jobs, paying an average of $22.99 per hour in wages and benefits, moved to Mexico, where the same package works out to $3.65 per hour.

Fewer than one half the workers were still on the job when the last refrigerator came down the line at the old plant and was shipped off to the local historical-society museum. In three layoffs over the previous six months, about sixteen hundred had lost their jobs, leaving eleven hundred to turn out the lights.

On the day the plant closed, workers finished their last shift and then, without ceremony or much of a look back, wandered over to the UAW hall across the street to the big, bare assembly room. There were plenty of free cookies and doughnuts and a lot of brochures on health coverage, pensions, and available benefits. One offered a glossary of benefit terms. Another was entitled "Need Help Paying for Medicine?" Flags and God Bless America signs adorned the hall. Lola Warren had come from the state unemployment office in Grand Rapids to tell the workers how to claim their benefits. The workers picked up the brochures, listened to Warren, watched her PowerPoints, asked few questions.

It was a somber, unemotional scene. This day had been coming for two years, and no one had much emotion left. The town government considered holding a ceremony to mark the big plant's closing, then decided against it.

I talked with some of the workers. Gilbert Jewell was fifty-four, with thirty-two years in at Electrolux. Steve Hammond had worked there twenty-seven years. Roger Richardson, at fifty-eight, had started building refrigerators forty years ago, then drove a truck, then came back to refrigerators. All said they planned to go back to school, "to be an electrician or something."

Maybe they will. Probably not. The state offers retraining and funds college courses. But fewer than one third of laid-off workers take the retraining available to them, and the Greenville workers are probably no different. First, no one knows what will be available: a fifty-five-year-old factory hand is not going to be retrained as a dental technician. Second, the dirty little secret of Midwestern manufacturing is that many workers are high school dropouts, uneducated, some virtually illiterate. They could build refrigerators, sure. But they are totally unqualified for any job other than the ones they just lost.

John Kreucher, a Michigan AFL-CIO officer, drove over from Lansing to offer advice and, in general, hold the workers' hands. "I've been closing plants for sixteen years," he told me at the union hall that day. "Most of these people, only a small percentage will take advantage of retraining. Mostly, they'll just disappear. They'll get a job with their in-laws, or something. They'll never find anything with benefits. Look, most of them have trouble reading or adding up a checkbook, but you can't bring them to the table to admit that they have trouble with this. The high-tech industry hasn't been invented that would employ them.

"It's the turn of the century, man," John Kreucher said. "Everything's changing."

As the end loomed, the local newspaper ran an editorial blasting NAFTA in general and Mexico in particular. On the same day, Mexican president Vicente Fox, in an interview in *Time*, lamented the departure of two hundred thousand Mexican jobs—to China.

In Greenville, no one could see beyond NAFTA. "It's all NAFTA," Gilbert Jewell said. "The first problem is letting foreign companies buy factories in the United States. The way things are going, places like Mexico and Japan are going to be ahead of us. We're going to be a Third World country."

"NAFTA is a hot issue," said Jim Hoisington, the local UAW president. "I feel betrayed by our own government. Employers want to be able to exploit people. Before, they couldn't do it in this country. They couldn't leave. Now Bush makes it possible."

This anti-NAFTA theme resonated in all the old manufacturing towns around the Midwest. China, being so far away, barely registers. Workers aren't dumb—they know something is happening to their lives—but the complexities of global finance are too deep to fathom. So workers and union leaders focus on Mexico and NAFTA and on George W. Bush, even though the NAFTA treaty was negotiated and signed by Bill Clinton.

Hoisington, like other labor leaders, wonder why business leaders aren't leading the demands for a national health system. At the Greenville plant alone, Electrolux paid $42 million per year for health care, $28 million for retirees and $14 million for active workers. "That's a big issue why corporations are leaving this country," Hoisington told me. "We've asked CEOs to help us lobby for health care reform." Any luck? "Not much."

When a town's economic heart fails, the rest begins to atrophy. Mike Huckleberry, proprietor of Greenville's most popular bar and restaurant, sat in his front window and pointed at vacant storefronts up and down Lafayette Street, the main street. "That's closed," he said, "and that's closed. And I'm down. I make my living off people who have jobs. I'm down from thirty employees to nineteen, and I don't know where the bottom is."

Huckleberry ran unsuccessfully for Congress as a Democrat, on an anti-NAFTA platform. He also started a Comedy Night, advertised with signs arguing Greenville Needs a Good Laugh. On the night before the factory closing, the place was packed to hear an imported comedian tell off-color jokes. Everyone laughed, but, as Huckleberry admitted, none of his customers worked at Electrolux. It wasn't that they didn't want to come. They couldn't afford it.

But since that day, Greenville has begun to revive. The Electrolux closure generated a lot of media coverage. Everybody knew that Greenville wanted new industry. One Michigan-based company named United Solar Ovonic took a look and decided to invest. The company plans to build at least six plants in Greenville to build solar panels. Each plant will cost $120 million and will employ two hundred people. The first plants are under construction and all six are to be online by 2010.

This means at least twelve hundred new jobs—maybe more, if United Solar Ovonic keeps growing. That doesn't replace the twenty-seven hundred jobs lost at Electrolux, but it's a start, a glimmer of hope, in a town that had lost all hope. Some of these jobs will go to the Electrolux workers, but most will probably not. Many of these workers don't have the education—a two-year college degree at least—to qualify for these jobs. About twelve hundred of them are taking advantage of retraining programs, at the local community college and elsewhere. But local officials say they just don't know how many of the handful of new hires so far at the solar panel plant used to work at Electrolux.

The town still is hurting. The last time I talked with him, Mike Huckleberry had had to fire seven of his restaurant's remaining nineteen workers.

Greenville will survive. The town may shrink. More residents will commute to Grand Rapids. But some jobs will remain, and for a change, this will be in an industry with a future.

On the very day the factory closed, President Bush visited Hyderabad, a high-tech center on the other side of the world, in India, and talked about globalization. "People do lose jobs as a result of globalization, and it's painful for those who lose jobs," Bush said. "How does a government or a society react to that? Losing jobs is painful, so let's make sure people are educated so they can find—fill the jobs of the twenty-first century. And let's make sure there are pro-growth policies in place. What does that mean? That means low taxes, it means less regulation, it means fewer lawsuits, it means wise energy policy."

The president was right about education. Those new jobs in Greenville will go to workers with a solid education, not many of whom worked at Electrolux. But if anyone in Muncie or Newton or Greenville thought their problems had anything to do with taxes or lawsuits, they never mentioned it to me. The unemployed workers are simplistic, certainly, in blaming everything on NAFTA. But they are not helped by a simplistic president who thinks that fewer regulations or lawsuits are going to restore a way of life to people— middle-class, middle-aged, Middle Western—who put in a lifetime making good refrigerators and now face an old age on the dole.

Education is also the vital ingredient in Warsaw, an astonishing little town in northern Indiana that thrives by doing what it's always done, and doing it better than anyone else in the world. Warsaw, with 12,500 people, rules the world of orthopedics. If you have an artificial hip or artificial knee, chances are it came from Warsaw. So probably did the tools that were used in the operation. Your surgeon probably spent some time in Warsaw, learning how to use those tools.

Warsaw is an example of "clustering." This happens when a number of companies in the same line of business set up shop in the same area. Technically competitors, these companies create a critical mass of expertise and ideas. Employees and executives from the different companies live next door to each other or chat at the grocery store or golf course. Mostly, it becomes easy to hire engineers and experts from outside because they know that, if the job doesn't work out, there are plenty of other employers in town. Silicon Valley fills this role in computers. For decades, the Midwest was a supercluster of auto companies.

Warsaw began with a natural advantage and a bright idea. The founding father, Revra DePuy, invented a wooden splint for broken bones in western Michigan. Western Michigan had heavy forests in those days—the reason it once reigned as the furniture center of

America—but so did northern Indiana, so DePuy moved to Warsaw in 1895 and founded the DePuy Manufacturing Company. Justin Zimmer, hired in 1905, became DePuy's star salesman before he broke away in 1927 to start his own company. In 1977, Dane Miller left Zimmer to help set up Biomet. The three companies—DePuy, Zimmer, and Biomet—remain orthopedics giants to this day. (The other two big companies in the field, Medtronics in Minneapolis and Stryker in Kalamazoo, are also Midwest-based.) DePuy is owned by Johnson & Johnson, but its headquarters remain in Warsaw. The other two are still locally owned. The cluster inspires spin-offs of orthopedic or support companies because the town is loaded with the expertise that such companies need.

Warsaw is prosperous and looks it, with modern buildings, good neighborhoods, and a lively downtown. The industry supports some six thousand direct jobs, plus service jobs in companies such as an executive search firm that specializes in orthopedic expertise. More than a hundred Ph.D.'s live in Warsaw; most of them, like the company executives, moved there from somewhere else. But most of the workers grew up in Warsaw, and the local high school offers vocational instruction in orthopedics. The companies prefer to do most of their own advanced training. In this business, ordinary employees must know how to read blueprints and program machines with great precision, because what they make ends up in the human body.

Warsaw has only 12,500 people, but its county has seventy-five thousand, and an amazing range of businesses—the world's largest duck processor, two big egg processors, a cereal mill, and a big printing plant. Lakes dot the county, and $2 million homes are not uncommon.

The near future looks great, the more remote future more uncertain. A generation of baby boomers is getting old. Most spent the past forty years jogging, and their knees are shot. In Warsaw, that's good news. These aging jocks will need all the artificial joints that Warsaw can turn out. Zimmer alone plans to add one hundred thousand square feet in research labs, plus four hundred new workers.

But there's a cloud on Warsaw's future and it's called biological regeneration. People need new knees and hips because their tendons and cartilage wear out. New techniques, some of them the result of stem cell research, may make it possible to repair and preserve this tissue, making joint replacement unnecessary. This could make Warsaw's economic engine as obsolete as the tintype.

The orthopedic companies know this is coming and are investing in tissue research, to stay ahead of the game. But no one knows what this will do to the operations of the companies and the people who work there. Ivy Tech, the Indiana vocational college system, is training biotech students today, to be ready for the industry of the future, but it's still a future that can only dimly be seen.

Is there a future at all for these Midwestern manufacturing towns and cities? A few will cope or even thrive, by excelling at one big thing, like Warsaw, or finding something new to do, like Greenville. Otherwise, the Midwestern landscape is littered with these civic relics, no longer working towns, not quite ghost towns, little civilizations that existed to meet the economic needs of a vanished era.

CHAPTER 5

Mega-Farmers

At sixty-nine, Melvin Stucke looks exactly like what he is—a typical American family farmer. But the typical American family farm these days is not what most Americans think it is.

Most people carry in their heads a romantic old image of farmers and the pastoral life. They picture humble plowmen tending a few hundred acres, most planted in corn or soybeans, with pasture for grazing cattle and a farmhouse next to a chicken coop and a pigsty. The hogs spend most of their day wallowing happily in the mud, while the chickens roam the farmyard, hunting seed and hoping they don't get grabbed for the evening supper. In this picture, the farmer and his wife work day and night, slopping the hogs and collecting the eggs in the morning, plowing the fields and reaping the crops by day, milking the cows by night. It's an early-to-bed-early-to-rise existence, enforced by the crowing of a rooster at daybreak. Once a week, they go to the nearest farm town to sell some produce, buy clothes, see friends, perhaps check in with their banker or the doctor.

These farmers were generalists, raising both crops and livestock, growing some of their own food, selling their produce on local markets. Few exist anymore. Today's farmers—both the very big ones and the very small ones—are specialists.

And Melvin Stucke is a specialist. On his farm near Versailles, in western Ohio north of Dayton, Stucke specializes in eggs—a whole lot of eggs. In two henhouses each longer than a football field, Stucke keeps 180,000 chickens. Each day these hens lay 165,000 eggs. The eggs are packed into giant cases—460 of them every day—and shipped to a cracking plant at one of the Midwest's mammoth egg companies. At the cracking plant, the eggs are cracked and poured into huge vats of liquid egg. Sometimes, the plants separate the whites from the yolks. The vats go to restaurants, especially fast-food places, where cooks can spend a lifetime making omelets without ever breaking an egg.

Each henhouse holds ninety thousand hens. You've never heard noise until you've been in the same room with that many chickens. The henhouse is 450 feet long and contains six narrow aisles. Each aisle is lined with four tiers of cages. Each cage is sixteen by twenty inches. Each holds six three-pound hens. Each hen spends her life in that cage, doing what hens are programmed to do, which is to lay eggs. It is an animal rights activist's vision of hell.

Each hen lays between five and six eggs a week, on average. The cages are slightly tilted, so the eggs, once laid, roll gently downhill onto a conveyor belt running the length of the henhouse. The belt carries them in a never-ending stream to packers filling those giant cases. I watched for a time and never saw a cracked egg.

These hens, like Stucke, are specialists. No roosters live on this farm. Not one of these hens will ever lay a fertilized egg that will hatch a chick. Nor will they end up on someone's plate. Other farms breed roasters or fryers with lots of the white breast meat that Americans love. Stucke's hens are slimmer, bred for their jobs. When Stucke's hens stop laying, they are slaughtered and become dog food.

Stucke is a "mega-farmer," which is what makes him typical. In the era of globalized agriculture, any American farmer who wants to survive has to be a mega-farmer—specializing in one branch of farming, such as eggs or hogs, or tilling vast spreads of land, two thousand acres or more. Each deals with giant global corporations under contracts that dictate not only price but almost every stage of the growing process.

Farming differs from state to state across the Midwest. Iowa grows more hogs, Minnesota breeds more turkeys, Wisconsin and Indiana milk more cows. But the globalization of farming affects them all, no matter what animals or crops they raise.

In this era of industrial farming, Stucke says he is actually a relatively small player, and more independent than most. Some egg farms have five million birds or more. A handful of companies, such as Cal-Main Foods and Rose Acre Farms, dominate the industry. Usually, these companies own the hens and provide the feed, insecticides, and other inputs. The farmer owns his land and has to build the henhouses and other facilities. The companies dictate how the chickens are to be housed and fed. In exchange, they agree to buy all the eggs at a fixed price for the term of the contract.

Stucke used to have a contract like this, with an Indiana firm called Midwest Poultry, and would like to do it again. "I'm totally dependent on the health of these birds," he said. "It's better to have a contract where somebody else owns the birds. Independence is nice, but it's a case of necessity from a risk point of view."

For the moment, the only contract Stucke has is to sell his eggs to nearby Cooper Farms. Stucke took out a $400,000 loan to buy all his own chicks, feed, and fuel. When I visited him, he was about halfway through the 110-week contract with Cooper Farms and was nearly ready to pay off the loan and start making some money.

For each dozen eggs, Stucke will net five cents—not much on a carton that will cost you $1.50 or so in a grocery store. But at 13,750 cartons per day, these nickels add up.

They add up in two ways. First, unlike most Midwestern farmers, Stucke is still in business. If mega-farming takes the romance out of farming, it lets surviving farmers keep their farms. Secondly, it clearly provides a good living. Stucke farms with his son, Mark, and his son-in-law, Luke Osterloh. Between them, they also till three thousand acres and raise cattle—steers, no cows. The families live near one another in graceful farmhouses. Millions of dollars in equipment keep the farm going: each henhouse alone costs nearly $1 million, and the six tractors can drink more than $1,000 in diesel fuel every day they are in the fields. The land itself is worth some $15 million.

In a mechanized and globalized world, efficiency rules and sheer size pays off. Thus is farming transformed. The reaping of crops and the raising of livestock are here to stay: land and climate aren't portable. But farms have become factories, and farmers have, increasingly, become little more than employees of the big agribusiness corporations, which in turn sell to giant supermarket chains.

William Heffernan, a rural sociologist at the University of Missouri, calls this an agricultural hourglass, "with thousands of farmers producing the farm products which pass through a relatively few processing firms before becoming available to millions of consumers."

Many critics rail against "corporate farms," as though corporations owned the farms. This is the wrong idea. Corporations control but do not own. Most farms are still owned by farm families, but these families work for corporations. In other words, ownership may be personal but control is corporate. As Drake University economist Neil D. Hamilton put it, "Why own the farm when you can own the farmers?"

What does this have to do with globalization? Just this—globalization has taken a century-long trend and thrown it into high gear.

Like most of the changes transforming the Midwest, this one didn't happen overnight. Technology—the steel plow, the railroad—defined and shaped the Midwest and its farming 150 years ago. Over the decades, the development of hybrid seeds, commercial fertilizer, chemicals, and modern equipment made it possible for each farmer to farm more acreage, leading to consolidation of land. For decades, giant corporations such as Cargill have amassed ever more market power. For thirty years or more, the raising of poultry and livestock has moved indoors, with cattle, hogs, chickens, and turkeys bred in confinement, a capital-intensive process that forced farmers to limit their risk by striking deals with corporations.

Now comes globalization, which is doing to farming exactly what it has done to manufacturing. It pits American farmers, tilling high-priced land in an economic and social framework that was formed in the nineteenth century, against farmers in places like Brazil, creating their own twenty-first century structure out of cheap virgin land. It demands the lowest possible cost. It outsources everything that can be outsourced.

In our mythology, we consider farming different from manufacturing, corn different from cars, cattle different from TV sets, eggs different from computer chips. They aren't. Globalization treats them all the same.

In Brazil and other competing Third World countries, everything—farm labor, land, shipping, processing—costs less than it does in the Midwest. Midwestern farmers can still compete for American markets, but their high costs hobble them in the vast and growing world markets outside the United States. This is crucial. Globalization is pulling millions of people, mostly in China and India, out of deep, grinding poverty and starvation. The first thing that happens when regions become prosperous is that people eat more meat. When meat consumption shoots up, so does the demand for feed grains for livestock. The Midwest grows feed grains for a living but faces increasing competition from Brazil and other countries, especially in soybeans. Some soybean farmers have actually emigrated from Iowa and Minnesota, where land prices are high, to Brazil, where land prices are lower and processing cheaper.

This revolution promises to be good for global agriculture, but Midwestern farmers may already have been priced out of this market.

To compete anywhere, Midwestern farmers need to be highly efficient and highly mechanized. This means huge investments, millions of dollars, both in equipment and in vast tracts of land to make maximum use of this equipment. No small farmer can afford this: instead, he sells out to the mega-farmer next door, making that mega-farm even bigger.

There were 3 million American farms in 1970; now there are about 2.15 million, possibly fewer. About five hundred thousand of them are in the Midwest, half as many as there were forty years ago. This sounds like a lot of farms, but 1.8 million of the 2.15 million bring in less than $100,000 per year in total sales, with an average income of only $20,000. Some tiny producers become successful "niche farms," selling ostrich meat or gourmet cheese by direct mail, striking contracts with city restaurants, or displaying in farmers' markets. Mostly, they are hobby farms for retirees or for workers who like to live in the countryside but work in town.

Another two hundred thousand farms are called intermediate farms, with total sales between $100,000 and $250,000; they average about $40,000 per year in net income. These are the endangered farms, the disappearing farms, too big to be hobbies, too small to compete in today's global market. People try to live off them. Increasingly, they can't.

At the top are "commercial farms," the mega-farms and their smaller cousins, all bigger than a thousand acres, some much bigger than that. They have average annual sales of at least $250,000, usually much more; the average big commercial farmer works sixteen hundred acres and produces nearly $700,000 per year. There are about 146,000 of these commercial farms, and about one third of them—the truly big farmers—have annual profits of $200,000 or more. Nationwide, commercial farms account for only 8 percent of all farms; in the Midwest, it's 11 percent. Together, they produce 68 percent of all U.S. farm output.

In Iowa, from 1987 to 1997, small farms under one hundred acres increased their sales by 18 percent; big farms increased their sales by 71 percent; farms in the middle saw sales fall, by no less than 29 percent. In short, American farming is doing fine but many American farmers aren't.

These farmers in the middle are going out of business. In Iowa, the number of medium-size farms fell by 23 percent between 1987 and 1997, and the trend is continuing. Between 1997 and 2002, the number of American farms larger than five thousand acres grew by 7 percent; in Iowa, they grew by 75 percent.

There are reasons for this. One is the federal farm-subsidy program. The program began in the 1930s, to provide a safety net for farmers trapped in the Depression. The subsidies were intended to smooth out market fluctuations and, especially, to keep small farmers in business. They failed. Commercial farms, barely 8 percent of the total, got 51 percent of all subsidies in 2003. In Iowa, the nine biggest farms got an average of $200,000 or more from 1995 to 2003. This makes the rich richer, in two ways. First, this capitalization shoves up the price of farmland. Second, and more important, it gives big farmers extra money to buy out their smaller neighbors. If the federal government wanted to speed up consolidation and mega-farming, it could not have found a better vehicle.

A second, bigger reason is globalization and the growth of global corporations. Some of the biggest global corporations, such as Cargill and Nestlé, are in the food business. Increasingly, they stand at both ends of William Heffernan's hourglass.

As farms get bigger, the corporations do, too, and no wonder. Mega-farms need massive amounts of equipment, seeds, feed, fertilizers, and other supplies. The big firms can supply them, faster and cheaper than any Main Street store in the county seat. The corporations deal in ever more massive amounts of grain, beef, pork, eggs, and poultry. Only the mega-farms can meet their demand for efficiency, on-time delivery, and standardized quality. As the *Des Moines Register* wrote, "Companies such as Cargill Inc. can call a farmer, order 20,000 bushels of newly-harvested corn and get it overnight. The processor gets the grain it needs to keep its plant running, and the farmer is paid a premium."

One result: no mega-farmer buys locally anymore. Another result: no corporation buys from small farmers anymore. The end result: farms get bigger and a few big corporations absolutely dominate American farming. They are most dominant in livestock, but they're growing stronger in grain, too.

Missouri's Heffernan has figured out the power of the four biggest corporations in each farm market. You'll notice that the same names keep popping up.

Among beef packers, Tyson, Cargill, Swift, and National Beef Packing Co. control 83.5 percent of the market. (In 1990, it was 72 percent.) Among pork packers, Smithfield, Tyson, Swift, and Hormel control 64 percent of the market. (In 1990, 40 percent.) Cargill ranks fifth. Among hog producers, Smithfield, Premium Standard Farms, Seaboard, and Prestage Farms control 49 percent of the market. Among producers of broiler chickens, Tyson, Pilgrim's Pride, Gold Kist, and Perdue control 56 percent of the market. Among turkey packers, Cargill, Hormel, ConAgra, and Carolina control 51 percent of the market.

Cargill, Archer Daniels Midland (ADM), ConAgra, and Cereal Food Processor control 63 percent of flour processing. Three companies—ADM, Bunge, and Cargill, have 71 percent of the soybean-crushing market. Four companies (Bunge, Cargill, ADM, and ConAgra) control 57 percent of dry-corn milling. Cargill and ADM, along with A. E. Staley and CPC, control 74 percent of wet-corn milling.

Internationally, the same companies dominate. Cargill, ADM, and Zen-Noh together control 81 percent of American corn exports and 65 percent of U.S. soybean exports. In Brazil, the new frontier of global agriculture, ADM, Cargill, and Bunge have 64 percent of the soybean-oil processing, even though none is a Brazilian company. Monsanto controls 90 percent of the country's transgenic (genetic modification) market. Cargill and Bunge dominate its fertilizer market.

Cargill is an economy all by itself. It accounts for 42 percent of all U.S. corn exports, is one of America's top three beef producers, and has the largest terminal capacity of any American company. It owns and runs a worldwide transportation business, with ships, trucks, barges, and railcars. It owns grain elevators. It owns a company that makes plastics from plant-based sugar. According to its Web site, it is an investor, broker, banker, and insurance salesman. As one of its corporate brochures put it:

"We are the flour in your bread, the wheat in your noodles, the salt on your fries. We are the corn in your tortillas, the chocolate in your dessert, the sweetener in your soft drink. We are the oil in your salad dressing and the beef, pork or chicken you eat for dinner. We are the cotton in your clothing, the backing on your carpet and the fertilizer in your field."

This is dominance, any way you cut it. Any farmer who wants to sell his produce knows that, whatever he's selling, there are four big buyers who own half to four fifths of the market and can dictate the price he gets. The same farmer knows that, when it comes time to buy the seeds and other supplies that he needs, the same companies are in control and can dictate the price he pays.

Monsanto and Pioneer, which is owned by Du Pont, control 60 percent of the American corn and soybean seed market. Mosaic, a company created by Cargill and ICM, sells 50 to 60 percent of fertilizer in the United States.

Eventually, much of this produce gets sold to consumers. Here again, dominance is the name of the game. Wal-Mart is the world's biggest supermarket, by a sizable margin in the United States and by an overwhelming margin in the world. In 2004, the five biggest supermarket chains controlled 46 percent of the market. Wal-Mart ranked first, with annual sales of $66 billion, followed by Kroger with $46 billion. Albertsons, Safeway, and the U.S. arm of the Dutch-owned Ahold finished the list. In the world, Wal-Mart reported $244 billion in annual sales in 2004, more than the next four chains combined.

The major suppliers to these giant supermarkets are none other than the giant processors—the Cargills and Tysons. This makes sense, because some 50 to 75 percent of net profits for these supermarkets come not from food sales but from retailer fees. These are the fees—for display and presentation—that supermarkets charge food companies just to put their wares on the shelves. Few small processors can afford these charges, so are beat before they start.

Here, then, is the new shape of food and farming, in the Midwest and the world. An egg company like Rose Acre signs a contract with a farmer like Melvin Stucke. Rose Acre, like Cargill or Tyson, is known in the business as an integrator, a company that controls all the links in the supply chain, from the artificial insemination that produced the chick to the placing of a dozen eggs on a supermarket shelf. Rose Acre supplies the chicks, feed, medicine, and pesticides and agrees to buy the eggs at a set price. The farmer builds the henhouse and acts as caretaker for Rose Acre's hens. Rose Acre packages the eggs, either in cartons or in liquid or dried form. Being a megafirm, it can afford to buy shelf space in Wal-Mart and other supermarkets.

The same process dominates hog farming in the Midwest. I drove around Iowa for two weeks and never saw a pig. But I certainly smelled them, every time I passed one of the long, low sheds where hogs are raised these days. Again, the integrator—the global firm—often controls every step. Some hog farmers raise tens of thousands of hogs at one time and are powers in the industry. But about half are small farmers who are little more than janitors, employed by the integrators.

Smaller operators raise an average of 2,000 hogs at one time. By contrast, one big farmer in North Carolina keeps 260,000 hogs. During their brief lives, all these animals are confined in the long, low sheds, raised on a standardized diet, By the time a hog is about forty weeks old, it has reached its desired weight, about 240 to 270 pounds, and is shipped to one of the giant slaughterhouses, almost all owned by integrators like Hormel or Cargill.

Over the years, hog farms have become bigger and fewer. There are now more than one thousand farms in the Midwest with five thousand or more hogs apiece. Small operations, with less than five thousand hogs, remain more typical, especially in Iowa. But almost all operate under a contract with Cargill or one of the other big corporations.

As Roger McEowen, an agricultural law professor at Iowa State, explains, it's a highly unequal contract. The integrator, a global firm, is looking for lowest cost and surest supply, to feed its unending food chain. The farmer often is not rich himself, possibly farming eighty acres or so, and is willing to do anything to hold on to his farm.

Under the contract, the farmer owns nothing but the hog house, having borrowed to build it according to the firm's specifications. The firm owns the swine-breeding operation, which produces the piglets, usually through artificial insemination. It provides the pigs, feed, and medicines and pays the veterinary bills. The farmer feeds the pigs and, twice a year, gets a paycheck. He gets to keep his farm but in exchange is utterly dependent on the corporation, which can cancel the contract, leaving the farmer with nothing but the bank debt on his hog house.

The loss of independence is, for most farmers, a price worth paying. It's important to remember that modern farmers, like factory workers anywhere, depend on regular income. True, big corporations have been known to break contracts arbitrarily. But for most farmers, the tie to the corporation makes life more predictable. The farmers know that the contracts, plus insurance, protect them from vagaries, such as weather or price fluctuations, that have driven earlier generations of farmers into bankruptcy. They still owe their soul to the bank, but they know that, at the end of the year, the paycheck will be big enough to pay off the loans. As with Melvin Stucke, the corporate tie enables them to stay on the farm.

As the hog farms grow bigger, they also grow smellier. Basically, these farms are just big sheds packed tight with hogs. Manure falls through slats into manure pits underneath. Fans pump the smell into the air outside. When the wind is right, the stench travels for miles. Small towns have banded together to keep hog farms from locating nearby. Health advocates claim the odor and pollution spread disease. Environmental groups fight to ban farms or pass legislation controlling their size and location. The disposal of manure is a big problem. Once, farms that raised a few hogs also grew crops, and the manure was used to fertilize the fields. Now a farmer usually does nothing but raise hogs, and state regulatory agencies fight running battles with farmers to keep the manure under control.

The same process—contract farming controlled by the integrating corporations—dominates the raising of chickens and, to a lesser degree, cattle. So far, farmers who raise corn or soybeans have more independence, but corporate control looms on their horizon, too.

I visited one of these macrofarmers, Ash Kading, growing corn and soybeans on a vast spread near Greenfield, Iowa. He is a young man, a graduate of Iowa State, educated and worldly, a big businessman whose business suit is blue jeans and whose limo is a pickup truck. Ash Kading's family history is almost a template for the history of Midwest farming.

With his father and brother, Kading farms ten thousand acres in Adair County, southwest of Des Moines. Ash, only thirty, is the seventh generation of Kadings to farm in the area.

"These big farms didn't start yesterday," Ash says. "My family came over from Germany in the 1880s. They started with small farms and big families, but when they started having smaller families, they were able to concentrate ownership. My great-grandfather, there were nine kids, with four boys. They were very poor and they all farmed. But my grandfather had one boy and three girls, and my father was the farmer. His brother had three boys and they all left. Another brother had one boy."

The same pattern held all over the Midwest. With each generation, families had fewer children, farming became more expensive, and fewer sons wanted to be farmers. And with every generation, the size of the remaining farms doubled.

"My grandfather retired with one thousand acres. It was the biggest farm in the township. This was in 1970. My dad was up to four thousand acres by 1997, when I came back from Iowa State. We're ten thousand acres now. Several people in the northern part of the county farm six thousand acres.

"A lot of people are nostalgic about the good old days on the farm. Well, those good old days didn't happen. Out of my high school class, there were ten guys who grew up on farms, and only two of them wanted to be farmers themselves."

This is the way the farms grow. A young man who wants to stay on the farm buys out his relatives, or his neighbors, who want the life in town, or who can't make a living. Often, farmers who sell out stay on as tenants or hired hands on the land they used to own. This is farming as big business. The Kadings have seven full-time employees and millions of dollars in equipment. They also are big beneficiaries of the federal government's crop-subsidy program—about $200,000 per year on average, going up to $500,000 in 2005, "an abnormally high year."

Despite this, Kading has nothing but scorn for the subsidies, because it gives the Department of Agriculture the right to tell him what to plant and where to plant it. "The only purpose is conservation, so you can have more pheasants and deer." He clearly doesn't think much of pheasants and deer, or of the people who would tramp across a farmer's land to hunt them.

Kading says he would gladly give up his subsidies. "On a ten-thousand-acre farm, losing two hundred thousand dollars hurts, but it's not that serious." Small farmers, though, need the subsidies, he says, if only to stay independent. While critics of the subsidy program say it gives big farmers the money to buy out their neighbors and become even bigger, Kading maintains that getting rid of the subsidies would drive down the price of farmland, which would make it easier for big farmers to buy out their neighbors and become even bigger. Either way, the era of mega-farms seems here to stay.

For these mega-farmers, the traditional life on a Midwestern farm is long gone. Once, farmers raised both crops and livestock. It was all-day, all-year labor. It was a hard life. Crops needed to be tended in season, but the pigs needed to be fed and the cows needed to be milked every day. There was no such thing as a day off.

No more. As Kading explains, a farmer who tilled 160 acres needed to raise both crops and livestock to make ends meet. A farmer who tills 2,000 acres has neither the time nor the need to raise hogs or cows or chickens. Instead, he specializes in one or two crops, while the factory farms, raising just hogs or cows, have taken over the livestock industry. Grain farmers must plant in the spring, spray in the summer, and harvest in the fall. In between is much more free time than the traditional farmers knew. Some farmers even hire out the spraying, leaving enough spare time "to go to Vegas for two months every summer," like one local farmer Kading knows.

Half the Kading land is in corn, half in soybeans. Ash says they could handle twice as much acreage, but it would be tricky because their land is broken up in two-hundred- or three-hundred-acre chunks. Erudite and articulate, Kading compares the family's balkanized holdings to the tiny principalities of Germany before that country's unification in 1871. He envies the vast land holdings in the Mato Grosso area of Brazil, where fifty combines can sweep side by side across a connected landscape.

Kading claims that corporations and integrators don't rule his life. It's true that consolidation hasn't taken over grain production to the degree that it dominates livestock or eggs. Independent grain elevators exist and compete for farmers' business, keeping prices competitive and demand negotiable. But even the independence of grain farmers is shrinking. As we saw, Cargill and the other agribusiness giants control large shares of seed and fertilizer sales, corn and soybean processing, and exports.

With ten thousand acres, Kading can afford to be independent. But even with an operation this size, the big corporations play a role. Kading actually worked for Cargill after college before returning to the farm; now part of his corn crop goes to a Cargill plant in Eddyville, Iowa, which makes ethanol, high fructose corn syrup, and other products. If ethanol plays a major role in the nation's energy future, it could absorb every ear of corn grown in the Midwest. Clearly, corporations like Cargill and ADM are preparing for that day. In the future, even huge grain farmers such as Ash Kading could end up as beholden to corporations as the Midwest's hog and chicken farmers are today.

There's no question that these giant corporations drive and shape Midwestern farming, even Midwestern society itself. Many farmers have become no more than hired hands. By linking farmers to the global economy, the corporations leave these farmers, like factory workers, vulnerable to low-cost foreign competition. By demanding the efficiency of size, they help drive small farmers out of business. As these farmers go, so do the small towns they once supported. An independent rural society is vanishing and probably won't come back.

But there's a historical precedent to all this. The corporations and big-business methods that are transforming Midwestern farming are not so different from the ones that made it possible.

In *Nature's Metropolis*, historian William Cronon describes the vital link between Chicago and its western hinterland, and the role that the city—with its railroads and markets, its canal and money, its transport and communications—played in turning the rich land of the Midwest into the world's breadbasket.

Key to this, Cronon wrote, were the railroads, the steam-powered grain elevators, and the Chicago Board of Trade. All were highly controversial in their day, and rightly so. The railroads gouged the farmers and the elevators cheated them outrageously; railroads and elevators colluded on price. The elevators set up cartels, gave farmers short weights, issued false receipts, and cheated on the grading systems that determined the price of crops. The traders themselves grew fat not by growing grain but by turning it into pieces of paper to be bought and sold by men who would never get dirt under their fingernails. But in fact, Midwestern farming would never have happened without these same railroads, elevators, and traders. The rough-and-tumble, even crooked, institutions of Chicago created a society.

"That farmers and merchants no longer needed to float rafts down prairie streams or haul wagons over muddy roads to sell their grain was due to the very railroads and elevators which now linked them so powerfully and troublingly to Chicago's marketplace," Cronon wrote. "The same traders who speculated or gambled in the golden products of the fields were also the people farmers depended upon to buy and sell their crops. Despite all the cries of fraud, corruption and monopoly directed against it, Chicago's immense grain market, with all of its speculative frenzy, served as a clearinghouse for the capital and credit that moved western crops to their final customers. It had improved the efficiency of trade and transport alike, so that many more farmers were able to sell much larger quantities of grain than ever before."

The big nineteenth-century meatpackers played a crucial role, possibly *the* crucial role, in shaping Midwestern farming. These packers connived and cheated and polluted on a titanic scale. They owned a virtual monopoly over their industry. They were accused by a congressional committee in 1889 of running a price-fixing cartel that kept prices down and drove farmers into penury. But these packers, Cronon wrote, not only created a reliable market for the ranchers and feedlots of the West and Midwest. They also created a whole new industry. They provided the market that made farming possible. Their innovations—assembly-line slaughtering, for instance, or refrigerated railcars—multiplied the supply of meat and revolutionized transportation. By supplying vast quantities of fresh refrigerated meat, they changed the way the country—and then the world—ate. In the process, they helped build a metropolis, the rich and noisome city of Chicago. "They had achieved these things," Cronon said in words that could describe today's corporations, "by creating immense, vertically integrated corporations capable of exercising managerial control over the food of many nations on a scale never before seen in the history of the world."

In other words, the businesses and capitalists of Chicago built the crucial bridge between Midwestern farmers and national markets. It's still happening. The corporations, like the railroads and elevators, do take every advantage of the farmers, and they do drive hard, sometimes ruinous bargains: cases abound of corporations canceling contracts, leaving farmers to pay for infrastructure, such as hog houses, but with no money to foot these bills. Like the meat-packers, they wield their great power ruthlessly.

But like the Board of Trade, they tie Midwestern farming to global markets. They provide the information from distant buyers and tell farmers what and how much to grow. They fix the price, arrange the shipping, put pigs into cans and corn into gas tanks. They make some farmers rich and drive others off the land.

At least a few of them have been playing this role for a century or more. Cargill was almost as much a powerhouse at the turn of the twentieth century, when it was one of the world's top five grain traders. Even in the turmoil of today's global economy, it seems, some things never change.

It's a savage but necessary process. A century ago, the railroads, elevators, and traders had to be reformed and regulated to expunge the worst abuses and create a tolerable civilization. As the giant corporations become all-powerful, buying and selling in noncompetitive markets, they, too, must be regulated, reformed, controlled, civilized. But like the railroads and the Board of Trade, they will not disappear. For good or ill, they are changing the Midwestern past into a far different future, and this future will not happen without them.

In this landscape of corporate mega-farming, it's nice to report that there are some micro-outposts, small-time farmers making a go of it in a big-time globalized world. Outside Freeport, Minnesota, which was the inspiration for Garrison Keillor's Lake Wobegon, I visited a farmer named Mark Hemker who raises exotic animals—impalas, zebras, oryx, elk, reindeer, penguins—on fourteen acres. The folks in town like to tell visitors that Hemker exports elk horn to China, where it is much prized as an aphrodisiac. Hemker just laughs and says his real exports are much more prosaic—animals to zoos in Japan, for instance. The Japanese have been good customers for Hemker's mountain goats and bighorn sheep ever since they found his Web site.

In Iowa, the number of farms smaller than fifty acres increased 10 percent between 1997 and 2002. There were 65 farmers' markets statewide in 1985; twenty years later, there were 170 of them. In Des Moines, Dang and Maiyang Lee, a Hmong couple who fled Laos in 1979, grow flowers on an acre and half and sell them at the Des Moines farmers' market.

Beth and Brent Eccles sell vegetables with an Asian flavor at the farmers' markets in Chicago, more than seventy miles from their farm in Starke County, near North Judson, in the flat countryside in northern Indiana. They grow the vegetables—Chinese and Korean eggplants and zucchinis, tart Asian greens, melons, specialty tomatoes, exotic beets and carrots, tiny peppers and hard-skinned shallots—on about a quarter of their 155-acre farm. There are forty-five farmers' markets in Chicago every week in the summer, served by seventy different farmers. The Eccles sell at five of them—three every Saturday, plus two markets near the city center on Tuesday and Thursday. It means leaving home at three a.m. for the drive to Chicago and getting home at six p.m.

Beth's grandfather came to America from Japan in 1917 and farmed in California before moving to Indiana in 1933, escaping the internment of West Coast Japanese in World War II. He bought a two-hundred-acre farm and raised five children by truck farming. Beth's father later took over the farm. Beth, now thirty-six, went to college and was working as a book editor in Indianapolis when she met Brent, a city dweller with country tastes. When her first daughter was born, Beth quit her job and began selling flowers in the Indianapolis city market. Soon a farm came up for sale near her parents' farm and they bought it.

"The first few years were pretty rocky," she told me when I visited the farm. Then they discovered the Chicago markets, "where the worst day can be one thousand dollars, and one day we made over eight thousand dollars." They began educating Chicagoans in the joys of Asian vegetables, and business grew. Most of their land is wooded or planted in rye, to withstand winds. Underground piping supplies irrigation. In the summer, they employ nine workers, all from Mexico. The Eccles and their two daughters live with a dog named Elvis in a solid farmhouse, but, when I visited, were building a splendid new four-bedroom home on the property. Clearly, there's a living to be made here.

Farming remains a precarious life, but perhaps less precarious for microfarmers than for traditional farmers. "When I was a kid," Beth recalls, "there were farmers in the neighborhood with two hundred acres, all growing corn or beans and working in towns. They all went bankrupt. This county was the largest mint producer in the nation. Farmers made tons of money. You could get sixty dollars for a pound of mint then. Imports from China undercut this. Now you're lucky to get twelve or fifteen dollars. You can't even grow it for that. People went bankrupt, all the kids I went to school with. Now the only people left around here have two thousand acres."

Microfarming won't save the Midwest. Starke County remains one of the poorest counties in Indiana. The average wage is well under the Indiana norm. About half the stores in North Judson are vacant, and the town has seen better days. More than half the workers in the county commute up to two hours each way to jobs outside the county. But the Eccles prosper by being throwbacks to an earlier generation of small Midwestern farmers who bring their produce to the big city and sell it directly to shoppers there.

On Saturday mornings, amid the daikon radishes and eight-ball zucchinis, Cargill seems very far away.

We know the future of Midwestern farming, because it's already here. Big corporations can be deplored, as the railroads and the Board of Trade were deplored in the nineteenth century, but they can't be wished away, because they are as basic to farming today as the trains and traders were in their day.

Technology will continue to drive consolidation. Already there are Iowa farms where nearly all the machines, including the tractors, run on autopilot. Using the Global Positioning System and kinematic guidance technology, farmers can use cell phones to get instant reads on moisture and yields, then relay back instructions on where and how to plant, fertilize, and spray. This is farming by remote control. Farm machinery manufacturers, such as Caterpillar, also are moving toward autopilot technology. Clearly, this increases efficiency, maximizes production, and enables one farmer to farm more land than ever, enabling the few remaining family farms to get even bigger, while driving smaller farmers off the land.

American farm policy will certainly change, eventually if not immediately. Big farmers and the American Farm Bureau carry enough power in Washington to block any real reform soon. But the changes must come, partly because the present system, with its huge subsidies to already rich farmers, makes no sense. Partly, the subsidies will change because they distort the country's trading relations—not with the Europeans or other rich nations, which subsidize their farmers just as mindlessly, but because they offend countries such as Brazil, Russia, and China, which are the emerging powers in global agriculture and can negotiate from strength in a world trading system once dominated by the United States and Europe.

Competition from low-cost farming in these countries—Brazil today, Ukraine tomorrow—will grow. Consolidation of farms will go on because, in a globalized world, size conquers. Farm population will dwindle, and so will the number of farms. In Iowa, half the state's farmland is owned by aging farmers. Within a decade or two, most of it will be passed on to heirs, assuming they want to farm, or more likely, will be bought by the big farmer next door or by an investor, a doctor or a dentist, in the county seat. About 175,000 farms produce most of our food now; many experts think we're heading for a day when this food is produced by 25,000 or 30,000 farms. On that day, Americans probably will have less variety in their food, but they'll also have more food, cheaper prices, and seasonal produce year-round. Some people will care about this and will seek out the niche farms that exist on the margins. Most won't: there's no evidence that the majority of shoppers are ready to abandon Wal-Mart and the other supermarkets. So both the farms and the corporations will get bigger and the brands more dominant. It takes no crystal ball to predict this. We're almost there right now.

There's a wild card, though, in the future of global farming: it's called bioscience. As we will see later in the book, many Midwestern planners see this new industry—plant and life sciences—as the savior of the Midwest economy. Crops and animals will become not only food but gas, medicines, chemicals, materials—anything that modern science can dream up. Much of this is already happening. Ethanol already uses much of the Midwestern corn crop, and soybeans are transformed into chemicals, inks, diesel fuel, biopolymers, resins for auto parts. Again, this isn't new. A century or more ago, Chicago's packinghouses were turning pigs into lard, glue, buttons, fertilizer, violin strings, candles, soap, brushes. The packers boasted that they "used every part of the pig except the squeal."

Whatever the future is, it will be expensive. Huge investments in research will be needed. Small companies can produce innovations, but no small company can afford the development and production costs. Most research will be done by the global corporations, working with the Midwest's major research universities. And this, too, is already happening. The same names that control agriculture—Monsanto, Cargill, Du Pont, Dow—already are bioscience and biotech firms, too.

This global future promises riches for much of the Midwest—its global cities, global farmers, global universities, global corporations, global citizens. But it also promises to leave much of the rural and small-town Midwest behind. In the conversation carried by e-mail and satellite phone from Chicago to Hong Kong to São Paulo, the old-style farming community will play no part.

This Midwest has lost its voice and is hard to hear. You have to go looking for it, in places like Eldon, Iowa.

CHAPTER 6

From Hometown to Slum

You've never heard of Eldon, Iowa, but you've seen it a thousand times. In 1930, an Iowa artist named Grant Wood passed through Eldon, a village in the southern part of the state, and saw a white wooden house, across the street from a cattle feedlot. The house was a graceful, simple place, five rooms, built in 1881 in a style called Carpenter Gothic. A gable with an arched Gothic window gave the house its character.

Back home in Cedar Rapids, Grant Wood painted the house from a photograph. In front, he posed his sister, Nan, and his dentist, Dr. Byron McKeeby, representing an Iowa farmer and his spinster daughter. Nan wore a period pinafore and a pinched look. McKeeby, bald and gaunt, wore coveralls and held a pitchfork that, like the window, pointed to the sky.

The result, of course, was *American Gothic*. It won a bronze medal and $300 at a show at the Art Institute of Chicago, where it hangs now. To this day, *American Gothic* remains the iconic image of the rural Midwest.

So, in a different way, does Eldon. The little house survives, a tidy place on the edge of town. A caretaker lives there, and tourists who find their way to it are encouraged to pose like Nan and Dr. McKeeby and have their picture taken. A Grant Wood Visitors Center is has opened: it created one job, for a manager. On the second Saturday in June, Eldon celebrates Gothic Days with a parade and a high school reunion.

But the rest of Eldon is decaying, not yet dead but losing signs of life. The town used to have two thousand people. It had a stately, old brick bank, doctors, a school, a grocery, a railway station, even an opera house. The population is down to about nine hundred now. The railway station is gone and so is the grocery; the nearest store is in Douds, an even tinier town nine miles away. The only local food shop is a Casey's General Store, part of a Midwestern junk-food chain specializing in doughnuts and frozen pizzas; the spare couple in *American Gothic* would be a lot paunchier today.

The feedlot across from the American Gothic House is closed. The nearest neighbors are a clutch of mobile homes. As usual in these old towns, the nicest building is a funeral parlor. The old bank and the opera house stand empty. The main street contains mostly shuttered stores and a few auction houses. Plans exist to reopen the opera house, someday, and to put a microbrewery in the bank. But these are only plans in a town where few dreams come true. On a Sunday afternoon, bearded men drink beer in the yards of mobile homes, beside rusted pickup trucks.

The stern rectitude and propriety of *American Gothic* seem far away. Eldon, in truth, is a tired and shabby place, left behind by an economy that like many former residents, has moved away.

Small farming towns like Eldon once defined the Midwest. The region was a galaxy of neat, prosperous villages, broadcast like seed across the soft, rich countryside, each a little civilization unto itself. These towns and villages were born 150 years ago when the logic of commerce—the demands of family farmers, traders, investors, railroads—decided they were necessary. The same logic, applied with a global spin, sees no need for them now. And so they are dying.

Chicago was the mother city that spawned farms, cities, towns, and villages in its vast hinterland. The markets of Chicago took in the grain and livestock of the Midwest, and so made Midwestern farming possible. The merchants of Chicago supplied the goods that these farmers and town dwellers needed, and so made Midwestern commerce possible. Along the rivers and railway lines of the nineteenth century, cities grew and gave birth to county seats and other larger towns, which gave birth to villages. As settlers thrived, they needed goods and services—stores, certainly, but also schools, doctors, banks, entertainment. Bad roads made travel hard, so the settlers wanted their commerce as near as possible. Because these settlers farmed small holdings, there were a lot of them, enough to support a little town every few miles. Doctors and dentists arrived, as did schoolteachers, storekeepers, café owners. By the middle and late nineteenth century, the Midwest was dotted with these towns, each one the center of the universe for the surrounding farmers and for the townies who served them.

When each farm amounted to about 160 acres, there were enough farmers and farm families to patronize the local grocer, to borrow from the local bank, to get supplies from the local feed-store, to see the local doctor, to send their kids to the local school. Each town had a few hundred or a couple of thousand people, and a thriving main street. It was "a great place to raise kids," everyone said, even when the kids grew up and moved away. Now that average farm may be two thousand acres or more. One farm family lives where ten or fifteen families once lived. That means one tenth as many customers for the local grocer, clothing store, and hardware store. It means one tenth as many patients for the doctor and one tenth as many students in the school. These big farms still need equipment and supplies, but, increasingly, they buy them from central suppliers, often the same global corporations that contract to buy their crops. Good roads make it easy to drive into the county seat, to buy groceries, see the doctor, go to church. One by one, all these stores and institutions die off. So do the people who ran them, the local pillars, leaving these little towns not only without commerce but without leadership.

What's left behind is a rural slum. Main Street stands empty. Sometimes a secondhand store and a bar survive. Sometimes not. The school closes, consolidated into a bigger one in the county seat. Sometimes a church lives on, sharing a pastor with other churches in other little towns. The last doctor dies or retires and no young doctor takes his place. A few neat white houses remain, with generous porches and gliders for summer sitting; old people live in them, waiting to die. The other houses are shanties or mobile homes with littered yards, occupied by people who work elsewhere and live there because it's cheap, or by welfare mothers who washed up there because their government checks go further here than in the city.

These little towns exist in a special, remote world, far from the metro reality of most Americans. Towns like Eldon define the rural part of the urban-rural divide: most of Wapello County voted solidly for John Kerry in 2004, but Eldon voted solidly for George Bush. They are suspicious of the cities where globalization has taken root, and they have reason. They are globalization's losers.

Iowa politicians say the split is not urban/rural so much as it is metro/nonmetro. Other small towns are close enough to larger, thriving metropolitan areas, such as Des Moines or Omaha, to become bedroom suburbs for workers earning good salaries. Some towns find themselves next to an interstate highway and live on the passing traffic. An Iowa town named Walnut, next to I-80, dusted off the region's old farm furniture and turned itself into "Iowa's Antique City." Sometimes, a local entrepreneur will be the savior. Woodbine, a little western-Iowa town that my great-grandfather helped found, has kept its population of fifteen hundred steady over the years partly because of Tommy Gate, a business started by a local man who invented a hydraulic hoist for pickup trucks. Even so, the biggest employers in Woodbine are the local school and the Rose Vista retirement home, not Tommy Gate. Iowa ranks first in the nation in the percentage of its residents over eighty-five; in these small towns, old folks outnumber youngsters and their care has become as important as schooling.

There is a greater loss here than the vanishing of a rosy past. With the disappearance of family farms and vibrant small towns, the Midwest loses an important part of its good young people. Traditionally, food scientists and researchers, not to mention the CEOs of big agribusiness firms, grew up on farms. Norman Borlaug, who won the Nobel Peace Prize for creating the "green revolution," grew up on a fifty-six-acre farm in northwestern Iowa. Henry Wallace, the future vice president who developed hybrid corn, came from a small farm near Orient, in southwestern Iowa.

Neither family farm would survive today. Most likely, young Borlaug and young Wallace would have grown up in town. Neither would have gone into agriculture. The world would be poorer, and hungrier.

A few small rural places in the Midwest are actually growing, for two reasons. Towns near the lakes and woods of northern Wisconsin and Michigan boom, thanks to retirees and second-home owners. And some towns, such as Storm Lake or Denison in Iowa, draw in thousands of immigrants, mostly Latino, who work in packinghouses. For all the social problems that immigration brings, it keeps these towns alive while surrounding towns disintegrate.

Ethanol plants have brought new zest to gasping towns like Eddyville, in southeastern Iowa. Not far away, Winterset thrives on tourists who want to visit the bridges of Madison County. One of the strangest, and most successful, little towns in Iowa is Fairfield, where members of the Transcendental Meditation movement arrived in 1974, bought a local college that had gone broke, and set up the Maharishi University of Management. Of the town's ten thousand residents, three thousand are meditators who, when not meditating, have set up high-tech businesses that created about two thousand new jobs. Fairfield may be the only town in Iowa where shops on the main square sell Jyotish gems with cosmic properties.

But hundreds of rural towns like Eldon are doomed. Ottumwa, the nearest city, is itself too depressed to offer an anchor. Most towns are too far from cities to permit commuting. High school graduates who go to college don't come back. The interstate is too distant to be useful. Any local inventor has trouble finding either funding or workers.

Globalization didn't start this trend. It's been going on for years. I went fifteen years ago to another dying village in southern Iowa, called Gravity. Once, Gravity was a thriving farm town with 1,000 people; by the early 1990s, it was down to 218. Not so many years before, it had a main street two blocks long, lined with two groceries, a drugstore, a jewelry store, a dance hall, two taverns, a movie, a bank, insurance offices, barbershops, and farm-implement dealers. There was a high school down the street and a gas station in the valley below the town.

By the time I got there, the main street amounted to three empty stores at one end, waiting to be torn down, and a closed bank at the other end. Between them were vacant lots, with weeds growing through foundations of stores that once served a close-knit community. The school and gas station still stood, derelict and unused. There was a café behind the post office, run as a nonprofit by some local women, just to give people a place to go.

A reporter on the *Des Moines Register* sponsored a charity fix-up day for Gravity, and hundreds of people came to paint houses and plant flowers. In the evening, four bands played at a town dance, the first since the school had closed thirty-three years before. This seemed sad, not festive, and I spent some time talking about it with Helen Janson, wife of the town veterinarian and the president of the county historical society.

"It was a busy town, but when we lost the school, things started disappearing," Mrs. Janson said. "You talk to every little town like Gravity, you find the same thing. The school was the center of activity." Without the school, everything else—potluck suppers, band concerts, Fourth of July parades, all the little rituals that hold these towns together—becomes too much trouble.

The charity dance was nice, she said. "It made you think of the times, many many years ago, when everybody attended all the functions in town. For years there was always a weekly dance here. Now there's nothing."

I was in the neighborhood in early 2007 and drove to Gravity. The three empty stores were gone. The bank still stood and still carried the sign Gravity State Bank; there's a small plant store inside now. On the vacant ground opposite was a marker honoring Mrs. Janson's husband, who died in 2000, and two signs proclaiming the town slogans, both rather grim: Gravity—We're Down to Earth and If Gravity Goes, We All Go.

Like any slum, Gravity has a few nice houses, well tended by people who care about such things, and a few sophisticated and educated people, who made their lives here. There are a couple of newer small homes, occupied by people who work in the county seat but choose to live cheap in Gravity. Most other houses are run-down shanties or abandoned. The tiny café behind the post office is still open. When I stopped in, a couple of old men were sitting around, drinking coffee, paying for it on the honor system, with a quarter or two in a tin can. Photos of Gravity's better days hung on the wall.

As Mrs. Janson had said, "It's depressing, if you let it be. To those of us who care, yes, it is depressing. It's a part of life that's gone that you wish hadn't gone."

There's a real nostalgia among Midwesterners of a certain age for the rituals and quality of life in rural America. Once a week, on Thursday or Friday or Saturday night, depending on custom or when the local factory paid its workers, everybody would drive into town to shop, sell some produce, see friends, chat a bit. In some places, people called it the "daughter and egg night," because farmers came to town to sell some eggs and show off their daughters to the local blades. The café would be full, the movie theater would do a good business, and, as I heard over and over, "You couldn't hardly walk down Main Street." Television helped kill this custom. So did the disappearance of the family farm: there aren't enough farmers to mount a decent "daughter and egg night" now. So did the movement of commerce: when the major stores moved from Main Street and the square to a strip mall on the highway, they carved the very heart out of their town.

Globalization may be the last act in the rural decline, but it didn't start it. In a way, rural America asked for it.

The Grangers and Populists were rural protest movements of the late nineteenth century that believed that the only true producers were farmers, who supported the rest of society. These agrarian movements not only demanded new regulations on railroads and traders but sought to upgrade rural life. What they wanted, as William Cronon wrote, "was to improve agriculture with science and to revamp education for farmers and farm children. New machines and new techniques would make farming more efficient and profitable. State schools of agriculture would put the findings of modern science at the disposal of farmers."

All this happened. They got what they wanted, and the result was a trend, now more than a century old, of scientific farming that made it possible for fewer farmers to farm more land, and of education that enabled farm children to escape the farm.

The rural Midwest has been losing population since the early twentieth century, when the collapse of farming presaged the Great Depression. This decline is most marked in the western Midwest, in Iowa, Illinois, Minnesota, and Missouri, where isolated little towns depended on farms and mines, with no nearby cities to cushion the blow. Ohio, Indiana, and southern Michigan have more small cities, with rural hinterlands that have turned into commuter belts. In these states, many small farmers support their farms with day jobs in factories, such as Delphi: as these factory jobs vanish, so will the farms.

Southern Iowa is an epicenter of decline, but northern Missouri, the other parts of Iowa, Illinois, and Minnesota look the same; so do the vast prairie reaches of Kansas, Nebraska, and the Dakotas. All are filled with little towns that are eighty to a hundred miles from the nearest city of fifty thousand or more—too far to commute to a new job. When farms consolidated or the mines collapsed, residents of these little towns had no choice but to move away.

Between 1960 and 1980, three fourths of Iowa's counties lost 40 percent of their population or more. The farm-debt crisis of the 1980s drove another nail into the rural coffin: in that decade, no fewer than ninety-two out of Iowa's ninety-nine counties lost another 25 percent of their people. Many of those who left were farmers, but not all: in the decade, two thirds of Iowa's counties lost town residents. Relatively, the smallest towns, of two thousand or less, lost the most.

In the nineties, another forty-five counties, all rural, lost population; from 2000 to 2005, another sixty-four declined. This time it was globalization that administered the coup de grâce. As farming declined, these little towns and counties had courted industry. Every county seat had its industrial park. Small-town mayors in the seventies and eighties commonly had business cards in English on one side and Japanese on the other. Towns of five thousand or so competed viciously with each other—with cheap rents, tax holidays, job-training programs—to land a factory. If the rural economy was to survive, it would be up to industry to do the job.

Many of these campaigns succeeded. The industrial parks filled up with small plants, often processing food or making parts for cars or farm equipment. Much of it was simple assembly work or other low-skill jobs. Some workers lived in towns; more lived on farms but farmed part-time, relying on their factory jobs to pay the bills. Being farm dwellers, these men and women knew machinery, and they knew how to work hard. They were punctual, educated, honest, relatively skilled. And best of all—they worked cheap, at least compared to city workers.

Manufacturing didn't just supplement rural economies. Over time, it came to dominate them. The majority of employment in seven out of eight rural counties now comes from manufacturing and other off-farm activities. Eighty percent of all farmers work other full-time jobs. More than 60 percent count on off-farm work for most of their family's income. If you think of Iowa as nothing but farms, think again. Iowa ranks fifth in the nation—behind four other Midwestern states, Indiana, Wisconsin, Ohio, and Illinois—in the share of its income that comes from manufacturing.

Just as Midwestern farmers now compete with farmers around the world, these small-town factory workers compete with workers in China, Latin America, Eastern Europe, or Indonesia. These global laborers also are relatively skilled, literate, punctual, diligent. And they are willing to work much, much more cheaply than any Iowan or Minnesotan ever could.

The Center for the Study of Rural America at the Federal Reserve Bank of Kansas City keeps the closest eye on this trend. It says, "Rural America's agricultural and manufacturing past was predicated on its ability to produce commodities with abundant, inexpensive land and labor . . . With globalization, however, overseas locations are rapidly becoming more competitive in the production of commodities, whether agricultural or industrial. Much as agriculture faded as an economic foundation for most rural areas during the twentieth century, rural factories are now closing at disproportionate rates relative to those in urban areas."

In other words, if manufacturing cities have it hard, these little manufacturing towns have it worse. Proportionately, rural areas have twice as many manufacturing jobs as cities do, according to the center's recently retired director, Mark Drabenstott. And not only do they have a lot of factory jobs, they have the wrong kind of factory jobs—low-tech and low-skill, the kind that Third World workers can do for rock-bottom wages. Of all rural manufacturing jobs, 48 percent are low-tech, requiring repetitive assembly-line skills; in the cities, it's only 32 percent. In the cities, 21 percent of factory jobs are high-tech, demanding knowledge of mathematics, science, and computers; in rural areas, it's only 5 percent.

"Since 2001," Drabenstott says, "forty percent of layoffs in the rural U.S. is due to factories closing. Part of the problem is jobs going to China. But a bigger part is the push for increases in productivity." To compete in the global market, American factories have to make more goods with fewer employees. As the best young people leave for better jobs in the cities, it gets harder for these Midwestern towns to invest or stay. The traditional argument—that a town like Eldon has good workers and is a nice place to live—doesn't hold much water anymore.

"Bragging about low wages and low property prices doesn't cut it in the global economy," Drabenstott says. "China has more of both, and better of both. Quality of life is fine, but it's not enough to have low crime rates anymore."

As a matter of fact, much of the rural Midwest can't brag about crime rates, either. Petty crime is rising but the real problem is drug use—especially the vicious synthetic drug methamphetamine, or *meth* for short. "It's the most addictive and controlling drug we've ever seen," Captain Gary Foster told me when I went to the Story County sheriff's office, east of Ames, to ask about it. "You try it once and you spend the rest of your life trying to duplicate that same high. It gives the most bang for the buck. Cocaine gives you a high for two to three hours. With meth, that high lasts ten to twelve hours." Now, he said, police are seeing a purer, crystalline form of meth, called ice, that produces an all-day, twenty-four-hour high.

Ice, like most meth these days, comes from Mexico, traveling up Interstate 35, which runs like a funnel straight from Laredo, Texas, to Minneapolis and Lake Superior, or on Interstate 80, which cuts across the country from California to New York. The two arteries meet in central Iowa, twenty-five miles south of Ames.

But meth was a homegrown menace before Mexican traffickers intervened. A synthetic, it is made in small makeshift labs. The labs reek, so meth is best made in cornfields or forests, far from inquiring noses. One ingredient is ammonia, often found in fertilizers. Other ingredients also are near at hand in rural areas. Along with cold remedies containing pseudoephedrine, the key ingredient, there's hydrochloric acid, drain cleaner, battery acid, lye, lantern fuel, antifreeze, denatured alcohol, and ether.

Meth, being relatively cheap, is the drug of choice in small towns and among the poor, but the sheriff's office has caught Iowa State University students in Ames using it. "It's mostly people nineteen to midthirties, but we've had seventy-year-old grandmothers," Foster says. No fewer than twenty-nine Iowa towns and cities have chapters of Moms Off Meth, a self-help group for addicted mothers. Not surprisingly, many users finance their habits with burglaries and other crimes.

The local meth labs are pretty much out of business since Iowa adopted a law, first passed in Oklahoma, that put pseudoephedrine under lock and key at drugstores. Customers have to produce identification and sign a log and can buy only limited amounts. But as this closed down the local chemists, it opened the market to imports of Mexican meth, and to a revival of the cocaine trade—a malaise that most Americans associate with cities, not with the bucolic reaches of the Midwest.

The rural pathology doesn't end with drug use. In any competition in a globalizing world, the rural Midwest—the remote and dying towns—already is far behind. The Fed's Center for the Study of Rural America has documented that people in rural areas are older, less educated, and poorer. This makes their towns bad places to do business. No one wants to invest in a place with few young, educated people. No store wants to stay in a town where most people are poor.

So new businesses don't come and the old stores go away. One store that goes, sooner or later, is the local grocery. Lois Wright Morton, an Iowa State professor, writes that many parts of the rural Midwest—supposedly the nation's breadbasket—have become "food deserts, places where few or no grocery stores exist." The reason is the globalization of agriculture and agribusiness—the trend toward domination not only by the big corporations like Cargill but the big supermarket chains like Wal-Mart. In the selling of food as in the raising of it, big is in and small is out. When a new supermarket opens in the county seat, small groceries close in the little towns around it. Iowa today has fewer than half as many small-town grocery stores as it did twenty-five years ago.

People who once had a decent grocery nearby now have to travel fifteen to thirty miles to do their shopping. Most rural residents own cars or trucks and willingly make this trek. But they don't make it as often: more people are shopping once a month instead of once a week, which means that fresh fruits and vegetables disappear from their diets. Older people without cars are stranded, relying on the kindness of neighbors.

It's hard to think of rural Midwesterners being hungry. But Morton reports strategies that small-town people use to make sure nobody starves. One woman said she "put in a garden, way too much fruit for the two of us, and I share. I give it to people . . . That's done quite a bit in this town." Another reported, "My in-laws go and they work on a farm. In lieu of pay we can raise hogs and cattle out there. That is how we get our meat." Churches hold potluck suppers and VFW halls have all-you-can-eat fish fries. Rotary Clubs raise sweet corn and sell it cheap—or give it away—at roadside stands.

When all else fails, there's always Casey's. Casey's General Stores is a chain, based in suburban Des Moines, that contributes to the Midwestern girth that so astonishes visitors to the region. Casey's started in my hometown of Boone in 1959 and now operates nearly fifteen hundred combination gas stations and convenience stores in nine Midwestern or Great Plains states, mostly in towns of fewer than ten thousand people. In many tiny towns like Eldon, Casey's may be the only store left.

A stroll through Casey's aisles is a dietitian's nightmare. The shelves groan with potato chips, candy, instant mashed potatoes, sugar-coated cereals, frozen pizzas, soda pop, and beer. Casey's makes its own fresh pizzas and its stores sell more than 27,000 of them per day. The chain also sells 269,000 doughnuts daily. At 250 calories per doughnut, that's around 70 million calories per day, many of which end up wrapped around rural Midwesterners.

Another competitive gap between rural and urban Midwesterners shows no sign of closing. The highway to the global economy is paved with broadband. If you have high-speed Internet access, you're plugged into the world. If you don't, you're not. The latest survey, by the Pew Internet and American Life Project, showed that 39 percent of urban and suburban Americans have high-speed Internet access at home, compared with only 24 percent of rural Americans. Partly, this "digital gap," like obesity, goes with being older, poorer, and less educated. Partly, it's the failure of companies to make this information technology (IT) available in rural areas, while charging inflated rates to those who get it.

Perhaps rural life wouldn't mesh with IT, even if it was more available. The Internet exists for people who compete in a 24-7 world. Most rural people are accustomed to an 8–5 world. They aren't lazy, just more tuned to the slower pace and long weekends. Global people want to do deals. Rural people want to go hunting. One activity requires IT, the other doesn't.

But as Edwin Parker, a telecommunications expert, has written, "Communities not connected to our emerging broadband network will suffer the same economic fate as many communities that were bypassed by the telephone network, the railroad or the Interstate highway system." They're being bypassed again, by the technology that will build the future.

Between these dying villages and the happier towns near cities, there are the places in the middle, county seats or rural centers, still alive and fighting to stay that way. From Gravity, I drove south to Bedford, the county seat of Taylor County, and dropped in on Jim Offenbacker, coordinator of the Bedford Area Economic Development Corporation. Bedford is a pretty little town, with sixteen hundred people, a stately redbrick courthouse, and—a rarity—a bustling main street, set in the rolling, achingly beautiful countryside of southern Iowa. Offenbacker retired to Bedford from a corporate career and takes a worldly and realistic view of the town and its challenges.

On the day I visited, the town's biggest employer, an upscale sportswear maker called Gear For Sports, had just announced it was moving to Colombia, where South American wage scales could save it $500,000 per year. Like so many small industries, Gear had been lured in eight years ago when the farm economy dwindled. Now it was taking its fifty-two jobs away, a real blow to a town of sixteen hundred people. A local grocery also was closing. Across the state line, a machining company in Albany, Missouri (a town of two thousand people), had just gone to Mexico, taking two hundred and twenty jobs. Across southern Iowa in Centerville (which has six thousand people), Newell Rubbermaid had announced that global pressures were forcing it to close its plant, at the cost of five hundred jobs, and consolidate the work in Kansas.

"There's got to be a bright side to this thing, this globalization," Offenbacker told me. "Now we just have to find it. This is rural America. Small towns like this, this is our world. But we're a long way from China, that's how people think. They don't realize what's going on."

Bedford, like many rural small towns with aging populations, has a special problem that it doesn't know how to solve. It's called wealth transfer: the owners of many of the area's farms and businesses are dying off, leaving their estates to their children, who have long since moved to Des Moines or Chicago. "That's a real challenge," Offenbacker said. "We have to attract some of that wealth back."

Offenbacker has clearly put thought into what Bedford needs. His sophisticated Web site touts the town's Long-Look Plan, which emphasizes local leadership and an emphasis on entrepreneurship. The idea is raise kids to start homegrown businesses, instead of competing with every other town and county to lure companies in from outside. The town has a fifty-seven-acre industrial park waiting to be filled. "We're not looking for companies from outside that are going to run overseas in four to five years," as Gear did. He hopes that some of the young people who left town after high school will want to come back. "They've been in the world for ten or fifteen years and they've done some thinking about it."

If anyone can save towns like Bedford, it's people like Offenbacker. But there are too few like him, and their resources are pitifully spare.

So far, solutions to this rural decline sound more like wishful thinking than plausible policies. Some small towns expect to remain cheap homes for workers who commute an hour or more to their jobs. But most of the Midwest except the big urban areas is losing jobs now, and unless a town is within an hour's drive of a city, its commuters will move away. Already, more than 35 percent of all rural residents commute to some other town to work.

This is the rural version of urban sprawl. As in cities, people are moving farther away from their jobs in search of affordable housing. As commutes grow longer, communities become more stretched out. In cities, some commuters get to work on public transport. No public transport exists in rural America. Instead, everyone drives along the straight four-lane roads that honeycomb the Midwest.

But this is a dream built on cheap gas. On the excellent, wide-open interstates of Iowa, a sixty-minute commute equals a sixty-mile commute. This means 120 miles per day or 600 miles per week. At $4 or $5 per gallon, the cost advantage of small-town living quickly erodes.

Planners like Offenbacker see a future in entrepreneurship and innovation. But this requires not only educated entrepreneurs and highly skilled workers, but the kind of climate where innovation happens. As the economist Richard Florida says, this climate exists where there are great numbers of creative people, bouncing ideas off each other. Florida cites diversity—ethnic, sexual, religious, intellectual—as a key ingredient in a creative climate: creative people, he says, prize diversity and diverse lifestyles and go where they thrive. If there's one thing that rural areas usually don't have and don't want, it's diversity. It's always possible that creative innovators can arise here and there from the noncreative soil of the rural Midwest, such as the Tommy Gate founder in Woodbine. But don't bet on it.

Almost every Midwestern state gives tax incentives or other breaks to businesses that move to rural areas. Illinois offers loan assistance to rural "microbusinesses" that want to expand. Indiana created an Office of Rural Affairs. Wisconsin set up ten rural development zones, modeled on Minnesota's Job Opportunity Building Zones (JOBZ). Minnesota claims it has generated twenty-five hundred new jobs—but most of them are near Minneapolis and St. Paul, not in the more remote north. These states are finding out something that Chicago and other big cities learned long ago, that you can't pay a business to go where it doesn't want to go. These cities set up enterprise zones, with tax breaks and other lures, to persuade businesses to invest in depressed inner-city neighborhoods. Most of the zones attracted little investment and, more important, created few jobs.

Some thinkers advocate rural economic "clusters"—towns and businesses clustered in a region around a key industry, allowing related businesses to feed off each other. Tourism is one such industry. So is the cluster potential for ethanol production and biochemicals: a biochemical plant can draw in other industries using its products. Lee Munnich, a professor at the University of Minnesota, sees a future in "rural knowledge clusters," built around existing skills and talents. Silicon Valley is the exemplar of this idea, but nobody plans to build another Silicon Valley in northern Minnesota, which has no research universities. What it does have is snow and people who know about snow. The result: a "knowledge cluster" around the towns of Roseau and Thief River Falls, which have collectively become the snowmobile capital of the world. A local man, Edgar Heteen, started Arctic Cat and Polaris fifty years ago, and they have grown to thirty-two hundred employees making not only snowmobiles but other all-terrain vehicles.

This is the regional approach to development. Offenbacker and other Iowans want to set up regions of three to six counties apiece, which would cooperate in luring businesses, encouraging entrepreneurs, working with community colleges, and advertising themselves. Having a college is probably essential. So is creating an economic niche, a specialty like snowmobiles. So is finding equity capital—capturing the "wealth transfer" that Offenbacker cited. So is having decent infrastructure, such as broadband. So is breaking down the bureaucratic boundaries between outmoded units of government, like counties—no small chore in towns and counties where bureaucratic jobs in courthouses and town halls depend on holding on to these outdated jurisdictions.

Will any of this work? For the most part, probably not. Rural America has too many strikes against it. It's too small, remote, poor, uneducated, uncreative—too nonmetro. In a world of the Next New Thing, devotion to biblical inerrancy and traditional values doesn't cut it. The global world is diverse, open, multinational, with no loyalty to place or places. The rural world is still white-on-white, local, fixed on itself as the homeland of all virtue.

The rural Midwest, in truth, existed for one era, and that era has passed. It responded to the economic demands of a single century, from 1850 to 1950, and has been withering ever since. Globalization only finishes the work of earlier decades. There is no place in a globalized world for the small town and the family farm.

The continued decline of the rural Midwest is probably inevitable, but sad nonetheless. These little towns and counties, where everyone knew everyone else and community really meant something, had a value, a particular civilization, that no city or suburb can duplicate. All of us who grew up in an earlier Midwest know that times have changed, but we can't be happy about it.

It's not that these little towns will all vanish. Some will disappear. Others, like Woodbine, will find a niche. Most will just continue to shrink, as their young people continue to leave and the others, left behind, continue to die.

In this, the rural Midwest resembles nothing so much as the black ghettos of Midwestern cities. Now, there's a thought. Rural whites and urban blacks would seem to be as far from each other as it's possible to get. African-Americans are as rare in most small Midwestern towns as whites are in the ghettos of Chicago or Cleveland. Politically, they stand on opposite sides of the red-blue divide.

But these two antagonistic clans have one big thing in common. They are globalization's losers, left behind, so far from the action—in education, life experiences, attitudes—that this new world will go on without them. Plenty of blacks leave the ghetto and make their way in a globalized world. Plenty of rural boys and girls leave the small town to find success in the cities. The ones that stay share too much—poverty, bad health, reliance on government handouts, high dropout rates, drugs, down-home religions, broken families, empty futures. If they ever sat down together, they would find many common enemies: free trade, immigration, the people who run the world that has cast them out.

We may, in fact, be creating a new underclass in our small towns and small industrial cities. It's a white underclass this time but in many ways indistinguishable from the black underclass of the cities. Both live where they do because there once were unskilled jobs in industry. Both were stranded when that industry collapsed. Both are unskilled and unlearned. Both want the best for their kids and no idea how to get it. Education—how much and what kind— is something they've never had to think about before. Both will subsist on welfare or poverty-level commerce. Both are prey to drugs. Both see the hallmarks of a decent community—good schools, medical care, stores—move away as their communities become less and less able to pay for them. Both see their best and brightest escape into the real world, leaving behind lumpen civilizations without leaders or role models. Their children will be left with nothing but dreams and no way to realize them.

Both the rural Midwest and the urban ghettos grew from the industrial era. We're in the global era now, and globalization is a harsh, uncaring force. Its race is to the swift. It is open to anyone with education, skills, imagination, creativity. It has little time for those who can't compete. Instead, it is creating a world that won't be flat at all, but will be dominated by aeries of global citizens, heedless of the ghettos and rural towns, which will be left in the valleys, out of sight and very much out of mind.

CHAPTER 7

The New Midwesterners

Father Eugene Weitzel never intended to become the de facto leader of the Mexican community in Beardstown, a tough little river town in west-central Illinois. For one thing, he was getting older and not looking for any new priestly duties. For another, he didn't speak Spanish.

The Mexicans started arriving in Beardstown in the early nineties to work at the big pork slaughterhouse owned by Excel Corp., now Cargill Meat Solutions, the second-biggest meat-packer in America. After a couple of years, they began to bring their families and settle down. One Sunday, Father Weitzel looked out on his normally all-white congregation at St. Alexis Catholic Church and saw a few Mexican faces. Pretty soon there were more, and they wanted their own mass, in Spanish, and to say confession. More important, they needed a champion, someone to stand up for them.

Beardstown, a blue-collar place, calls itself "redneck" with pride. Well past midcentury, it was one of those Midwestern towns called sundowners, where the unwritten law decreed that no African-American be caught in town after dusk. Now Beardstown was on its way to becoming 30 percent Mexican. Worse, the Mexicans were there to take jobs, at low wages, that the whites of Cass County used to do for high wages. It was a recipe for trouble, and the Mexicans needed Father Weitzel's help.

The priest learned to say mass in Spanish. Confession was trickier. "But they're speaking to God, not me. The rules say I have to hear confession, but they don't say I have to understand it. I just ask them in Spanish if they're sorry and they say, '*Sí, sí.*' "

In the fifteen years before his recent retirement, Father Weitzel became the spokesman and defender of Beardstown's Mexicans. There are now about two thousand of them, possibly more: many lack legal documents and no one knows for sure how many there are, but they're at least one third of the people in town, probably half. Most work at the same place, Cargill, but this community remains disorganized, lacking leaders or institutions. Formal contact between Beardstown's native Anglos and new Mexicans barely exists. So St. Alexis became a clubhouse for the Mexicans and Father Weitzel their leader by default.

It hasn't been easy. St. Alexis has lost Anglo parishioners, just as Beardstown has lost some of its older residents, mostly German or Irish in heritage. Many people in Beardstown resent Father Weitzel, feeling that if he had not made the Mexicans welcome, they might have gone away. More than 350 Mexicans attend mass at St. Alexis now, compared to only 160 Anglos. Father Weitzel has masses in both English and Spanish. Neither congregation attends the other's mass.

For Beardstown, then, the Mexicans present problems the town would prefer not to have. The Mexicans like their music loud, leave their front doors open, let their kids run wild, at least by Beardstown standards. They take jobs that Anglos used to work. They park their cars on their front lawns. They speak Spanish in a town that has always spoken English. They overload city services, such as police and ambulances. They have forced the town to hire translators. They eat different food. They even dress differently. "Just last Sunday," the old priest recalled, "a girl came into mass wearing just a couple of straps above the waist. When she came up to Communion, both Jesus and I got an eyeful."

Especially, in a town with a racist past, Mexicans look different Almost nobody in Beardstown likes them very much. Almost everyone wishes they weren't here. Except for one great big fact: the Mexicans and the packinghouse where they work have saved Beardstown. The old railroad roundhouse is closed. So are the refrigeration plant and the glove factory. Young people go off to college and never come back. The old folks die and are not replaced. From Beardstown, it's sixty miles to Springfield, eighty miles to Peoria—too far for most people to commute. If not for the Cargill plant and the cheap labor that keeps it there, Beardstown would shrivel, perhaps die.

Everywhere in the Midwest, small, old blue-collar towns, isolated and out-of-date, left behind by globalization, are simply withering away. And everywhere in the Midwest, exceptions exist. Most of them are meatpacking towns that have drawn in thousands of Mexican workers. These towns are growing, even thriving. Hispanic enrollment in local schools is surging, bringing with it new problems ranging from bilingual education to the tracking of students whose parents move every year. But it also brings huge increases in state aid and, often, brand-new schools in a region where most towns struggle just to keep schools open.

If these towns have a future—indeed, if the Midwest has a future—it depends on immigrants. Midwestern cities know this. Every urban area is losing native-born residents. The only cities that are growing and thriving, such as Chicago and Minneapolis, are pulling in immigrants and building a future.

Midwestern states know it. Iowa has been losing population for decades. A local author, Stephen Bloom, has written that "Iowa's greatest export isn't corn, soybeans or pigs: it's young adults." Iowa's former governor Tom Vilsack ignited controversy with a public campaign to draw immigrants. But Vilsack, like other governors, knew he simply needed immigrants to take the place of young people who were leaving—in short, to do the work that must be done to keep the Midwest functioning. Towns with immigrants are growing. Towns without immigrants are shrinking. It's as simple as that.

But that's pretty much where it stops being simple. Immigration in the Midwest is immensely complicated—in its legality, in its politics, in the economics behind it, in the reactions to it.

Certainly, it's not a pretty process. The Midwest is the whitest part of America, Europe transplanted to the New World. Outside the cities, the Midwest is largely a social system based on everybody looking and acting like everybody else. It also is a social system based on respect for the law. Now come millions of immigrants, mostly Hispanic, largely dark-skinned, about half of them in the country illegally, without valid documents. Their very presence mocks the law.

In the small towns, most of them work in meatpacking plants, which may be the most dehumanizing job in the country. Into these slaughterhouses come truck after truck of pigs, turkeys, chickens, or cows. Outsiders are barred from entry, but I stood outside a slaughterhouse one evening, listening to the shrill shriek of the machinery inside: then I realized the shriek wasn't the grinding of machines but the squeal of pigs.

Inside, the animals go to the killing floor. A device is put on the back of a hog that sends a fatal shock to its heart. Cows are killed by "knocking"; a metal pin is loaded into a steel cylinder and fired into the animal's forehead with a .22-cartridge charge; the pin is reusable. Then the animals are hung on hooks and chopped apart on "disassembly lines" by workers who need no English, only strength. Their job titles describe what they do. *Knockers* kill the cows. Their workmates are called stickers, bleeders, tail rippers, flankers, gutters, sawers, head backers, tongue trimmers, and plate boners. The floors run with blood, water, and fat. The work tools are sharp, dangerous knives or band saws, including a little hand-held saw called a whizzer knife. The pace is relentless, heedless of safety. A big plant can slaughter and disassemble eleven hundred hogs every hour, twenty-four hours a day. By all accounts, the injury rate is appalling: after commercial fishing, meatpacking is reckoned America's most dangerous job. But no statistics exist because the workers, being undocumented and fearing not only unemployment but deportation if they file reports or complaints, keep quiet. Indeed, this is why Cargill and the other companies employ them: not only are they willing to work cheap, they are the most docile workforce imaginable.

This is exploitation squared and cubed. But Americans aghast that anyone should have to suffer such conditions must take a deep breath and think again. The Mexicans and other workers come to Cargill and the other plants for the same reason that the

Lithuanians and Poles came to the legendary and equally appalling stockyards of nineteenth-century Chicago: they dream of a better life and are willing to do anything to get it. The Mexicans literally risk their lives to get these jobs: in 2002, eleven smuggled immigrants were found dead in a sealed Union Pacific railcar in Denison, a meatpacking town in western Iowa. Laborers in these plants earn $12 or $13 per hour, a decent wage for the rural Midwest and vastly more than they would make back home.

As small Midwestern towns lose the factories that kept them alive, the meatpacking plants, once concentrated in cities, move in. Even apart from their mistreatment of workers, they are usually terrible corporate citizens, giving little to their communities and doing nothing to alleviate the problems in health and education created by their hiring policies. The old manufacturing giants—the Maytags, Fords, and Balls—not only paid the wages that supported their towns but lavished their philanthropy on them, with parks and schools and arenas. There is no Tyson Park or Cargill School in the Midwestern meatpacking towns of today.

In most towns, the locals, lacking any guidance, cope in their own way. In Beardstown, immigration just seemed to happen; problems get solved as they arise, but no one has tried to organize a civic response to coordinate these solutions. In other towns, such as Storm Lake, Iowa, the town first ignored what was happening, then got together in a concerted effort to bring the natives and newcomers together. Neither approach is totally successful. But an outsider, more used to the posturing of politicians and ideologues around the issue of immigration, has to be awed by the honesty and thought with which these small-town Midwesterners dealt with the changes in their lives. Cities, too, are coping with twenty-first-century immigration in their own way. But no city has been transformed so completely, so visibly, as the little meatpacking towns like Beardstown and Storm Lake. Visits to these towns tell a lot about the future face of the Midwest.

If Beardstown is known at all, it's as the home of the Beardstown Ladies, a group of local women who won national fame—not entirely deserved, as it turned out—for their acumen at playing the stock market. I went to see one of the Beardstown Ladies, Buffy Tillitt-Pratt, a vibrant woman in a Stars and Stripes blouse who runs a local real estate agency. Some of her best customers, she said, are Mexicans buying houses in the $40,000 to $50,000 range and fixing them up. In Beardstown, that buys three bedrooms, a yard, and a garage. Some Mexicans buy rental properties. All pay on time. "I think they're wonderful people," Tillitt-Pratt says.

Not so the waitress who served me a plate of catfish down by the river. "There's a Mexican who lives next door, and he came over and destroyed my trampoline in the backyard. I tried to get them to pay one hundred dollars to replace it and they just said, *'No comprende.'* "

In a small town under stress, a local newspaper can set the tone. Bill Beard, a local historian who owns the weekly *Cass County Star-Gazette*, does a noble job putting immigration into its global context and urging tolerance. Mostly, he knows that in any small town, the most important institution is the school. When it comes time to run the annual page of pictures from the senior prom, Beard makes a point of including both Anglo and Mexican kids in the photos. It sounds small, but everyone notices.

Nobody seems to mind, he told me. "At least they haven't burned my place down."

Those Mexican kids amount to 27 percent of the high school enrollment, 40 percent at the grade school level, and no less than a majority—54 percent—in prekindergarten. This pattern repeats itself in most packing towns. Before long, the school enrollment at all levels will be majority Hispanic. Someday, the towns themselves will be majority Hispanic.

It sounds like a problem, and it is. Many classes have to be bilingual. Many of the Mexican parents lack classroom education themselves and don't see why it is important for their children to go to school. The Beardstown school employs Spanish-speaking emissaries, called parent educators, to go into Hispanic homes to contact parents. Band concerts and student plays are staged two times or more, so that parents working the night shift at Cargill get a chance to see their children onstage. Twenty percent of the students are transient and may appear or disappear in the middle of a school year.

It's worth it, for both the students and the schools. The state pays $5,000 for each student. Enrollment in Beardstown, unlike most towns, is rising, and revenue with it. In addition, towns like Beardstown take their schools seriously, no matter who's being educated there, and local voters passed a bond issue that paid for an impressive new high school.

"Would I rather have declining enrollment and the problems that go with that," the superintendent, Robert Bagby, asked me, "or would I rather have this beautiful new school?"

Trevor Cottle is the bilingual coordinator at the school and deals with the day-to-day problems of educating children from two very different cultures. To hear him tell it, he has less trouble with the students than with the Beardstown teachers, who consider this melding of cultures nothing but a distraction from the normal classwork.

Cottle works with another bilingual coordinator, Julio Flores, in an office decorated with American and Latin American flags and a picture of the California farmworkers leader César Chávez. "Within the school, we're considered fun and games," he said. "The other teachers say we take away from the English-language instruction. We tried to develop a forum on integration, but even the teachers don't have enough knowledge about this phenomenon."

Cottle told me something that I found astonishing. In the decade that Hispanic children have been going to school in Beardstown, no one at the school ever considered using the local influx of immigrants to teach Beardstown children about Mexico, or the outside world, or the way that globalization can affect even the smallest and most isolated town. This changed during the spring of 2006, at the time that Mexicans were marching in American towns and cities to protest new laws restricting immigration. The Mexican students at Beardstown wanted to march, too. School officials said no, but suggested that they instead hold a forum on immigration. It was a good idea that ended badly.

"We were delighted to have this forum," Cottle said. "We

didn't have any way to find out what the kids thought about the world around them. In the end, it scared hell out of our administration. The first part went okay—why immigration happens, what the immigration bill was all about, that sort of thing. Then came the comments. It started well and escalated into accusations. The Anglos accused the Hispanics of taking their jobs, of not paying taxes. They'd say things like, 'My brother went to Cargill and they wouldn't hire him because he's not Mexican. They're stealing jobs from my brother.'

"Some of the Hispanic kids were crying. Some of the others were answering back, but they were in the minority. We learned there's a lot of division." Only five teachers attended the forum, Cottle said. And though the school planned more such assemblies, there haven't been any.

Bob Walters was a ham boner and union representative at the meatpacking plant back in the days when it was owned by Oscar Mayer and employed mostly local people. Now he's the mayor and has presided over the transformation of his town. He says what he thinks and seems to have made everyone mad at one time or another. He's a tough old guy, a believer in the dignity of the working man, a staunch Democrat—his office is a shrine to John F. Kennedy—and a blue-collar community leader who wrestles daily with his own past and prejudices to come to terms with a confusing new world. Among other things, he's a self-proclaimed redneck, which he defines as someone who says, "Do it my way or no way."

Beardstown's way of doing things—at least the old way—ended in 1986, when Oscar Mayer closed the plant. Cargill bought it in 1987, hired 250 former Oscar Mayer employees, then quietly began sending recruiting agents to Mexico, to bring in Mexican workers to take most of the other jobs. In 1990, the census recorded thirty-one Hispanics in town. Now, Walters says, "We're a town of fifty-nine hundred people by the census and about eight thousand truly." All the rest, he says, are illegals. He doesn't like it much, but he knows he doesn't have much choice and has to deal with it.

"A lot of people in town say they wish to hell they'd leave," Walters told me late one afternoon after he drove back from his regular job with the state government in Springfield. "Come on. Let's be realistic. They sustain the town.

"But it's a redneck town. Don't think we ever had any blacks here. We've always been closed to outsiders. Here we've got generation after generation after generation. But it's a new economy now. We can't keep our brightest and our best. We had four kids from our graduating class, they went to West Point at the same time. But they'll never come back."

A lot is changing, including attitudes. The presidential primary season was just beginning and Bob Walters and I talked politics a little. What Democrats did he like? What about Hillary Clinton? No, he said, his part of the world isn't ready yet for a woman president. Who, then? Well, he said, a ticket of Al Gore and Barack Obama would look good.

Obama? Come on, I said. I know the history of this town. Not so long ago, you wouldn't let a black man stay in town at night, let along elect him president.

"Oh," the mayor said, "we've kind of gotten over that black-white stuff now. What we have a problem with is the Mexicans."

Cargill is the biggest employer for seventy-five miles around. It employs twenty-five hundred workers, most of them immigrants, and three hundred persons in management. It's not only Beardstown's biggest employer by far but the biggest taxpayer, turning in some $500,000 per year. It's unionized—"even the illegals belong to the union"—and pays good wages, about $13 per hour.

So what's not to like? Well, Oscar Mayer paid $13 an hour, too, according to the mayor, when it closed. When Cargill reopened the plant, it paid about $7 per hour, and wages for the exploited and docile workers are only getting back to where they were twenty years ago.

"This is legitimized slavery," said Walters, the old union man. "If there weren't illegals here, they'd have to raise the wages. They need them here so they can abuse them and underpay them. It's a guest-worker thing. This is corporate America telling the worker to kiss my lily-white ass, or I'm going to tell the immigration people. It's corporate America at its worst."

I heard this echoed across the meatpacking towns of the Midwest. Virtually everywhere, the packers are hated—and no one knows what they'd do without them.

Feelings about the Mexicans themselves are equally ambivalent. According to the mayor, the Mexicans run up Beardstown's bills for police and medical care, especially because the town has to provide translators. The biggest problem, he said, is that no Hispanic will step forward and take leadership. No immigrant ever attends city council meetings. The Mexicans don't mix in the community. About thirty-five Mexicans voted in the last election. If the mayor needs to contact the Mexican community to discuss mutual problems, there's nobody to talk to.

In his once all-white town, he can't get used to deciding what to call himself. "I'm an *Anglo?*" he asked me. "I'm just a good ol' boy."

So what are the positives? Many workers bring their families, settle down, have children, send them to school, buy homes, become good neighbors, even on phony documents. "We've got maybe half a dozen businesses and stores opening up," the mayor said. "The ones that have families here and buy a home, they're here for the long haul. They've bought some terrible homes and fixed them up, did a real nice job." The Mexicans live all over town and there's no ghetto, no Little Mexico. In 1996, a Mexican who worked at Excel shot a local man in a dispute over a woman, then fled back to Mexico. Beardstown hunkered down for a Mexican crime wave—which never happened. That was the last murder. "There's not much crime, other than no seat belts or no driver's license," Walters told me. "We got no crimes of violence or property. The illegals, you know, they want to stay out of trouble, so no one notices them, and those who want to live here, they don't want to step out of line." There's some drug use, mostly methamphetamines, but that's true in most blue-collar Midwestern towns.

In the mayor's view, legal immigrants are okay and illegals aren't. But, as he says, what are you going to do about it? "People want to shut the border down and stop immigration. I've got no problems with the legals being here. But forty percent of the plant is illegal workers. There's a Mexican store over on the corner.

Give me two hundred dollars and I'll go over there right now and get you your two forms of ID."

Bob Walters agonizes openly about this. He hates the illegality and, in a letter to the local congressman, wrote, "Amnesty does not set well with me. But I am a realist and have yet to hear of a reasonable plan that would work in removing the 11 or 12 million illegal immigrants already here if we deport them." To me, he said any plan to build a thirty-foot wall along the border would only result in a boom of Mexican-made thirty-five-foot ladders.

"It's a world economy now, and that's the way it's going to be. Sometimes, you don't like it much. If you're working-class, you're competing with Mexico or China and you're just going down. Most people in this town didn't have any exposure to other ethnic groups. But now, we're paying more attention to the rest of the world. It's hard. Look at Galesburg. They closed that Maytag plant there and took it to Mexico. Now you've got all these Mexicans busting their butts to get here.

"People don't understand it. Is it good or bad for the town? The jury's still out. You can't have change in a community without losing something. Where would we be without them? But where are we going to be in the future? Someday, the mayor of this town will be Hispanic."

Dark-skinned immigrants are moving into the Midwest, but it's uneven. In Iowa, the Hispanic population shot up by 153 percent between 1990 and 2000, according to official census figures. But still only 3.3 percent of the total population is foreign-born. More important, most Iowa towns and villages don't have a single immigrant. Others, meatpacking towns like Beardstown, are 30 percent Hispanic or more. These are places like Denison or Marshalltown or Columbus Junction.

Or Storm Lake. Storm Lake, Iowa, calls itself the City Beautiful, and it is, in truth, a pretty place, sloping down to the shores of its eponymous lake. Low, wooded hills surround the shore, and in the distance the graceful metal arms of a vast wind farm turn slowly. The town lies in northwestern Iowa, by far the most conservative part of the state, beholden to the Republican Party and the Farm Bureau. It is a blue-collar town and, despite the lake, never got the tourism that has sustained Okoboji and the other meccas for vacationing Iowans.

One reason may be that, if you stand beside the lake when the wind is from the north, the breeze smells like a thousand pigs. Storm Lake, too, is a meatpacking town. The Tyson pork slaughter-house and the Sara Lee Bil Mar turkey-processing plant employ, be-tween them, about twenty-five hundred workers and are by far the town's biggest employers. Officially, there are 10,700 people in Storm Lake. The true figure is probably 12,000 or more, and about 5,000 are Hispanic.

In both Storm Lake and Beardstown, the big plants and their employees utterly transformed the town and the lives of the people who live in it. But the two towns are handling the transformation very differently.

Beardstown just let the wave of immigration wash over it and tried to cope without taking too much action: "We're not that kind of town," Buffy Tillitt-Pratt told me. To this day, there have been no public forums, no diversity committees, no civic attempts to ponder the changes. Storm Lake, by contrast, has thought hard. Townspeople have banded together to help police, schools, and hospitals react to the new pressures. Civic leaders have emerged. Storm Lake still has problems, but it seems to have them under control. The immigrants here, as in Beardstown, came to take jobs that the local whites always had. This was explosive—but no ex-plosion happened. No riots, no KKK, no violence of the sort that has tarnished immigrant towns in France or Britain.

Not that the immigrants, especially the Mexicans, play any real role in the town, any more than in Beardstown. Attempts to bring the two communities together, socially or politically, have failed. Anglo leaders say they have no idea who speaks for the Latino com-munity. The Latinos keep a low profile and seem to like it that way. One night, the town closed off Lake Avenue, its main street, and in-vited the lieutenant governor for a ceremony announcing a new re-sort and water park to be built just southeast of town. This is a big deal, an attempt to draw in tourists and diversify the economy away from the packinghouses. About two hundred townspeople showed up to eat pork-tenderloin sandwiches and hear the speeches, but I saw not one Hispanic or Asian face. The next day, I drove into the Sara Lee plant as the shifts were changing. The workers were Mexican, African, Asian, women in chadors, with not one Anglo in the lot.

Art Cullen is the editor of the weekly *Storm Lake Times*, which, like Bill Beard's paper in Beardstown, sees its mission to help its readers understand the new globalizing world they live in. Cullen was part of a local mission to Santa Rita, in central Mexico's Jalisco state, where most of Storm Lake's Mexicans began their journey north. His story on life there, spread over six pages of the paper, was a first-rate job of public education. He found people who had lived in Storm Lake, and many more who wanted to go. He reported that meatpacking jobs in Santa Rita pay $40 per week, one tenth the wage in Iowa. He described 30 percent unemployment and 50 percent illiteracy. He compared schools, hospitals, groceries.

Underneath he found a crucial similarity: Buena Vista County in Iowa and Ayotlan County in Mexico are both "isolated rural counties depending on razor-thin margins in agriculture, trying to become something more . . . Santa Rita and Storm Lake are two little rural towns far away from anywhere. They are enmeshed in the center of a huge international complex involving politics, economics and culture that neither city can do much about but try to understand. So we set off."

"People here are conflicted," Cullen told me. "They're conflicted about the plants. It's not simple. People like to bitch about the Mexicans or about Tyson. But what would Storm Lake be without Tyson? We'd be Newton, that's what."

Meatpacking came to Storm Lake in 1935, as part of the companies' great exodus from the Chicago stockyards to the cheaper, less congested, nonunion towns to the west. (All these plants, in towns and small cities scattered across the Midwest and Great Plains, employ Mexicans today.) Until 1981, the big Hygrade pork-packing plant employed mostly white men who spent thirty years or more there and typically earned around $30,000, big money then. Hygrade closed the plant in 1981. The next year, IBP took over, broke the union, turned down most of the Hygrade workers who applied, slashed wages by half or more, and began hiring outsiders, including immigrants. (Tyson bought the plant in 2001.)

Storm Lake already had some experience with diversity. In the late 1970s, twenty four families of Tai Dam refugees were resettled there from camps in Thailand. After them came a wave of Lao refugees: about three hundred ended up working at IBP. Like the Tai Dam, the Lao settled down, worked hard, sent their kids to school, and saw them move away into better jobs, including the professions—the American dream in action.

Then came a group of Mennonites from Chihuahua state in Mexico, German-speaking Mexicans recruited by agents in Texas. In the early 1990s the recruiters began bringing in other Mexicans, some straight from Mexico but more from Los Angeles, Miami, and other cities. If Storm Lake welcomed the Tai Dam and Lao refugees and tolerated the Mennonites, this wave of Mexicans came as a shock.

"Some of these guys were just out of the Dade County jail," Art Cullen recalls. The Storm Lake crime rate spiked. But these newest Mexicans, being drifters, drifted away. They were replaced by Mexicans who came directly from Jalisco state, mostly recruited from the town of Santa Rita; once here, the new arrivals sent word home that jobs awaited in Storm Lake. Storm Lake and Santa Rita became part of a transnational human pipeline, two stations on a global railroad. Storm Lake had been losing its young people, its best and brightest, to the cities, to Des Moines or Chicago. Now Santa Rita was losing its most ambitious young people—to Storm Lake. Suddenly the two towns were linked by a lifeline across a bristling border.

The farmers from Jalisco ended up on the disassembly line in Storm Lake, because of NAFTA, which, among other things, brought American corn and American ways of farming to Mexico. Storm Lakers who have been to Santa Rita say that more and more cornfields there display signs for the same American seed companies, such as Garst or Pioneer Hi-Bred, that bloom from cornfields in Iowa. NAFTA has opened Mexico to investment by

American firms, and the big seed companies have moved in with their high-yield seeds and fertilizers. These modern farming methods produce the same result in Mexico as in the Midwest—more food, of course, but also the consolidation of farms, as farmers who can afford to get big buy out those who can't. As in rural America, small farmers are driven off the land. In Iowa, these dispossessed move to Des Moines or Chicago. In Jalisco, they move to Storm Lake.

When large numbers of Mexicans arrived, Storm Lake citizens, alarmed by the changes, formed the first diversity task force to try to understand what was happening and decide what to do. Several such task forces over the years have provided a useful forum but seem to have achieved little themselves. They did, however, ignite action by various local leaders who were in a position to do something. By all accounts, the local hospital responded. So did the schools. So did the police force.

The local police chief, Mark Prosser, is a white cop from the mostly black town of East St. Louis, Illinois. His parents had been part-time missionaries in Guatemala. He knew something about different cultures but had no idea, when he arrived in 1989, that this background would come in so handy.

The police force hired civilian community officers to work with immigrants. An unarmed Spanish-speaking officer is a liaison between new immigrants and the police. Neighborhood watches were formed. Policemen learned Spanish. Prosser initiated diversity training—not exactly a traditional priority in most Iowa small-town police forces.

"We're very strict," he told me. "No use of hate words. Officers say, 'I've talked this way since I was a kid. I can't change,' and I tell them, 'Well, I talked that way, too, and I know you can change.' "

So far, so good. The crime wave peaked and dropped. Storm Lake is about 30 percent Hispanic now, and Prosser figures that this population commits about 30 percent of the town's crimes, no more and no less than everybody else; though among young people, about 60 percent of the crime stems from immigrants.

It's a new kind of policing. Getting evidence is hard: immigrants, fearing officialdom in general and the police in particular, won't talk and won't testify. Forged documents are a growth industry: one raid turned up a box of blank county birth certificates. Prosser helped federal officials stage two raids on illegal immigrants in the 1990s but won't do it anymore: "In a matter of days, most of them were back. It was a waste of money and resources."

Much policing arises from a clash of cultures. Storm Lake residents call the police to complain about loud parties and public intoxication. Then there's machismo—"they think it's okay to beat on their wives. We handle domestic violence the way we're supposed to. Women will call us to get us to stop it, but then they don't want us to arrest the husband, and they won't call us again. It's a learning curve."

Churches and local attorneys hold classes on weekends on education, health, or housing. The Lutheran church has a Hispanic outreach program. The Catholic church has a separate Spanish-language mass. The Presbyterians and Methodists cosponsored a Southeast Asian Christian ministry. Because of the Lao, there even is a Buddhist temple, the first in Iowa—a yellow farmhouse out on Rothmoor Road, with a statue of a golden Buddha in the forecourt, surrounded by prayer flags, a patio with a Weber grill, and a small, yellow wooden shrine in the field behind.

Renea Seagren, a local nurse, went to some of the diversity task force meetings. She already knew that 95 percent of the local tuberculosis sufferers were immigrants. She learned that most of them were uninsured: the local hospital took heavy losses by treating them. Mexican women never saw a doctor between the confirmation of their pregnancy and the delivery.

"Doctors here say that everyone is seen, and I guess they believe it," Seagren said. "Yes, they'll see anyone who gets into their examination rooms, but they don't understand what goes on over the phone. The hospital has interpreters, but doctors demand that patients bring their own interpreter. Usually this means the patients have to take their kids out of school. So the children miss school, and it's scary, if the illness is serious. Do you want kids talking about the mother's menstrual problems, or their father's prostate?"

Seagren, backed by sixty local leaders, applied for a federal grant to open the United Community Health Center—basically a clinic for immigrants. In 2005, she got $650,000, renewable annually, and a year later opened up shop in a retired surgeon's office. The clinic has interpreters on staff, helps drive patients to the office, and charges on a sliding fee scale: "We don't ask them if they're legal or illegal."

The grant covers about 40 percent of her costs. She thinks the packing plants could help with donations, since many of the patients picked up their ailments—carpal tunnel syndrome, bad backs, rotator-cuff injuries—on the disassembly lines there. "But they say no—it's not in their budgets."

The hospital supports the clinic, Seagren said, but local doctors see it as competition and refuse to help. At least two doctors in Santa Rita have reported getting calls from Santa Rita natives in Storm Lake. Seagren says some Mexicans in town go to a *curendero*, a Latino shaman or faith healer—not a specialty taught in most Iowa nursing schools.

What Seagren really needs is a Spanish-speaking doctor and a couple of nurse-practitioners. So does virtually every packing-house town. When I got back to Chicago from Storm Lake, I asked leaders of the city's vast Mexican community if they knew any Hispanic doctors who would like to live in a pretty, quiet little town in Iowa. I was told that the flood of immigration into the United States has burdened health systems everywhere, including cities. Chicago needs every Spanish-speaking doctor it can get, and Storm Lake has to stand in line.

But the immigrant children can't stand in line for an education. As in Beardstown, the schools are where everything—language, education, culture, family strains, the future—comes together. I spent some time with Lori Porsch, the curriculum and special-education director for the school system, talking about how the schools are coping. As we talked, I was struck by the sheer determination, quality, and decency of so many people in small and troubled Midwestern towns who take their responsibilities seriously.

Those responsibilities are growing. In the junior and senior high school, 54 percent of the students are locals and 33 percent are Hispanic. In kindergarten through fourth grade, Hispanic children make up 72 percent of the enrollment. Storm Lake schools have forty bilingual instructional assistants, Porsch told me. The schools have set up networks to draw in Mexican parents. Federal grants fund preschool English-language programs that teach both toddlers and their parents at the same time; as a result, 90 percent of Hispanic kindergarten students speak English. About 25 percent of the students are transients who move from town to town, often without records. "This starting and stopping just kills us, and the record-keeping is still a nightmare," she said. "But we have to educate the kids that are here now.

"Some families go home for 'holidays'—and that can mean two or three months. We had one kid who had missed forty days. We found out that her father had left and her mother, who didn't speak English, was trying to hold a job. The least of her worries was keeping her daughter on grade point." With all this, the school has a 6 percent dropout rate. In Chicago schools, the dropout rate for both Hispanic and African-American students is closer to 50 percent. I asked Porsch how she did it.

A lot of it seems to be the kind of personal attention that small-town schools offer. But part of it is an imaginative charter school program that allows senior high school students to take courses linked to classes at the local community college and to a local university, Buena Vista. By delaying their high school graduation, the students come out with something approaching higher education.

Porsch said, "Many of these kids are the first kids in their family to graduate from high school. Mostly, they're Hispanic. Their families don't dream of college for their kids. But we have to help them figure out that school is really necessary. We have to encourage them to want more than to work on the line at Tyson. Their parents can't afford college, and some of them are undocumented kids who are not going to get financial aid. So these students, there's about fifty of them, decided not to graduate but to stay with this charter program, taking a general course in science and math, or construction, or health, or audio mixing. At the end, this gets them a two-year degree."

Unlike Beardstown, Storm Lake makes diversity and immigration part of the curriculum. It seems to be paying off. "We have a larger number of kids living here in Storm Lake with languages, or who are going into foreign affairs. We've just had two kids go to Ivy League schools. They already understand globalization—because we've living it."

All these good things are happening in a town that is represented in Congress by one of the nation's more vitriolic foes of illegal immigration, a Republican named Steve King. King, a Storm Lake native and a contractor by trade, has designed his own version of a wall to keep immigrants out. His Web site claims that "thousands of Americans die at the hands of illegal aliens every year." Without illegal immigration, he says, the import of methamphetamines would fall by 80 percent. "The lives of twelve U.S. citizens would be saved who otherwise die violent deaths at the hands of murderous illegal aliens each day. Another thirteen Americans would survive who are otherwise killed each day by uninsured drunk driving illegals. Our hospital emergency rooms would not be flooded with everything from gunshot wounds, to anchor babies, to imported diseases, to hangnails, giving American citizens the day off from standing in line behind illegals. Eight American children would not suffer the horror as a victim of a sex crime." There are no statistics to back any of these claims, and many Iowans agree with the *Des Moines Register*, which has called him "an embarrassment to Iowa."

King's district embraces not only Storm Lake but other towns—Denison, Sioux City, Council Bluffs—that depend on industries, such as meatpacking and casinos, that employ mostly Hispanic immigrants. Natives of these towns know they need these immigrants and, most of the time, work hard to absorb them. Then, once every two years, as they did in the 2006 congressional elections, the same natives go into the voting booth and reelect King by 60–40 margins. It's easy to see this as a reflection of the way the people really feel about immigrants, and this is partly true. On the other hand, northwest Iowa is yellow-dog Republican territory, where any GOP candidate will win big. Both the traditional churches, like the Dutch Reformed, and the growing ones, like the Evangelical Free, are solidly conservative. King brings pork into the district: he claimed some of the credit for dredging Storm Lake to make way for the new water park. But mostly his reelection is an example of the gap between the anti-immigrant rhetoric in Washington and the reality of immigration politics back home.

Down at the newspaper, Art Cullen tries to put this into local context. "Most people here know they don't want their kids working in the packinghouse, and somebody's got to do it, so we guess they [the immigrants] are okay. But when King says we have to police borders, this does have some resonance. This is one of the states that gave birth to the populist movement. People accept that somebody's got to slaughter those hogs. Storm Lake needs to be a pork-producing center, and if it takes Mexicans to do it, okay. But they don't like it, so they vote for Steve King."

In fact, most polls show that hostility to immigrants is greatest in towns and regions that don't have any. In towns like Storm Lake, immigrants are not some vague looming threat but a real presence, for better or for worse, a fact of life, the devil people know. In towns without immigrants, they are a dark-skinned menace whose arrival would signal defeat. These are dying towns that have lost not only their economic purpose but their very character. Jobs have gone. Main Street is crumbling. All the town has is its character, its identity, which is usually based on a common heritage, a common religion, a common face. In other words, the immigrants are disliked less for who they are than what they represent. What they represent, to people who have lost everything else, is the loss of identity.

In this choice between identity and survival, some towns choose suicide. Plans to put packing plants into two other northern Iowa towns, Spencer and Iowa Falls, fell through in the face of local protests. According to Mark Grey, a professor at the University of Northern Iowa and the state's leading expert on immigration, townspeople in Iowa Falls posted signs asking, "Do you want to be like Storm Lake?" "Do you want more TB?"

The state government split over the issue. In 1975, after the Vietnam War, a Republican governor of Iowa, Robert Ray, was the only governor to respond to President Ford's plea to states to take in Southeast Asian refugees. Thousands of Laotians, Cambodians, and Vietnamese became new Iowans. Then, in 2000, Governor Vilsack, a Democrat, recognized Iowa's shrinking population and desperate

need for new workers. Vilsack proclaimed Iowa "the Ellis Island of
the Midwest," sent out a call for hundreds of thousands of immigrants, established regional Diversity Welcome Centers, and chose
three towns—Marshalltown, Fort Dodge, and Mason City—as
"model communities" to seek immigrants.

It didn't work. Public opinion polls showed that most Iowans
opposed immigration on this scale. Vilsack, facing reelection,
muted his enthusiasm. The legislature, in a meaningless but hostile
gesture, passed the Iowa English Language Reaffirmation Act of
2002, making English the official state language; in polls, 86 percent of Iowans cheered.

Of the three "model communities," Fort Dodge actively opposed the program and never spent the state money it got to imple-
ment it. Marshalltown, on the other hand, already had a packing
plant and civic leaders who were coping effectively with five thousand new immigrants. When the Marshall County supervisors
voted to make English the county's official language, the Marshalltown city council passed a resolution proclaiming that English
might be the official language of the county but not its county seat.

After an initial burst of enthusiasm, the program in Mason City
"died a quiet death," Mark Grey told me. City leaders kept their
hands off it. A New York–based anti-immigration organization
called Project USA didn't help by rolling a hostile "truthmobile"
through town. Long-term planning waned and vanished. Such a result in Mason City was an irony not lost on Iowans. Mason City is
"River City," the town immortalized as the epitome of Iowa by a
native son, Meredith Willson, in his musical *The Music Man*.

Remember?

> *Oh, there's nothing halfway*
> *About the Iowa way to treat you,*
> *When we treat you*
> *Which we may not do at all.*

Back in Beardstown, St. Alexis Church has a new priest, a
Chicagoan named Richard Sheehan, who spent most of his career
in Texas and speaks Spanish. Someday, the church will need a

Hispanic priest, but, like Hispanic doctors and other professionals, the available ones are seized by cities like Chicago. Towns like Beardstown have to wait.

In retirement, Father Weitzel is campaigning to bring in a movie theater—Beardstown has none now—that would show movies in both English and Spanish. He wishes the local Mexicans would try harder to learn English, but is clear on what they have given the town.

"There are two kinds of towns in the Midwest," he said. "There are bedroom communities with the potential for growth, and there are towns like Beardstown, which are too far from anywhere to be bedroom communities. Beardstown would have died out if the Hispanics hadn't come. If Cargill stays, this town will become a Hispanic town. If it goes, we better buy a casket big enough to bury the town."

CHAPTER 8

New Blood for Cities

Chicago, too, has an immigrant problem. No less than 22 percent of the city's population is foreign-born. There are 1.5 million Latinos, immigrant or American-born, in the Chicago region, most of them Mexican. The city holds more than fifty thousand foreign-born residents from each of eight different countries, and only one of them, Poland, is in Europe; the rest are Mexico, Guatemala, China, India, Korea, the Philippines, and Palestine. Calls to 911 can be answered in any one of 150 languages, including Hmong and Pashto.

Chicago's problem is melding all this diversity and division into one coherent whole. How do you plug all these newcomers into the city and put them to work? How do you find them jobs and homes? How do you find bilingual cops, doctors, school principals? How do you make sure their kids go to school and stay in school? How do you induct them into the mysteries of banks, urban politics, voting? How do you educate kids in a school that by necessity holds bilingual classes in Spanish, Gujarati, Arabic, Vietnamese, and Serbo-Croat? What do you do when you need every last one of those immigrants and some 25 percent of them broke the law to get here?

And then you think—these people saved the city. Thirty years ago Chicago was a decaying has-been of a city that was bleeding people and jobs. Today it is booming, and the immigrants—not just Latino but Asian, African, Arab—are a big part of that boom. Put simply, Chicago's veins pulse with new blood.

Cleveland, on the other hand, has a bigger immigrant problem. It doesn't have any. At one point, Cleveland was 50 percent foreign-born—Italians, Germans, Slovaks, Poles. Today, immigrants account for barely 4 percent of the city's shrinking population. Population has been falling for years. Cleveland is about half as big as it was after World War II. Today it is an empty, dull place, lacking new blood and, hence, lacking life. "We even have a hard time attracting illegal immigrants," Ronn Richard, president of The Cleveland Foundation, told me.

We saw in the last chapter how most Midwestern towns and counties outside the glow of metro regions are shrinking—except for meatpacking towns where thousands of immigrants, mostly Mexican and often undocumented, have generated new life. We also saw how these towns struggle with the many pressures and problems these immigrants have brought with them for the towns' schools, hospitals, police, taxes, and, especially, their very identity.

Cities, too. Almost all major Midwestern cities are losing population. Those that hold their own, such as Chicago, make up for the loss of native population, mostly white, with the arrival of immigrants, mostly Hispanic. Everywhere, these immigrants create severe strains on schools, health care, job markets. A lot of political and economic energy goes into absorbing these new Midwesterners.

It could be worse. The new Midwesterners might not be coming. Now *that's* a problem.

As Art Cullen said in Storm Lake, "People are conflicted." Across the Midwest, birth rates are down. Young people are leaving. The Midwest desperately needs people to fill jobs at the top, in the sciences and the professions, and at the bottom, on construction crews and in restaurants. It needs Ph.D.'s from India and farm boys from Mexico. It needs the ideas and ambitions that immigrants bring.

For all the public controversy over immigrants, few urban experts dispute their contributions. They not only bring jobs and skills.

They bring global viewpoints, vital contacts with other nations, ethnic restaurants and neighborhood festivals, new art and different music. They make cities richer and more fun. Cities that are booming—New York, Chicago, Boston, Toronto, Denver, Portland, San Francisco, Atlanta—all have big and growing foreign-born populations. Cities in trouble—Detroit, Cleveland, Pittsburgh, Baltimore—do not. Successful cities draw immigrants, which make them more successful yet.

The Midwest was first settled by restless and hungry foreigners. These immigrants built the Midwest. In the century and a half since then, the region lost this restlessness and hunger—and must recapture it. For all the stresses they cause, the Midwest simply needs as many immigrants as it can get.

But that means the Midwest needs to break the law. To thrive, it needs to import criminals—that is, people who come here, work here, and live here illegally. The Midwest has work for almost all the immigrants arriving now—and only about 15 percent of them come in through the front door. Without the illegal immigrants, whole chunks of the Midwestern economy, from Chicago to Storm Lake, would seize up. But even Midwesterners who want immigrants gag on the issue of the illegals—or the undocumented, to use the more polite term.

Talk about being conflicted.

This chapter will deal with the view from Midwestern cities, both those with immigrants and those without, and the impact of immigrants on jobs and wages. It will look at the needs of the Midwest as a whole as it faces a global era and will argue that those needs are clear. The only immigration policy that will help the Midwest is one that opens the door as widely as possible. And that means rethinking America's whole approach to immigration.

"Immigration laws are like the Prohibition of our time," Allert Brown-Gort, a Mexican-born professor at Notre Dame, said. "The law itself is broken. The problem isn't the people who break the law, it's the law itself. You know a law is broken when the cost of obeying it is much higher for most people than it is for breaking it." By "most people," Brown-Gort meant not only undocumented

Mexicans sneaking across the border into Arizona, but most Mid-westerners who rely on Mexicans to do many of the jobs that keep their civilization afloat.

Before Chicago was a city, it was a labor pool. The great industries that built the city first imported workers, mostly from Europe, to run the plants and factories. Unlike in European cities, no single tribe or nationality ever dominated the city. Instead, it was a salad of tribes, thrown together by the industries but fiercely separate and suspicious, bristling with hostilities imported from abroad, but too tightly jammed together, too interdependent, to permit replays of the tribal wars that many of them had come to escape. During the Balkan wars, I asked a Macedonian kiosk owner, the purveyor of some of the city's best Polish hot dogs, how he got along with the other former Yugoslavs who have come to the city. "The Serbs in Chicago?" he said. "I hate them and they hate me. But, no, we don't fight here, like they're doing back home. We're too busy making money."

In other words, Chicago is no model of unity, not then and not now, no New World nirvana where refugees from foreign poverty or pogroms come to live in sweet harmony. But in the city itself, immigration is not much of a political issue. It's only when you get to the farther suburbs, where immigrants are settling for the first time, or into the exurbs, where there aren't any, that politicians played the immigrant card in the 2006 elections. (There's no evidence that immigration played a decisive role in the elections, at least in the Midwest. The region's leading anti-immigration congressmen, such as Iowa's Steve King and Wisconsin's Jim Sensenbrenner, won handily, but both held solid Republican seats.)

The city has always specialized in the "wretched refuse," people who got tired of being hungry. This was true in the nineteenth century, the homesteading era. At that time, the government was giving land to anyone willing to farm it, and few of those newly minted farmers could be lured off their land into the factories. So the early entrepreneurs—men such as Cyrus McCormick and George Pullman—sent agents to Europe to announce that anyone willing to work would always find a job in Chicago. Thus came the Germans, Poles, Lithuanians, Irish, Slovaks, Croats, Italians—the great waves of European immigration who built industrial-era Chicago. Mexicans, Cubans, Chinese, and Jews came, too, and the city thrived. When heavy industry died after World War II, immigration declined: at one point immigrants made up barely 10 percent of the city's population. There were no jobs, so why come?

Now they're coming again, to take the jobs offered by a global city. This time, though, it's different. The early immigrants were fodder for the city's factories, a vast proletariat that, after years laboring in the mills and stockyards, achieved a middle-class standard of living while still carrying a lunch pail. Some of today's new immigrants, especially those from Asia, are more likely to come with education and, often, a native command of English. Chicago's health system and schools would collapse without its immigrant doctors, nurses, and teachers. One third of the students at the University of Illinois at Chicago and 60 percent of its engineering graduate students are foreign-born. The student directory at Northwestern University lists more students named Kim, Park, and Chang than Jones, Smith, or Johnson. An Egyptian runs the city's leading international human-rights law institute. An Iraqi is the chief lobbyist for a new Chicago airport, and another Iraqi heads the cardiac department at the University of Chicago. An Indian is dean of Northwestern's Kellogg School of Management. At the University of Chicago's medical school, a Nigerian leads the cancer genetics program; another Nigerian is chief AIDS researcher at the leading public hospital, and yet another directs the environmental program at the city's Field Museum. Chicago's most prominent novelist, Alexander Hemon, came from Croatia as a teenager, barely speaking English. Lucent Technologies employs six hundred Indians, and so many Indonesians work at the financial markets on LaSalle Street that an Indonesian church has been installed in a nearby skyscraper. The city has 130 non-English-language newspapers. At one high school, the student newspaper is published in English, Spanish, and Urdu. In the same neighborhood is a Romanian Pentecostal church that used to be a Korean Presbyterian church and, before that, a synagogue; on one block is the *Korean Times* newspaper, two law offices with nameplates in Greek and Arabic, and the Holy Land Grocery, which used to be a Jewish restaurant called The Bagel.

The city's Polish-born population, which was 137,000 in 1920, had fallen to 55,000 in 1970; since the fall of Communism, a new wave from Poland has brought it back up to 137,000, precisely what it was almost ninety years ago.

This new European and Asian immigration is dwarfed by the flood of Hispanic immigrants—1.5 million of them, including 1.3 million Mexicans. Only half live in the city itself, in neighborhoods such as Pilsen, which, as its name implies, began life as a neighborhood for Czech immigrants. Pilsen's Twenty-sixth Street now ranks second only to glitzy Michigan Avenue as the city's busiest shopping street. The other half live in the suburbs, in towns like Aurora and Waukegan, where earlier immigrants established a beachhead. In some of these suburbs, entire apartment buildings contain Mexicans from a single town or village in Mexico, just as immigrants from Santa Rita head immediately for Storm Lake. Priests from Mexican towns travel regularly to Chicago to perform wedding and baptisms in these northern outposts of their parishes.

The earliest immigrants were largely working-class and stayed that way, even when they achieved a middle-class standard of living. Today's immigrants are more likely to split into two classes. At the top are scientists, doctors, professors, engineers, managers, largely from Asia. At the bottom are the laborers, often barely educated and largely Hispanic, who make the beds in hotels, tend the city's gardens, park its cars, hang drywall on construction crews, work in small factories, or, especially, man the stoves in Chicago's restaurants: any Chicagoan who goes out to eat Chinese or Indian or French will probably get a meal cooked by a Mexican.

The average Asian family in Chicago makes about $10,000 per year more than the citywide average, even more than white residents. Asians are not only professional but entrepreneurial. Indians own almost all the Dunkin' Donuts franchises in Chicago. Most of the city's dry cleaners are Korean. By contrast, the average Mexican makes only $15,000, placing him well below the poverty line (although the average Mexican household income is $45,000, because most homes include several workers). Many Mexicans are day laborers who gather beside streets or in parking lots every morning, hoping to get picked for a few hours' hard work.

Rob Paral, Chicago's leading immigration demographer, says this split, in class and education and income, simply matches the demands of the economy. Over the next ten years, he says, more than 30 percent of new jobs will require a college or junior-college degree. Another 58 percent will be at the bottom—the sort of jobs that can be learned with a few hours' training. In the middle will be the jobs that really require a high school diploma—but they amount to only 12 percent of the openings.

The trouble, Paral says, is that most Americans—more than 80 percent, and the figure is even higher in much of the Midwest—have a high school diploma, but only 15 percent have a college degree. That puts these Americans in the middle, where the new jobs aren't. The economy is going to need a lot of dropouts and Ph.D.'s, and we will need to import both.

This means that, in a global economy, the Midwest relies on immigration just to fill the available jobs. It's already happening. Asians and Africans keep Chicago's industries and health systems going. At the bottom, anyone with eyes can see that Chicago's lakefront parks, construction boom, and tourist industry rely totally on Mexican immigrants.

"This is the flip side of outsourcing," Allert Brown-Gort says. "We may be outsourcing some jobs to India, but we're insourcing workers for other jobs. We're not going to send dishes to China to be washed or chickens to India to be plucked."

The problem is, there are nowhere near enough legal immigrants to fill these jobs. Yet the jobs are being filled. No mystery, according to Paral. Some 305,000 Mexicans arrived in Illinois in the 1990s, and only 79,000 of them were legal immigrants. More recently, he estimates that fully 85 percent of all new arrivals from Mexico are undocumented. This means that, of the 1.3 million Mexicans in the Chicago area, both foreign-born and American-born, some 25 percent are there illegally. Most of them got here with help from earlier, legal immigrants or are living with relatives who may be here legally but are breaking the law by helping their illegal cousins.

"That means that half of Pilsen is affected by this," Paral says. "Are you going to criminalize half of Pilsen?"

Sheer numbers make this impossible. Economic realities make it stupid. The Mexicans in Chicago own fourteen thousand businesses, employ forty-two thousand people, generate $2.4 billion in sales. No city can afford to obey a law if it means paying that big a penalty.

Amazingly, some of this entrepreneurship and homeownership comes from undocumented—illegal—immigrants. The Mexican consulate in Chicago and in other cities issues a card called a *matrícula consular*, which is an alternative form of identification for people without any ID. With the *matrícula*, as it's called, an otherwise undocumented immigrant can open a bank account, get a mortgage, or buy a car. The *matrícula* also acts as a tax number, enabling the immigrant to pay taxes. Part of those taxes go for Social Security, even though an undocumented immigrant will never collect Social Security, because he's probably registered under a false name.

It's a sort of don't-ask-don't-tell approach to immigration, a vast gray area that keeps the economy going but that exploits the immigrant while involving two governments—the Mexican and the American—in a transnational scam. The Mexicans give identity numbers to immigrants who are here illegally; the Americans accept taxes and Social Security payments from the same immigrants. Both say they want immigration reform, and both pursue policies that make this immigration possible. Legally, this shouldn't happen. Realistically, it has to.

The whole debate carries an air of unreality. No one really knows how many illegal aliens live in America—estimates vary between seven and twenty million—because of the obvious impossibility of counting them. All attempts to block undocumented Mexicans at the border have failed, and no expert believes new measures will work any better. Immigration reformers suggest "guest worker" programs that would allow a Mexican to work here legally for two or three years, then go back. This "reform" would be worse than any problem it could solve: it would guarantee a permanent floating population of unsettled immigrants. Worse, it would be unenforceable: no Mexican worker is going to go back voluntarily once the legal temporary stay ends.

The history of immigration in Chicago, like that in most of America, has always followed a three-generation pattern. The first generation comes to work, learns a little English, sacrifices for its children. The second generation graduates from high school, is generally ashamed of its old-world parents, and gets good, solid jobs. The third generation goes to college, becomes dentists or accountants, and moves to the suburbs.

The Americanization of the new wave of Mexican immigrants may be trickier and take longer. Traditionally, immigrant parents have leaned hard on their children to get an education. But as in Beardstown, many immigrant Mexican parents in Chicago, barely literate themselves, don't understand the value of an education. Usually, both mother and father work, sometimes at two jobs, often at odd hours, and play almost no role in their child's schooling. Chicago public schools, hampered by union rules, have been slow to expand school hours or make other accommodations to their students' parents. The upshot is a high dropout rate—about 50 percent for Mexican children. It seems unlikely that this huge dropout population will produce many suburban dentists. In short, Chicago and its immigrants have problems. Most other Midwestern cities wish they had problems like these.

Successful cities attract. They attract tourists, investment, scholars, jobs—and immigrants. Immigration follows success and generates more of it. This is true everywhere. "If a city develops successfully, you can't stop immigration," Kemer Norkin, an adviser to the mayor of Moscow, told a Chicago meeting.

By that standard, many Midwestern cities fall short. Only 9 percent of Milwaukee's population is foreign-born. In Des Moines, it's only 5.3 percent; in Detroit, 7.5 percent; in Indianapolis, 3.5 percent; in St. Louis, barely 3 percent. Compare this to the true global cities, such as New York or San Francisco, where about 35 percent of the population was born in other countries.

But let's be fair. New York and San Francisco have always been immigrant gateways, with large foreign-born populations. This gives those cities their character. Midwestern cities like Indianapolis and Des Moines don't share this heritage. They are more homogeneous, more all-white, and took their character from this sense of stability and belongingness. In recent years, some areas have opened their arms to refugees or certain national groups: Vietnamese have settled in Des Moines, and Bosnians in St. Louis. Russian Jews play an important role in Cleveland, and the largest Arab community in the United States is in Detroit. But the Midwest has far to go before it begins to reflect the diversity of the coasts. Even if that time comes, the social and political tensions might not be pretty.

This is the lesson from Minnesota. For the first time, that state faces substantial nonwhite immigration. In trying to absorb these strangers from strange places, Minnesota is facing a backlash that challenges the character of the state and has already changed its politics.

Minnesota, with its Twin Cities of Minneapolis and St. Paul, has always been seen as one of the most progressive societies in America. The state was largely settled by Scandinavians and Germans, who brought a strong social conscience and a powerful sense of social responsibility with them from the old country. They also brought a trust in government that dominated Minnesota politics for decades. This produced a strain of populism, a belief that government has the right to regulate and control the big corporations, which were seen as the real threat to the public well-being. With this went a strong welfare state and an acceptance of high taxation. The Democratic-Farmer-Labor Party, or DFL, set the high-minded and progressive tone and produced such politicians as Hubert Humphrey and Walter Mondale. Even Republican governors such as Elmer L. Andersen accepted the tradition of a strong state government and social responsibility.

Minnesota corporations, like Minnesota politics, were different from those in the rest of the country: a 1978 study showed that, of the thirty-seven American corporations that gave 5 percent of their pretax profits to charity, thirty-three were based in

Minnesota. The state passed early laws on child labor and workmen's compensation.

In most of the Midwest, the big cities and their suburbs exist in mutual hostility; only the Twin Cities and their suburbs have worked out a tax-sharing arrangement that acknowledges their stake in each other's prosperity. To the rest of us in the Midwest, Minnesota and Minneapolis always seemed more high-minded, cleaner, more reasonable; smug perhaps, but a superior civilization.

That's changed. Minnesota and its cities are learning that it's easier to take responsibility for your fellow man when he looks like you and everybody else. Immigration into Minnesota—from Asia and Africa and, more recently, from Latin America—has been rapid, mostly since 1990, and it has undermined the state's cohesion and its sense of shared responsibility. It also shifted Minnesota politics to the right. Once one of the most reliably Democratic states in the nation, Minnesota now is a swing state: it voted for John Kerry in 2004 but elected a Republican governor, Tim Pawlenty. Among American governors, Pawlenty is among the most hostile to illegal immigrants. He pushed a policy of tough controls on illegal immigration, including a fine for companies that employed them; only when opponents protested did he couple this with increased spending for legal immigrants. In 2006, Pawlenty bucked the Democratic trend to win a narrow reelection. There was more to his reelection than immigration. Friends in Minnesota told me he is seen as a good guy, genuine, "a guy you'd like to have a beer with, whether you agree with him or not." But his stand on immigration didn't appear to hurt him.

"It's been difficult for people here to adapt to diversity," a Minneapolis journalist named Carl Goldstein told me. "There's a liberal tradition here, but as the color mix has changed, the overall climate has grown more unfriendly to our liberal traditions—what used to be the Minnesota Way. As our population has changed, the old idea of the importance of strong social programs has frayed. There's a shortsighted view now of the community's obligation to maintain a strong educational system. The idea of Minnesota as a whole was based on that German-Scandinavian culture. Now, with the racial mix, that consensus has broken down."

The pollster Stan Greenberg did a study for the Humphrey Institute of Public Affairs at the University of Minnesota and came to the same conclusion: "Minnesota is changing. In a state where the storied 'consensus' once meant a high degree of civic engagement and shared vision for economic, social and educational betterment in the state, we see divisions into increasingly irreconcilable camps."

There is more to this than a backlash against immigrants, Greenberg said, but immigration plays a major role. "There is a great deal of ambivalence, if not at times outright hostility, in Minnesotans' feelings toward immigrants," he wrote. "They express a strong commitment to openness and community spirit but hold deep concern about increasing immigration to the state. Many in exurbia, in particular, see them as having a detrimental impact on the state, in particular the provision of public services. This negative view, in turn, has become an important component of the case that Minnesotans make against government: hardworking Minnesotans are frustrated by alleged 'handouts' for immigrants. In principle, people support the notion that Minnesota is an open and tolerant state—embracing the notion of 'Minnesota nice.' But below the surface, there is clear resentment."

Greenberg's polls found that the growth in immigration ranked a close third, behind high taxes and weak schools, as the "most discouraging" aspect of life for Minnesota exurbanites: 21 percent cited immigration, compared to 23 percent citing taxes and schools. By contrast, concerns over immigration came in last among the worries of city dwellers: only 7 percent mentioned it.

More vivid feelings came through in Greenberg's focus groups. Some of the comments were confused, others bitter:

"Too many . . . it's really gotten out of control."

"If you're coming over here with the intent to live the American dream, it's one thing, but if you're coming over here to hang your country's flag in your front yard, and if you're coming over here trying to make me change, or I've got to stand up and apologize for who I am because you don't speak my language or I don't understand your religion . . . I think that's crap. I think this is America."

"Diversity, are you kidding? I see other people coming up here to work at the plant. They are only up here to have their babies, to get the money, they are here illegally."

"We're letting a lot more minorities from other countries into this country . . . The groups are getting very large . . . They get all this help. They get this, they get that, they get this, they get that, and those of us who live in this country, who have paid our taxes, and those of us who have fought for our country and in this state are the ones that are paying for all those breaks, and our children and our lifestyles are not increasing. They are staying stagnant."

(Greenberg identified his focus-group members only by gender and town. This last comment came from a woman in Anoka, which is Garrison Keillor's hometown. Minnesota today feels a long way from Lake Wobegon.)

Much of this is anecdotal and, by the rhetorical standards of other states, pretty mild. Minnesotans make poor Klansmen. But Greenberg's polling, which is taken seriously by most political experts in Minnesota, gives statistical shape to a drift that is transforming the way the state governs itself.

One result is the breakup of the old support for an active government. Both polls and voting patterns indicate that Minnesotans no longer see government as an efficient and necessary means to even out life's inequities. There is a feeling that citizens are paying taxes to support programs for immigrants who refuse to be integrated into the life of the state.

Minnesota, once a cohesive place, is splitting in two, with the dominant Twin Cities confronting a hostile alliance of impoverished rural areas and thriving exurbia. Long after Chicago and other cities experienced white flight from a growing African-American population, Minneapolis and St. Paul are going through the same process, as whites flee to the suburbs and exurbs, partly to escape the increasing diversity in the cities. "These concerns are strongest in exurban areas, where residents are trying to escape the perceived challenges of urban living—poor public schools, increasing racial and ethnic diversity, crime, and a high tax burden," Greenberg said. "Here, we find the greatest skepticism about government and the role of immigrants in society, as well as the greatest reluctance to make a public investment in helping the disadvantaged." It is hard to imagine a sharper rejection of the Minnesota Way.

All this, he said, "is altering the social and political landscape of Minnesota." The rural areas remain the most rock-ribbed conservative, but the exurbs tend to be more Republican, while the cities remain solidly Democratic. The result is a state that is, overall, deep purple but splits between the blue urban core and the sea of red outside it.

Minnesota is far from unique. In fact, it resembles the rest of the nation now more than it ever has done. But it has changed, and the change dramatizes the ability of immigration and the global forces behind it to alter not only the demographics but the psychology of a state and a region.

The surprising thing about this is that, compared to other states and cities, Minnesota and the Twin Cities don't have that many newcomers. It's a northern state, far from the usual immigrant gateways. Even today, only 6 percent of its people are foreign-born, half the national average; even in the Twin Cities, this population is barely 16 percent. There is a growing African-American population, but non-Hispanic whites still make up no less than 87 percent of the total population. By New York or Chicago standards, this seems hardly noticeable. But in Minnesota, it's noticed.

It's not the totals so much as the rapid change. The number of blacks, Asians, and Hispanics nearly doubled between the censuses of 1990 and 2000. Another factor is the number of refugees: Minnesota is home to large colonies of Hmong, Somalis, and Sudanese, many of them war victims who were brought to the state by church groups. From 2000 to 2005, the number of white students in Minnesota schools fell by forty-three thousand; the number of black, Hispanic, Asian, and Indian students grew by twenty-eight thousand.

A third, and critical, factor is that so much of the immigration is concentrated in a few places—not only the Twin Cities but meatpacking towns such as Worthington, Willmar, Austin, Faribault, and Albert Lea. In places like Worthington, about half the kindergarten students are minorities, mostly Latino and Somali. These towns are on the way to becoming "majority minority" towns, a change in the state's complexion so radical that many Minnesotans simply can't come to terms with it.

David Goodhart, the editor of the British magazine *Prospect*, has identified the problem as the "progressive dilemma." Progressives, he said, idealize both diversity and social solidarity. But maybe you can't have both. Progressives favor increased immigration, to open society to more and varied people. But they also want a generous welfare state financed by a progressive tax system. The problem, Goodhart said, is that people are more likely to sacrifice and share with other people who look like them, have similar backgrounds and values, and face problems that they themselves could face. Immigration enriches a society but fragments a common culture. It "asks a question as old as human society itself: who is my brother?"

Goodhart wrote, "The diversity, individualism and mobility that characterize developed economies—especially in the era of globalization—mean that more of our lives is spent among strangers. We must not only live among stranger citizens but we must share with them." This immigration is breaking down the common culture in Britain, he said, which is becoming more like America. In the United States, "you have a very diverse, individualistic society where people feel fewer obligations to fellow citizens." In parts of America, certainly, this is true. But much of the Midwest, and especially Minnesota, were more like Europe—were indeed patterned on the welfare states of Scandinavia and Germany.

In all these places, Europe as well as Minnesota, the welfare state is on the run. Everywhere, this no doubt has much to do with the economic pressures of globalization: nations, states, and corporations are all finding it harder to pay for social spending, especially when they're in competition with countries with no welfare state at all. But this financial squeeze only makes it easier, if not mandatory, to keep our hands in our pockets when faced with the new needy, who, unlike the deserving poor of old, don't happen to look like us.

Opponents of increased immigration argue that immigrants—especially the uneducated and unskilled immigrants from

Mexico—take jobs from Midwesterners, both the white packing-house workers in rural towns and the unskilled blacks of the inner cities. By working for low wages, they say, the immigrants drive down wages for everyone. Supporters of increased immigration retort that the Mexicans do jobs that Midwesterners don't want to do and claim there's no evidence that they drive down wages. One side claims that immigrants raise taxes by demanding services from schools, hospitals, and welfare agencies; the other says the immigrants pay far more into the tax system than they take out.

To say these issues remain unsettled puts it mildly. Each side marshals statistics, rhetoric, and experts to prove its point. Neither convinces the other. But the country's immigration policy depends on making a choice. Any choice must include the Midwestern point of view, because the Midwest has too much riding on the issue to remain silent.

Months of travel and study through the towns and cities of the Midwest have made up my mind. The Midwest needs all the immigrants it can get. This is true of the more educated Asians and Africans and even more true of the uneducated Latinos. Everyone would be happier if all the immigrants, especially the Latinos, had entered the country legally. But most haven't, and they are too integrated into the Midwestern society and economy to send home.

Wherever they have gone in the Midwest, immigrants have enriched their new homes—occasionally, even saved them from a slow death. The Midwest has a long way to go to integrate these immigrants, but that is no reason not to recognize what they've done for us. This means conceding that the critics make some good points. In the small meatpacking towns, immigrants hold poorly paid jobs that used to be held, for higher wages, by white local workers. Certainly, low-skilled immigrants compete with low-skilled African-Americans for some jobs in cities and probably drive down the wages for those jobs.

But in most of these meatpacking towns, unemployment rates are low, 4 percent or so. The workers who used to work in the plants moved on. Certainly, some local workers would jump at jobs in the plants if they paid well and offered solid benefits. But those jobs are gone. The plants themselves would probably pick up and move to Mexico if forced to offer the kind of jobs that most Americans would take. This says a lot—not much of it good—about the meatpacking companies and globalization and the world we live in. But for both the towns and the Midwest, it is a matter of survival. The plants and the immigrants provide jobs and workers where otherwise there would be neither.

There is no evidence that immigrants drive down wages for Americans with education or skills, for the simple reason that they don't compete with them. At the top, there aren't enough American scientists to fill the demand: the Asian Ph.D.'s are here because they're needed. At the bottom, few Americans with high school degrees would do the work the Mexicans do. Theoretically, Latinos may be competing with uneducated African-Americans for these jobs; in fact, the employment chances of these African-Americans may have been doomed the day they dropped out of school. The solution to their problem is education, not immigration control.

David Card, an economist at the University of California, has argued that, despite all the immigrants, most U.S. cities have fewer unskilled workers and higher wages than they had in 1980. The reason: despite the high dropout rate in cities, more Americans than ever have high school diplomas and are simply unwilling to take the minimum-wage jobs that immigrants fill. Certainly, these American workers have problems: median wages in this country have been nearly stagnant since the early 1970s. But work by Card and other economists makes it hard to argue that the immigrants are hurting American workers. If these workers face job losses or lower wages, it has more to do with other aspects of globalization—especially outsourcing—than with competition from immigrants.

Most economists concede that, at the very bottom, uneducated immigrants hold down the wages of uneducated Americans, especially African-Americans. But as noted above, the solution is a high school diploma. Even then, African-Americans would probably lag because many employers prefer Latino workers; much of this is the result of racial prejudice, which, however despicable, can't be blamed on immigration.

The evidence is even thinner for the proposition that immigrants take more from American society than they give. In Chicago, 65 percent of the region's Latinos are citizens. Fifty-two percent of all Latino homes are owner-occupied. The immigrants are family-oriented: Latinos are half as likely as whites to be single persons living alone, and some 56 percent of Latino families have children at home, compared to 30 percent of white families.

Most Latino workers pay taxes, and there is no evidence they use public services more than other workers; illegal workers use them far less, because they fear any contact with officialdom. There is one exception—schools. Immigrants have lots of kids, and in cities as in small packing towns, this puts pressure on over-crowded and understaffed schools. But in areas like the Midwest with declining populations and birthrates, these children represent the future. Investing in the future means investing in these Latino students. Both the expense and the problems are great, but the payoff is greater.

The Latino dropout rate is huge, and the college attendance rate is low. The Chicago public schools try to combat this by offering a "college bridge" program that lets good students take classes at one of twelve area colleges and universities while still in high school. The school system covers the costs, and the students get college credit. One leading university, DePaul, has already awarded thirty-six degrees through this program.

Integrating immigrants is more complicated than just fixing the immigration laws. Mexican immigrants travel back and forth between their two homes and exist as foreigners in two countries, never really sinking roots. Many send money back home, helping families in Mexico to build homes or open businesses; in Illinois alone, these remittances amount to about $2.6 billion per year. This is great for the folks back home, but adds up to $2.6 billion that doesn't get invested in their new country. Like most immigrants, Mexicans here harbor dreams of working a few years in the Midwest, then returning to Mexico. In fact, most get married, buy homes, have children and grandchildren, and never go back. Many Mexican community leaders argue that it is time for these immigrants to decide that they are here to stay. The title of a recent study on Latino Chicago, issued by the Institute for Latino Studies at Notre Dame, said it plainly: "This Is Home Now."

American banks are beginning to realize that the huge Mexican community offers rich pickings. Many immigrants are "unbanked"—they have no bank account or other relationship with banks. But increasingly, others are opening accounts, taking mortgages, drawing loans, using banks to send remittances back to Mexico. Some American banks, such as Wells Fargo, have led the way into Mexican neighborhoods. The Federal Reserve Bank of Chicago has run programs urging local banks to follow suit. In Milwaukee, the Mitchell Bank, a local institution, is so active in the Mexican community that it has opened a branch in a local, heavily Hispanic high school and hired some of the students as tellers, in an attempt to reach Mexican families through their children.

Despite this, the community still starves for decent financial services—not only banks but legal advice, accountants, and the like. Hispanic-owned businesses in Chicago do $7.5 billion in business every year, existing on the fringe of the city's economy. Both the Mexicans and the city need to provide the services that could make this potential bloom.

All this could happen—in fact, it *is* happening—with no change in the immigration laws. But those laws remain unrealistic and unenforceable, and most solutions suggested so far won't fix things. A thirty-foot-wall will, as the mayor of Beardstown said, only lead to a market for thirty-five-foot ladders. Tougher border enforcement doesn't keep illegal immigrants out of the United States. Instead, it keeps them in. An undocumented immigrant who is already here is much less likely to go home if he fears he won't be able to get back in again.

The last major revision of immigration law took place in 1965 and opened the American door for the first time to large numbers of non-European immigrants. But as demographer Rob Paral points out, no one in 1965 could foresee the future—the invention of cheap communications, the advent of low-cost air travel, the destruction of much of Mexican farming by NAFTA, the boom in

the demand for unskilled labor, and above all the birth of globalization and its ability to erase national borders. In an era when
everything else—money, goods, jobs, ideas—flies across frontiers
as though they don't exist, it's unrealistic to think that people can
be fenced in or fenced out.

So long as millions of immigrants desperately want to come to
the Midwest, and so long as the Midwest desperately needs them,
no law or wall will keep them out.

Most debate over immigration reform isn't rooted in economics
at all. Instead, it rises from the push and pull of political con-
stituencies, from fear of terrorism, from anger at the wholesale
breaking of immigration law, from outrage over the exploitation
of immigrant workers, from dread among a white majority that it
will soon be a minority, from threats to traditional culture, from
the itch of employers to get cheap labor, from black opposition to
competition for low-wage jobs, from outright racism, from the
age-old hatred entrenched Americans feel toward immigrants,
whether they be Irish, Jewish, Italian, German—or Mexican.

The exact shape of any new immigration law will emerge from
the welter of political motives. In the end, there are only two ways
to solve the problem of illegal immigrants. One way is to round
them all up—all twelve million of them—and send them back to
Mexico, and this just is not going to happen. The other way is to
legalize them all. Opponents will object that this is amnesty that
rewards millions of law-breakers, and they're right. But there is no
other solution that has a chance to succeed. At the moment, of
course, this open-door policy is politically impossible to pass, but
that doesn't make it wrong. Quotas, especially for Hispanic workers, should be quadrupled or quintupled. Green cards should be
easy to get. Border enforcement should be focused on the real
problems—catching terrorists and intercepting smuggled goods,
including drugs: both will be easier, because it is simpler to record
and search a legal immigrant, entering with a passport, than to
catch an illegal immigrant crawling beneath a fence.

There will still be more Mexicans wanting to come to America
than quotas will permit. But this is true of immigrants from many

other countries, and a liberalization of laws will bring this supply and demand into better balance.

Any immigration reform must be coupled with serious programs to improve the Mexican economy. It's not only Midwestern factory workers who feel damaged by NAFTA. American imports have ravaged the Mexican farm and industrial economies, leaving workers no choice but to seek their fortune north of the border.

Mostly, when it comes time to write a new immigration law, the Midwest needs to speak with one voice in demanding that Midwestern needs for more workers and citizens are met. No one can complain that this will change Midwestern society: that's already happened. No one can say that there are enough Midwesterners to do the jobs available: there aren't. Everyone knows that assimilating these new Midwesterners—economically, politically, socially, economically—will be tough: so what else is new?

The only real point is that, in a global world, we have no choice.

CHAPTER 9

Global Chicago and Other Cities

Twenty-five years ago, Chicago hit bottom.

The city had peaked sometime in the 1960s, not long after the first Mayor Richard Daley took office. At that time, it symbolized the industrial age, a strong, pulsing city proud of its production, pollution, and paychecks, unaware that this astonishing potency, like the age that supported it, was about to end. The next two decades saw a long, slow decline into the Rust Belt. In the 1970s, Chicago lost 361,000 people and 153,000 manufacturing jobs; it was to lose another 188,000 of these jobs in the decade to come. When a factory closed, so did the corner bar where the workers drank, and the grocery store where their wives shopped, and the gas station where they filled their tanks, and the office of the doctor who took care of their kids. All these people and businesses paid taxes, and when they went, so did their tax dollars. Suddenly, the city had less money to plant trees or stock libraries or fix streets and sewers or run bus lines: in short, it didn't have the money it needed to make itself attractive to the people and businesses who might reverse this slide.

But, oh my, it was something while it lasted.

For a century, Chicago had been that toddlin' town, Sweet Home Chicago, the city that worked, a brawling, noisy place, almost magical in its sudden wealth, its gangland guns, its Machine politics. Its politicians had names like Hinky-Dink Kenna and Bathhouse John Coughlin. Nelson Algren called it "the city of all cities most like Man himself." Loving Chicago, he said, was "like loving a woman with a broken nose. You may well find lovelier lovelies. But never a lovely so real." Most memorably, Carl Sandburg came to town from downstate Galesburg and proclaimed it "Hog butcher for the world / Tool maker, stacker of wheat / Player with railroads and the nation's freight handler / Stormy, husky, brawling / City of the big shoulders." Sure, it had its culture, its art institute, and its nonpareil orchestra, but these were, as Saul Bellow once told me, "only the ransom that the rich guys paid to their wives." Mostly, it was as Algren described it, a city on the move, where no one really belonged but everyone came to make his pile, "a drafty hustler's junction in which to hustle awhile and move on out of the draft."

"If you have to be an American, you might as well live in Chicago," Tom Geoghegan, the most lyrical of local lawyers, wrote. "Do it right. Embrace your fate." An enchanted place, Geoghegan called it, almost mythical. Some exuberant part of the American character achieved full bloom in Chicago. It reigned as the capital of the Midwest, the place where, as Sandburg said, the farm boys came to be lured by the painted women under the gas lamps, and stayed to make it big, or at least to get a job in the mill, buy a bungalow, and settle down.

If you wanted work, brother, Chicago had work for you.

Then it ended. The myth lived on, of course: it was all we had. Chicagoans told their Al Capone stories, celebrated their crooked aldermen, pretended they still lived in the city that worked, even when it had stopped working.

I returned to Chicago in 1976, after nearly two decades abroad, and found, beneath the braggadocio, a grim and sour place, sliding downhill fast. Publicly, civic leaders kept up the old Chicago boosterism; in private, they admitted that the city had had its day. As one urban expert told me, "Chicago is not going to disappear, but all the trends that I see are against it. I see very little hope for locating economic activities here again."

And then it reinvented itself. Twenty-five years after its collapse, the French author Bernard-Henri Levy came to Chicago and exulted over "this magical, beautiful city, perhaps the most beautiful city in the United States." In the eighties, the *Economist* wrote that Chicago's skyscrapers were no more than "a façade" hiding urban decay; in 2006, the magazine devoted a special section to the city,

unironically entitled "A Success Story." "Chicago," it said, "is un-
doubtedly back . . . This is a city buzzing with life, humming
with prosperity, sparkling with new buildings, new sculptures,
new parks and generally exuding vitality." Shoppers and tourists
thronged in. So did companies and universities and, especially, new
residents—mostly young singles and empty nesters but some professionals, many with families, to fill the town houses and lofts that
bloomed where, not long ago, only empty warehouses and parking
lots stood.

In most listings of "global cities," Chicago ranks in the top
twenty, sometimes in the top ten. Its streets and parks teem with
flowers and statuary, and one neighborhood after another revives,
as the children and grandchildren of the people who first fled to
the suburbs come back to the city. The town's old lefties, who
made careers out of fighting the first Mayor Daley, Richard J., grit
their teeth and concede that his son, Richard M., the mayor since
1989, is doing a great job.

Chicago's rise has everything to do with its fall. To a great degree, its new prosperity is based on the industries that made it rich
in the industrial era—but it had to get rid of those industries to
thrive in the global era. It is a classic case of new wine in old bot-
tles, of a city reinventing itself with the raw materials at hand.

As the British urban expert Peter Taylor wrote, "Globalization
takes place in cities and cities embody and reflect globalization."
In the global era, metro areas dominate the wealth, the people, and
the action. But they have to do it without the heavy manufacturing
that once sustained them. For better and for worse, Chicago exemplifies this new emerging city. Its global reach extends from a
regional base. The tools of its trade are money, business services,
hospitals, universities, tourism, communications—the industries
that have replaced manufacturing as the new masters of the global
heights. By paying attention to amenities, such as parks and good
restaurants, it is drawing in the rich and the brainy—the modern
equivalent of Carl Sandburg's farm boys—to run those industries.
In the process, like most global cities, it has become a place of vast
inequalities, between the global citizens at the top and the left-
behinds at the bottom.

No other Midwestern city has transformed itself from industrial powerhouse to global center. Minneapolis has some global status, but it is an outlier in Midwestern history, never having had a heavy industrial base in the first place. All Midwestern cities struggle to cope in the global era. Some won't make it. Detroit certainly won't. Cleveland probably won't. St. Louis and Milwaukee may not. Others, such as Indianapolis and Grand Rapids, may succeed. Des Moines and Omaha are doing well, but both, like Minneapolis, had no heavy-industrial legacy to overcome. All look to Chicago, hoping to learn its secret.

In their youth, all Midwestern cities—Chicago most of all, but also Detroit, Cleveland, Milwaukee, Akron, Gary, St. Louis, Dayton, Flint, Toledo, Grand Rapids, Peoria—embodied American industrial dominance. Chicago symbolized meatpacking, Detroit ruled the auto world, Gary made steel, Akron produced tires, Grand Rapids dominated furniture making, Peoria grew rich on whiskey distilling. As Purdue historian Jon C. Teaford wrote, "An exciting energy pervaded the heartland cities, making them the envy of the world. They were the birthplace of the automobile revolution." In the late nineteenth and early twentieth centuries, they were "youthful marvels, growing at a breakneck pace and brimming with vitality." In the twenties and thirties, they matured but remained the hubs of the nation's commerce, even as California and the South claimed some of the vigor.

Not only that, these cities were social laboratories and hotbeds of political reform, the places where industrial barons and urban idealists both did their best work. Mayors such as Hazen Pingree in Detroit, Samuel M. Jones in Toledo, and Tom L. Johnson in Cleveland saw the city as the natural home of justice and democracy. Dayton led the movement toward city-manager rule. American socialism achieved its greatest success in Milwaukee. (Chicagoans, then as now, prized effective government and the ability to get a drink over democratic ideals. Paddy Bauler, a notorious alderman and saloonkeeper, danced a tabletop jig in his tavern after a Machine victory in 1955 and crowed, "Chicago ain't ready for reform yet." Things aren't quite that raw now. But given their city's relative success over the years, Chicagoans suspect that civic virtue may be overrated.)

If the cities of the Midwest once prospered together, they declined together after World War II, becoming, as Teaford put it, "the capitals of the Rust Belt, a decaying industrial swath that was no longer the nation's pride but instead had become a national problem." Heavy industry decamped, first to the suburbs and the hinterland, then to the Sun Belt. So did workers, following their jobs to the suburbs or to Dixie. Black workers from the South took their place, turning whole neighborhoods from white to black in a decade. Racial turmoil followed: white flight at best, race riots at worst.

Detroit and the great Auto Alley from Flint through Indiana to Dayton lived on cars; the Japanese challenge wiped out a region that is only now hitting bottom. Cleveland and Gary lived on steel; first Japan, then Third World nations such as Brazil, learned to make steel that was just as good and a lot cheaper. St. Louis lived on steel and shoes. Chicago was more diversified: it slaughtered steers, made steel, manufactured railroad cars and radios; none survived.

The Chicago I rediscovered in the midseventies fit this glum picture. The Loop, the city's central business district, survived more or less intact: the first Mayor Daley, by allying himself and his government with Loop businesses, ensured that this core remained. But twenty years of decline had left Chicago with a dumbbell economy—lumps of prosperity in the Loop and the suburbs, with not much in between but the expressways holding them together. Steel mills closed, leaving sad neighborhoods without jobs and, after a while, without people. Chicago deserved its reputation as the most segregated American city, the place that defeated Martin Luther King, a place where, twenty years after *Brown v. Board*, the black poor remained imprisoned in savage housing projects and rotting ghettos. Schools were both segregated and terrible, probably the worst in the nation. Daley deserves credit for saving the Loop and preserving the business-government alliance that drives the city. But otherwise, he presided over the city's decay, all the

while proclaiming that he ruled "the city that works." His supporters were Loop businessmen, his troops were the patronage
workers in a corrupt city government, his friends sent their children to parochial schools; outside these charmed circles, the city
slid slowly into a future as cold and gray as its lake. If great events
are a city's chance to show itself to the world, it was fitting that the
bloody 1968 Democratic National Convention displayed Chicago
as it truly was.

Not that Chicago was alone. The other great Midwestern cities
declined as rapidly into the same pathologies. Chicago's problems
were not worse, only bigger. Chicago has never been a small-*d*
democratic town. But it did exemplify a sort of social contract
that, through the years, suited most Chicagoans. The big-*D*
Democratic Party and its machine delivered services—jobs, decent
schools, safe neighborhoods, parks, street repair, garbage
pickup—in exchange for votes. But these services cost money. As
businesses and workers and taxes fled the city, Chicago had less
money to keep up its end of the social contract. The machine first
cracked when a flamboyant maverick named Jane Byrne won the
mayoral election after a vicious winter in which unplowed snow
clogged streets for weeks, a symbol that city government no longer
worked. It collapsed four years later when black Chicagoans, the
prime victims of the city's decline, rose up and elected a black congressman, Harold Washington, mayor. Washington fought a bitter
racial battle with white aldermen for four years, won reelection
and vindication, took a firm grip on the reins of power, and then
died at his desk. Two years later, in 1989, Daley's son became
mayor of a city in crisis.

Chicago, Lord knows, still has its problems—struggling
schools, isolated black ghettos, congested traffic, industrial neighborhoods that never recovered from industry's flight. Corruption
persists in city hiring and contracts, and Daley struggles to stay
free of federal investigations. But it would be ridiculous to call
Chicago a city in crisis. It is, as the *Economist* said, a comeback
city, a magnet. One study has found that, of all American cities,
Chicago draws the most young people, aged twenty-five to thirty-
four, to live near the center of the city—a sure sign of civic vitality.

Flowers bloom in planters down the middle of the city's boule-
vards, and the new Millennium Park—a gigantic undertaking of
theaters, fountains, promenades, gardens, sculpture, all set on a
lawn built over railroad tracks—has given the divided city a common, a sort of Tuileries, where all races and classes come to play.
This being Chicago, the project ran over schedule and way over
budget. Almost nobody cares.

What's going on? Globalization, that's what. Chicago ruled the
industrial age. When that age crumbled, so did Chicago. Now
we're in the global age, and Chicago has become a global city.

As the above should make clear, this is an uneven, even cruel, process. The city as a whole is doing great. Many of its people are not.
Many Chicagoans live better than ever, in safe housing in vibrant
neighborhoods, surrounded by art and restaurants, with good public transport whisking them to exciting jobs in a dazzling city center
that teems with visitors and workers from around the world. These
are the global citizens, hardworking, well-educated, well-paid, well-
traveled. And many Chicagoans live worse than ever in the old ghettos or, worse, are being shoved by gentrification out of the ghettos
into destitute inner-ring suburbs: the old housing projects, lying in
the path of the Loop's expansion, are knocked down and their inhabitants scattered to the civic winds. These are the global have-
nots, separated by class and education as much as by race from any
of the benefits of a global economy. In the middle are the global servants, immigrants, mostly Mexican, who perform the services—
valet parking, gardening, dishwashing, dog-walking, busing in
bistros, low-level construction—that the global citizens need.

All this, the rich and the poor, is on display in Chicago. Once a
broadly middle-class city, where factory workers owned their
homes and shared in the dream, Chicago today is a class-ridden
place, with lots of people at the top and lots of people at the bottom and not that much in between.

What is a global city, and how does it differ from the old, familiar
industrial city that carpeted the Midwest with its factories, rail
yards, solid working-class neighborhoods, and union halls? The difference is fundamental. An industrial city makes things. A global

city does things. We are what we do—people and cities both. A global city makes its living in a brand-new way, and the result, in many respects, is a new city.

Once the economy was local, or national at best. The old Midwestern factories sat rooted in one neighborhood. The same space housed workers, assembly lines, offices, research labs, bookkeepers, sales reps. Next to the factory stood rail lines, ready to carry goods to customers a hundred or a thousand miles away.

Over the years, some of these factories, led by Midwestern giants such as Ford, Caterpillar, and John Deere, became "multinational." They not only began to sell overseas but to set up factories in other countries. Usually, they moved their headquarters into a skyscraper downtown, housing the white-collar employees, including an international department; periodically, the international vice president drove to the airport and flew to Germany or Brazil to visit the far-flung parts of his company's empire.

Today, most companies don't even have international departments, because their entire operations are international. Manufacturing can be entirely overseas, more likely in China or Poland than in Germany. Everything else—R&D, sales, accounting, personnel—may be overseas, too, in whatever town or country makes the most economic sense. In short, the company has gone global. What once was a tight, local operation is strewn across the globe.

But these global operations don't run themselves. No matter how scattered a corporation may be, it still needs a headquarters. With most of its operations somewhere else, this headquarters can be relatively small: when Boeing moved its headquarters from Seattle to Chicago, it created barely five hundred new jobs, one third of 1 percent of its global workforce. Given the miracles of modern communications, these headquarters people can be in touch with their outposts wherever they are, anytime they want.

But given those same modern communications, this headquarters theoretically could be anywhere in the world—on a mountaintop or beside a lake, so long as a satellite dish stood nearby. For a while, people thought that the big corporate jobs would indeed end up out in the country, with plenty of fresh air, just a quick drive from home. But that hasn't happened. Instead, these headquarters or their main branches are setting up downtown, in the hearts of cities—often the same industrial cities that seemed set to die.

Saskia Sassen, a sociologist at the University of Chicago and probably the world's leading theorist on global cities, has figured this out. Sassen says that global cities—probably no more than thirty or forty of them worldwide—are the "command points in the organization of the world economy." Global corporations, she says, have outsourced everything, including their lawyers, accountants, consultants, advertising and PR people—everything that we now call business services. Businesses can't operate without these services. Again, theoretically, businesses could go sit by a lake and talk with their lawyers, accountants, etc., by phone or e-mail. For routine stuff, that's what they do. But more often, businesses want to talk with their lawyers and accountants in person.

Even in a global era, face-to-face is important. It's a matter of information, Sassen says. There's a lot of information—stock market reports, trade figures, who just got hired or fired—that you can get on the Web. But really important information only comes face-to-face. This isn't what happened today, but what's going to happen tomorrow. It's who's up and who's down. It's what companies will merge, which divisions will be sold, which CEO will be fired, what new drug will be introduced. It's the latest idea, the hottest innovation, the new new thing. It's gossip. In a fast-moving world, it's not good enough to learn something after it happened. You have to know it before it happens, and you only learn that in a whisper, a nod, a confidence over a good meal.

In short, global citizens like to have lunch. So the businesses and the business services are gathering in one place, where they can meet and talk and eat and stay one jump ahead. That one place is the center of great cities. They are where the global economy is run, the hands that hold the global reins.

These cities can be measured, and a new academic discipline is growing up to measure them. It's an imprecise science, and the measurements vary. The prominence of the nearest international airport is vital; so is the number of international flights and international passengers that pass through it. Foreign tourists mean foreign exposure, and the big tourist cities—New York, San Francisco, even Orlando—have a global claim. It's important to have big universities with lots of foreign students, foreign researchers, and foreign faculty. Los Angeles makes and exports much of the world's entertainment, so Los Angeles is a global city.

But the real measure is the number of those reins that a city holds, the power it wields over the global economy. This means the number of global lawyers, accountants, consultants, financiers, investment bankers, traders, public relations people, and other global citizens that operate from a city's core, and their links to other global managers around the world. The global conversation takes place between these cities.

Some cities hold more reins than others. At the top stand New York, London, and Tokyo, plus maybe Paris and Hong Kong. These are the true world capitals of global law, global communications, global markets, global banking. They have bigger airports, more international airline flights, more international e-mail messages, more foreign students, usually more immigrants. Like London or Paris, they might also be capital cities, but this isn't important. Governments are national, not global. In a globalizing world, capitals count for less than global business centers. New York and Hong Kong aren't centers of government. But they are centers of everything else.

Chicago has a place in this league. It ranks in the top ten internationally for global lawyers, accountants, consultants, advertising people, and other professionals; it is weak only in banking. Most lists of global cities put Chicago solidly in the second tier, with such cities as Frankfurt, São Paulo, Los Angeles, Milan, Singapore, San Francisco, Toronto, and Sydney. Brussels sometimes makes the list. Washington, a one-dimensional company town if there ever was one, never does.

These cities form a network, often more in touch with each other than they are with their own backyard: Chicago probably deals more, daily, with Frankfurt or Tokyo than it does with Indianapolis. Witold Rybczynski, a leading thinker about cities, says this network looks like the old Hanseatic League on a global scale, a confederation of city-states running their commercial world. Today's global cities, of course, exist within nations, Rybczynski says, but their global network "appears to be supranational, unaccountable to national control and strikingly autonomous." In other words, they aren't independent city-states but neither are they traditional regional centers. Like global corporations, global cities are breaking national bounds. Almost unnoticed, they have become something new in history.

Many new global cities were also old industrial centers: New York, London, Tokyo, Chicago. Others, such as Toronto or Frankfurt, were backwaters before the global wand touched them. Some titans of the industrial age—Detroit, Manchester, Essen— have dropped out of the global running. Being big is not enough: none of the world's ten most populous cities, from Mumbai on down, leads the global league. Nor is growth a help: the fastest-growing cities, from Lagos to Las Vegas, attract the uneducated, not the global citizens that every city wants. Among fifty major metro areas, Las Vegas ranked first in the 1990s in percentage growth of young adults, but it ranked last in the share of its young adults with a college degree.

Clearly, determining which cities can be called global can be pretty impressionistic, almost a party game, but not to the cities themselves, which crave this recognition. The new economy and the business services that power it have revitalized these cities and the lives of people who live in them. All of them, including Chicago, buzz with businesses—not just lawyers and accountants but all the services and stores, from Quiznos to Kinko's, that serve them. All of them draw in young professionals, who work hard, hate long commutes, and want to live where the action is. All blossom with good small restaurants and boutiques. All have a lot of jobs, both good and bad—for global citizens and global servants. In all, the arts boom. So does education: universities are opening downtown campuses. More than fifty thousand college students go to school in Chicago's Loop.

Chicago indisputably is booming. But its population is still falling—not by much, but falling. Perhaps this tells us that being a global city is great, but it's not enough.

Globalization may be creating jobs, but no one knows yet how many. Can global industries—the headquarters and business services—spin off enough jobs to support a city like Chicago? The mills and factories created hundreds of thousands of jobs: this was mass manufacturing, by the masses for the masses. The global economy creates mass employment in Third World factories, but it's still the property of the elite in the cities of the First World.

Between 1986 and 1998, Chicago added forty thousand positions in advertising, investment banking, law, accounting, and consultancies. Not bad. But thirty years ago, a single steel company, U.S. Steel, employed that many people in the Chicago region; almost all these jobs are gone now.

Globalization has transformed the way global cities are governed. Once, mayors like the first Mayor Daley worried most about jobs and who had them. Now mayors like his son worry most about amenities, about flowers and parks and good schools and enjoyable neighborhoods. The idea is to draw in the kind of people who will move to Chicago because they like it, then start a company after they get there.

Chicago had a choice between reinventing itself or dying. But in this reinvention, Chicago built the new on the foundations of the old. As Sassen points out, industrial-era Chicago specialized in heavy industry and agriculture, and it created financial, legal, and accounting experts who knew how to handle the agro-industrial sector. That sector may be global now, but it's still important, and it needs bankers, lawyers, and accountants who understand it. Chicago has them, so has become the global go-to town for these industries.

Probably the most dramatic example of this is the city's commodities and financial futures markets. These markets, arrayed along LaSalle Street, are the cornerstone of Chicago's place in the world economy, and they owe everything to its agricultural past. As we saw earlier, the markets were born in the nineteenth century to buy and sell crops and livestock raised by the pioneer farmers of the Midwest: futures contracts developed in Chicago made Midwestern farming work. In the twentieth century, these same markets moved from pork bellies to financial futures. Then, with an intellectual shove from the University of Chicago, they invented the global money market and derivatives—highly complex financial instruments that are as crucial to the global economy as farm futures were to the farm economy.

Chicago also is the leading Internet hub of the western hemisphere: more e-mail messages pass through it than through any other city in the Americas. This, too, is a result of history. First, Chicago was the main railroad city of the heartland. Then it became a communications center because telephone companies laid their lines along the railroads. Later, fiber-optic cable for digital transmission was laid along the old phone lines—which is to say, through Chicago.

In the second decade of its revival, Chicago has become what much of the rest of the Midwest wants to be. This is because, in much of that Midwest, reinvention has barely begun.

Nothing says that cities, any more than rural villages, have to live forever. Too many other Midwestern cities are beginning to look like new versions of Potosí.

If you've never heard of Potosí, don't feel bad. Almost no one has. But once, Potosí was the biggest city in the western hemisphere. It's a Bolivian city, thirteen thousand feet up in the Andes, that once supplied the Spanish conquistadores with a fortune in silver. Potosí peaked about four hundred years ago. It's still there and still produces a little silver and tin, but it's been a couple of centuries since anyone outside Bolivia paid any attention to it.

Potosí belongs to the legion of cities—like Tyre, Babylon, Ur—that once projected fabulous wealth and power and now exist, if they exist at all, as backwaters, far from the action. Some, such as Venice or Ragusa (now Dubrovnik), remain beautiful if shrunken places that thrive on tourism. But it's been centuries since anyone looked to them for trade or ideas.

A city is an organic thing. It is born usually for economic reasons: Potosí existed to mine and sell silver. If the economic base vanishes—if a mine gives out or a port silts up or trade goes elsewhere—so does the city's reason for being. Great cities reinvent themselves, over and over, finding new ways to support themselves and their citizens. They don't necessarily disappear—Potosí today has about one hundred thousand people, historic Venice about sixty thousand—but they stop counting for much.

The Midwestern landscape is littered with has-been towns. Until 1860, Cincinnati was the Queen City of the West and the biggest city in the Northwest Territory. Among the dozen biggest were Steubenville, Ohio, and New Albany and Madison, Indiana—all then about the size of Chicago. All were river ports and lost their purpose when the railroad came in.

Virtually all of the greatest Midwestern industrial cities owe their wealth to water—either rivers (St. Louis, Cincinnati, Peoria) or, more often, lakes (Chicago, Cleveland, Detroit, Toledo, Milwaukee). All are where they are today because goods once moved by water. When the railroads arrived, all reinvented themselves as industrial powerhouses. Iron and coal lay nearby. Nineteenth-century tool shops became auto plants. The factories needed steel, so steel mills grew. Everywhere, as in Chicago, a new and mighty economy grew from the base of the past.

This economy—mostly autos, but not just autos—is dying. Steel survives in northern Indiana, but employs one tenth as many workers. What's left of heavy industry declines by the year. In a global economy, cities earn their living by moving services and ideas, not goods. Geographic location can still count—Chicago proves that—but is no longer decisive. The cities of the past must reinvent themselves if they want to be cities of the future.

So far, many of the once-great Midwestern cities are failing that challenge. Detroit's plight is best known. Once the auto capital of the world, it is a destitute city today, with a forlorn core centered on casinos, surrounded by vast neighborhoods of poverty. The city, which is 82 percent black, has never recovered from a 1967 race riot. Once the fourth-largest city in America, it has lost more than half its population and is so empty that parts of it may be plowed under and returned to farming. In the last half century, Detroit has symbolized urban decline and decay. It won't vanish: houses last longer than people, Harvard economist Edward Glaeser has written, and some people—the poor, unskilled, and hopeless—actually move to cities like Detroit because of the cheap housing, keeping the cities both alive and impoverished.

There is no reason to expect Detroit ever will reemerge as a center of economic life or civilization. Southeastern Michigan has the expertise and facilities to reinvent itself as a center for automotive research and innovation, if not manufacturing. But this rebirth will take place—indeed, is already taking place—away from Detroit and nearer Ann Arbor, where the future is as bright as Detroit's is grim.

Detroit remains the best-known civic disaster zone in the Midwest. But it's not the only one. Like Detroit, Cleveland and St. Louis once ranked as economic powerhouses; both, like Detroit, lost more than half their peak population and struggle to survive.

Until the Civil War, St. Louis was considered the Midwestern city most likely to succeed. As late as 1870, it claimed to be the largest Midwestern city. But it bet too heavily on the future of its north-south river, the Mississippi, and delayed laying the east-west train tracks that would have linked it to New York and the East Coast. Chicago bet on the railroad and won. St. Louis remains a perplexing place today, all sprawl and no center. It is a doughnut city, with a hole where its heart should be, surrounded by a relatively prosperous region. The downtown is barren, cut off by ugly highways from its natural waterfront along the Mississippi River. Most downtown buildings are government offices, a sign that no one wants to do business there. Another sign is the presence of a ballpark—in this case, Busch Stadium, home of the Cardinals—in the heart of the city: it takes both a lot of cheap land and civic desperation to plop a huge stadium downtown, where shops and offices should be. St. Louis did it twice—first in 1966, during the Rust Belt era, and then again in 2005, on the same site. Traffic downtown peps up on the eighty nights or so when the Cards play at home. Otherwise, a visitor has the feeling that he could lie down in the middle of any downtown street at two o'clock on a weekday afternoon in perfect safety.

But St. Louis plans a future in biosciences and may succeed. It has a lot going for it—local money, a first-rate research school at Washington University, a lot of focus and drive. St. Louis may be better than it looks.

Cleveland, by contrast, now ranks officially as the poorest big city in the United States and may stay that way. According to a Brookings Institution report, its poverty rate is no less than 32.4 percent, even worse than that in Detroit, St. Louis, Dayton, Youngstown, or the other symbols of Rust Belt collapse. But when I went to Cleveland, I found not alarm but complacency. In a city that is being destroyed by global forces—its industry and best young people are fleeing and are not being replaced—I found almost nobody willing to actually talk about globalization or global challenges. In a city crying for answers, no one even asks the questions.

This is strange. A century ago, Cleveland was one of the three or four richest cities in America, the home of Rockefellers, an industrial powerhouse. Now its median household income of $26,000 per year lags far behind that in more vibrant Midwestern cities such as Indianapolis ($42,000) or Chicago ($39,000). Euclid Avenue once ranked with Fifth Avenue in New York as the most elegant street in the country: when the Rockefellers and the Hannas lived there, it was known as Millionaire's Row. Cleveland used to be the fifth-biggest American city; now it's thirty-ninth.

"You have to remember, this is a city built for a million people that only has half that many now," a friend told me. We had just come out of his office on Superior Avenue at five thirty p.m. on a Thursday. It should have been the rush hour. Instead, the streets were empty of traffic. A few stragglers headed for their cars. The sun still shone but Cleveland had closed for the night.

After years of neglect, the central business district remains a stately place. Many of the buildings are neoclassical gems, many built a century ago from a 1903 civic plan. From a distance, you can see how grand it used to be. But it's an eerie, echoing space now, all past and no future, splendid buildings with no one in them, noble streets faced by locked doors and cracked windows. I walked down Euclid, with its graceful and vacant buildings, empty stores, sagging gates blocking entrances that are no longer used. The existing shops sell cheap clothing or fast foods. The many For Rent signs look as if they've been up a long time.

Outside the downtown is a vast sweep of poverty, more than half-black, with abysmal graduation rates producing badly educated young people totally unfit for the global age. Everyone who can flee has fled—most of the whites to the exurbs, the better-off blacks to Shaker Heights, the poorer ones to near-in suburbs. Cleveland's police and firemen are even suing to overturn the law that keeps them from moving out.

What happened? "We stopped innovating," Ronn Richard, the president of The Cleveland Foundation, told me. "We missed the IT revolution. We missed it because we were so fat, dumb, and happy with our prowess in heavy manufacturing." Back in the 1980s, the Rand Corporation looked at Cleveland, saw it was falling behind, noted that manufacturing employment was going down, and suggested a switch from industry to services. Twenty-five years later, the Federal Reserve Bank of Cleveland reported that nothing had changed. After the Rand report, some people wanted to push Cleveland toward more changes, but others wanted to stay with manufacturing. The Fed report said that people are still divided.

In all my travels through the Midwest, Cleveland was the only place, big or small, that seemed heedless of the global challenge. Only 4 percent of its population is foreign-born, in an era that demands new blood; the city government isn't sure it wants more. One of its leading economists told me, "You can't kill manufacturing— that's stupid," but manufacturing is fleeing and cities need new ways to support themselves. In an era of global connectivity, only one nonstop flight per day, to England, links Cleveland to the world. The first-rate Cleveland Clinic is expanding, but every Midwestern city is building up its health industry: few actually count on it to carry the city's economy. The *Cleveland Plain Dealer* ran an excellent series, "The Quiet Crisis," on the declining economy; one editor told me that many of the articles excited reader interest, but the two on globalization and immigration "just landed with a thud."

Cities like Cleveland, St. Louis, and Detroit raise the question, is it possible to have a strong urban region with a weak city at its core? The obvious answer is yes—at least economically. All three centers are surrounded by vibrant suburbs and exurbs, run by people who are only too glad to get away from the cities and their problems. But much is lost: if globalization is happening in cities, then these places are missing out. Global business has revitalized the centers of New York, Toronto, and Chicago. The global conversation, as we've seen, is face-to-face and depends on proximity. Sprawling suburbs can hold a lot of routine commerce, but when this global conversation takes place, they're out of earshot.

And it's a funny thing about poverty. It moves. People who moved to the suburbs to get away from the central city are finding that the poverty and destitution that they thought they'd left behind are moving out, too. Across the Midwest, the poor—especially African-Americans—are moving out to the inner-ring suburbs, where the whites first went when they fled the city. Many Hispanic immigrants are moving straight from Mexico to the suburbs of Northern cities. According to the Brookings Institution, there are now more poor people in the suburbs than in cities. What is an affluent suburbanite to do, except to move farther and farther out?

Finally, cities are—have always been—the core of civilization. Even today, Cleveland and Detroit still boast two of the nation's five great orchestras, relics of better days. But patrons drive to concerts from the suburbs, park their cars, hear some marvelous music, and then drive home, seldom pausing to enjoy the cities that once throbbed there. Cities have museums, universities, zoos, theaters, stadiums. They are the literal heart of their regions. You can put a stadium in one suburb and create an orchestra in another, but if there is no critical mass, no center holding the region together, there is no true civilization.

So these cities, which helped build the Midwest, are moving to the fringe, economic powerhouses for one season only, like Potosí. Such cities become backwaters, living in a globalizing world that is run by somebody else. As with the cities, so with their regions. To live in the hinterland of a nonglobal city is to be condemned not necessarily to poverty. Just irrelevance.

In talking about globalization around the Midwest, I kept hearing two theories attached to two names. One was the "flat world" metaphor coined by Thomas L. Friedman, arguing that everyone in a global world is competing with everyone else. The other was the "creative cities" concept of Richard Florida, which says that the world isn't flat but "spiky," that there are global winners and global losers and the winners usually live in places, such as global cities and university towns, that perch on the peaks of the global landscape. Everyone else, Florida says, is down in the valleys of this nonflat world, out of touch and out of luck. These mountaintops, Florida says, are "creative cities" that draw in the "creative class" of people who are winning the global race.

Florida is a charismatic professor at George Mason University, like Friedman a good writer and riveting speaker, who has been spreading his gospel in such books as *The Rise of the Creative Class* and in speeches in cities around the country. Cities that fail the Florida test fear they have already lost.

"Florida says that you need a culture of creativity to be successful, and Indiana doesn't have that culture," a morose civic leader in Indianapolis told me. "He says you have to have a culture of embracing difference. Not just a toleration of difference, but rather prizing people because they're different. Tolerance is one thing, but it's pretty minimalist. It's better than intolerance. But Florida's basis is that you're excited by the way that people are different from you. You're glad that some are gay or belong to other races. Indiana isn't glad. It's more tolerant than it was when the Ku Klux Klan was here. But glad? Not yet."

"What matters today," Florida says, "isn't where most people settle, but where the *greatest number of the most-skilled* people do." If population growth were all there was to it, places like Phoenix or Las Vegas—or Lagos or Calcutta—would be leading the global charge. Instead, the key is a city's attractiveness to the "creative class"—the large number of designers, architects, scientists, artists, entrepreneurs, dreamers—whose main creation is ideas. Such people powered classical Athens and Renaissance Florence. They are the inventors who made Detroit and Dayton throb a hundred years ago and Silicon Valley boom in the 1990s. They patent drugs, customize cars, invent new products and wrap them in new packaging. They're the people who bring you everything from extreme sports to 125 different kinds of tea.

We've always had this creative class, Florida says, but it's been an intellectual elite, maybe 5 or 10 percent of the population. Now, though, it's driving the economy and it accounts for about 30 percent of all workers. There are creative lawyers and doctors, just as there are creative musicians and journalists. And their defining characteristic is that they like to be near other creative people, because that's where the fun and the action are.

Where they like to be, he says, is in cities—small cities like Madison and Cambridge, or big cities like San Francisco and Boston. Florida takes Saskia Sassen's ideas one step further. Sassen says global cities exist as a meeting point—a big bistro—for global lawyers, accountants, and other providers of services to global corporations. Florida agrees, but says they're really big coffee shops for creative people of all kinds, whose wild idea today is the new new thing tomorrow. Like Sassen's global citizens, these people thrive on face-to-face contact, because that's how ideas get bounced around. Creativity seldom thrives in isolation; instead, it happens only when creative people come together in the kind of density that sparks creative flames.

That density, Florida says, is the creative city. Every city, it seems, wants to be a creative city now. Michigan governor Jennifer Granholm even set up a Cool Cities program, a rather desperate attempt to make some of her state's tired towns "creative" by funding art galleries and pedestrian zones. As Florida notes, it takes more than a few bicycle paths and coffee shops to make a creative city. More important than what a city has is what it is— open, diverse, tolerant, "proactively inclusive."

"Courting divergent ideas and inputs isn't about political correctness," Florida wrote. "It's an economic growth imperative. My research finds a strong correlation between, on the one hand, places open to immigrants, artists, gays, bohemians and socio-economic and racial integration and, on the other, places that experience high-quality economic growth."

Florida has even adopted measures, such as the "bohemian index" and the "gay index," that hold that there's a link between the number of gays and artistic types in a city and its economic success. Not that bohemians or gays themselves are necessarily creative or productive, although many are. Rather, creative people like to be in places that actively embrace all lifestyles, and the gay culture, for instance, is a good way to measure it. Many traditional economists scoff at this as pop economics, but Florida boasts a following in the cities themselves. It's no accident that Chicago's current Mayor Daley sponsored gay-pride decorations in the city's "Boys' Town," along North Halsted Street, and takes part in the annual Gay and Lesbian Pride Parade, a public gesture that would have been unthinkable for his father, the first Mayor Daley.

In the global era, Florida says, creative cities are the ones that make money, just as manufacturing cities made money in the industrial era. The reason is the same for both—exports. Cities, like people, have to earn their livings by selling something—goods, skills, labor—to somebody else who is willing to pay for them. They have to draw in money from outside; otherwise, they stagnate, just taking in their own washing.

Before, the Midwest exported things, and got rich. Chicago exported steel, meat, metals, and railroad cars: shoppers came from all over the Midwest to buy things in its stores. Detroit exported cars. Akron exported tires. Newton and Galesburg exported refrigerators.

Midwestern cities—indeed, most American cities—still have to export to live, but they don't make things as much these days. Instead, the successful ones export services and ideas. The world needs biotechnology and information technology and is willing to pay for the brains to make them work. Boston exports the products of its brainpower, and thrives. Seattle exports the ideas of Bill Gates and his colleagues. Los Angeles exports movies and television shows. New York exports finance: every day, the world sends billions to Wall Street. San Francisco and Silicon Valley export the computer technology that powers the information age. Medical centers such as Rochester, Minnesota, export health to people who are willing to come from around the world to pay for it. Great universities—Stanford, Michigan, the Massachusetts Institute of Technology—are in the export business, even though what they export is no more than the thoughts in the heads of the people who work there.

Chicago, as we saw, exports business expertise. Global corporations that need advice and guidance on global law, global accounting, or global advertising hire Chicagoans and pay money for their knowledge, just as the world once paid money for Chicago steel.

Florida's point is that none of this happens in isolation. It happens only when creative people in a field come together to bounce ideas and inspiration off each other—that global coffee shop. The ideas and inspiration can deal with something as somber as the law and accounting, or as big as Google, or elusive as design or pop music. Creative cities are where this happens. They're where creative people want to be. If there are enough of them, they'll support a city as surely as a steel mill or auto plant ever did.

Mostly, this is bad news for the Midwest. A few college towns, such as Madison and Ann Arbor, are indisputably creative. Chicago gets high marks from Florida, who proclaims it probably the best mixture anywhere of a tough old factory town and creative city. Des Moines has been sprucing itself up. Milwaukee has a vibrant downtown, surrounded by economic distress. Indianapolis is the economic powerhouse of Indiana but still dies at night.

But the "creative class" are citizens of the postindustrial age, and most Midwestern cities still suffer an industrial hangover. These are "materialist places," assembly-line cities, where a century of good, steady jobs leeched out the itch to be new or different. These cities say they want to be creative, Florida says, "but continue to pour resources into recruiting call centers, underwriting big-box retailers, subsidizing downtown malls, and squandering precious taxpayer dollars on extravagant stadium complexes."

All this describes St. Louis, Cleveland, or Detroit. These are places that still compete for factories. Creative cities compete for people.

Like creative people, smart people like to gang together. A creative city has lots of college graduates. Nearly half the people in Seattle and San Francisco have a college degree, almost double the national average. In Minneapolis, 40 percent have degrees, in Omaha 30 percent, in Chicago 27 percent—about par for big cities like New York and Los Angeles; more than two thirds of the residents in downtown Chicago, like those in midtown Manhattan, have degrees.

But only 19 percent of residents of St. Louis own degrees. This percentage plunges to 18 percent in Milwaukee, 17 percent in Toledo—and barely 11 percent in Cleveland and Detroit. Only 5 percent of people in Cleveland and 4 percent in Detroit have advanced degrees; in Seattle, it's more than 20 percent.

Harvard's Edward Glaeser agrees: "As smart places get smarter, they're leaving everyone in the dust." Once, the corporate titans such as Henry Ford employed mostly unskilled workers who made up in diligence what they lacked in imagination. Today, the corporate titans are Bill Gates and Michael Dell, and the workers they hire are highly educated—and creative.

These people sometimes live in uncreative places, but they don't stay long. Ted Waitt founded Gateway in Sioux City, Iowa, but eventually moved it to California. Marc Andreessen dreamed up a Web browser called Mosaic while a student at the University of Illinois in Champaign-Urbana. But he felt he had to go to California to develop it. The university, instead of trying to help him, protested that they owned the name Mosaic, so Andreessen changed it to Netscape—and helped invent globalization.

As the Netscape story shows, not even college towns are a sure bet to be "creative," in the Florida sense. It takes a critical mass of creative people. The reason: had Mosaic stayed in Champaign and grown, it would probably have had to bring in skilled engineers from outside. But it was a chancy, experimental company, and most potential hires would want to go somewhere with lots of creative companies, just in case they needed a new job. Lots of creative companies require lots of creative people. Austin, Raleigh, and Madison have them, and so draw in even more. Champaign doesn't, and doesn't.

Every Midwestern city likes to huff and puff about its "revival" or its "renaissance." Some are probably beyond reviving. Others, such as Indianapolis, are prosperous enough but bland, empty at night, dull by day. Each civic booster, wondering if his town is "creative," should ask himself, "Would I go there if I didn't have to?"

Would you go to Cleveland or Dayton or St. Louis? Well, you

might go to see a game or hear a concert. But would you stay, walk around, window-gaze, eat a leisurely meal, spend the night? Or would you get in your car and drive home as soon as you could, leaving behind a city that had nothing else to keep you?

In a global era, cities must carry entire economies by themselves. As small towns and cities lose their industry, they'll become part of a metro region, bedroom suburbs for people who drive into the big city to work. Once, places like Newton and Anderson supported themselves; now they're part of the Des Moines or Indianapolis region. If these regions are to survive, the big cities must provide enough lifeblood to do it.

Des Moines is doing fine: with its river walk and downtown condos, it looks good and has one of the country's lowest poverty rates. But can it carry the whole state of Iowa? Minneapolis–St. Paul are Midwestern success stories, but the rest of Minnesota isn't: can the Twin Cities hoist an entire state? Chicago is booming, and it's doing what it's always done, which is to lure the farm boys, to draw in the young people from around the Midwest. Can Chicago, no longer the City of the Big Shoulders, support an entire region?

Probably not. Chicago's big, but it's not that big. The Midwest has a handful of global cities and creative cities, and it desperately needs more.

CHAPTER 10

Left Behind

Globalization, the force of the future, is leaving millions of impoverished African-Americans stuck in the ghettos of the Midwest's cities and in the dying neighborhoods of its smaller manufacturing towns. The contrast between the verve that new immigrants bring to the Midwest and the torpor of these inner cities could not be greater.

The industrial age brought blacks north into the great manufacturing cities of the Midwest—Chicago, Detroit, Cleveland, Milwaukee. The North in those days was no paradise of desegregation. The blacks were herded into ghettos or public housing, barred from white schools and white neighborhoods, and burdened by discrimination and substandard public services. Nevertheless, the road north meant escape from the Jim Crow South and the opportunity to earn a good living in the stockyards, steel mills, auto plants, and parts factories that cared less about a man's education or skills than about his strength and willingness to work hard. The years after World War I and World War II were good. Though blacks were confined to the ghettos, most of them had jobs, belonged to unions, raised families, owned a place in stable societies; these cities, being totally segregated, produced ghettos that held not only the working class but doctors, lawyers, preachers, teachers, artists. They lived a hard life, surrounded by the hostility of a racist society outside, but certainly a better one than they had left behind down South.

In the 1950s and 1960s, two things happened. The first was the beginning of the Rust Belt era and the hollowing out of the Midwest's industrial cities. At the start of the decline, factories

moved from the old industrial neighborhoods of the cities out to
the suburbs. Blacks, poorer than whites, usually lacked cars and
had no way to follow their jobs; in fact, companies often moved
out of the cities deliberately to get away from black workers and
black neighborhoods. They wouldn't admit this publicly, of course,
but in my reporting days I heard executives, after a couple of
drinks, proclaiming how glad they were to be away from the inner
cities and the people who lived in them. Many factory owners kept
blacks away by putting their suburban factories well away from
public transport; then they chartered buses into Hispanic neighborhoods in the cities to bring the preferred Latino workers to and
from their jobs. In time, Midwestern factories began to move to
the South, to cheaper, nonunion locales—a cruel irony for blacks
who had left the South to seek work, only to watch that work flee
to their former home.

The second thing that happened was the civil rights revolution.
In the South, the civil rights movement broke the legal chains that
bound Southern blacks. In the North, it struck down an edifice of
unwritten law that had made even educated African-Americans—
in the Midwest as in the rest of the North—second-class citizens.
These upper-class and middle-class blacks suddenly had access to
integrated education, entertainment, jobs, and especially homes in
formerly all-white areas. But along with these positive effects
came at least one unintended one. Those who could flee the ghetto
did so; most never looked back. Those who couldn't leave were
left behind. Invariably, these were the poorest, the least educated,
the least skilled. No longer did they live in racially segregated but
economically integrated neighborhoods, with teachers next door
and doctors a block away. Now they—and their children—lost
role models, the idea of social mobility. Lacking educated neighbors, they lost the idea of education. Lacking visible emblems of
success, they lost the idea of ambition.

Many of these left-behind blacks had already lost their jobs
when the local factories moved out. The Rust Belt economy put
men with no skills but a strong back on the unemployment line.
But the same economy opened new opportunities to black women,
in stores and offices: men who had earned their livings on blast

furnaces or loading docks couldn't be trained to be secretaries, nurses, or salesclerks. But their wives could, and they became the breadwinners: this is the economic wedge that broke so many black families.

Thus were born whole neighborhoods of people who were not only poor but hopelessly poor, generationally poor—that is, families that had been so poor for so many generations that children grew up never knowing anyone who held a steady job. This new underclass showed every symptom of poverty—high dropout rates, high drug use, high unemployment, low education, low skills, single-parent households, low life expectancy, high infant mortality. Of Chicago's fifteen poorest neighborhoods, twelve are mostly black. Forty-six percent of the black high school freshmen in Chicago—and no less than 55 percent of the black males—will drop out before their senior year; perhaps 5 or 6 percent of those freshmen may eventually get a college degree.

Economic distress spans all races in the Midwest. Many cities losing jobs and industry to global pressures are mostly white—Anderson and Muncie, Indiana, come to mind, as does Newton, Iowa. But the fact remains that the ghettos of Midwestern cities hold millions of blacks who were the first to lose their jobs and have been out of work longest, in cities with the bleakest hopes of recovery. The cities with the biggest problems—the highest unemployment, the lowest incomes, the worst schools—all have big black populations. African-Americans make up 40 percent of the population in Milwaukee, 43 percent in Dayton, 51 percent in Cleveland and St. Louis, 53 percent in Flint, and no less than 82 percent in Detroit, which ranks with Cleveland as the poorest big city in the nation. Globalization is hitting all these cities hard, but scattered around the Midwest are other sad and forgotten towns that died years ago, long before globalization's arrival, and aren't coming back. These, too, are largely African-American. Gary, Indiana, is 84 percent black; Benton Harbor, Michigan, 92 percent; East St. Louis, Illinois, 98 percent.

Many big Midwestern cities are among the most segregated in the nation. Cory Nettles, a black lawyer in Milwaukee who used to be the Wisconsin secretary of commerce, told me that his city is so segregated—"hypersegregated," he called it—that black neighborhoods exist almost outside the local economy. In the city's old Bronzeville district, seven out of every ten black working-age men are unemployed, disabled, or in jail. The big employers—railroads, breweries, and foundries—are long gone. In 1970, median African-American family income in Milwaukee was 19 percent above the national black average; thirty years later, it was 23 percent lower. Jobs programs train young black men for factory jobs that no longer exist; meanwhile, high-wage welding jobs go begging.

"A lot of people have been left behind, and their kids, too," Nettles said. "The school system is a mess." Public school enrollment is 80 percent "brown," he said, and 80 percent of that is black. Up to 60 percent drop out before graduation; maybe one in ten makes it to a college degree.

But no one is willing to clean up this mess, he said. According to Nettles, "Deeply entrenched political constituents oppose any change"—an accusation I heard in many Midwestern cities. What it means is that the schools are controlled by politicians, administrators, and the teachers' unions, all of whom fight any reform that might erode their power. These reforms include longer school days, longer school years, higher pay for better teachers, increased power to fire bad teachers, and the streamlining of bloated school bureaucracies. In most cities, teachers' unions have become politically powerful: elected officials tamper with teachers at their peril. In Cleveland, Ronn Richard, the president of The Cleveland Foundation, which funds programs in that city, despairs of school reform. "You've got to destroy the system and start from scratch," he said. "Unions are appropriate in steel and autos. Unions are inappropriate in education."

Peoria, Illinois, is a relatively prosperous city, but many of its African-Americans, who make up about 25 percent of the population, don't share that prosperity. I met Dave Koehler, the director of the Peoria Area Labor Management Council and a Democratic state senator, at an office in the middle of one of the town's black neighborhoods. He told me that, as industrial jobs shrink, so do the ways that his neighbors can earn a living.

"Most people in this neighborhood don't have a full-time job," he said. "They work downtown, maybe, as janitors or as night maintenance people. The industrial jobs are out on the edge of town, but the bus service closes down at ten p.m. There are a lot of part-time jobs. Hotels are always going to need to be cleaned. It takes about $9.80 per hour to live here, so people are really scrambling. Most of them don't have health care. Our dropout rate in school is about fifty percent, and if you can't read or write, what are you going to do?" As the Harvard sociologist William Julius Wilson said, the underclass is in the ghetto because it's black, but it stays there because it's poor and uneducated.

The underclass is America's single insoluble social failure. This is a nation that believes in success and never admits that some problems may be beyond fixing. It is a belief rooted in our immigrant history: generation after generation of poor immigrants have flowed into the United States, suffered, toiled, and, within a generation or two, succeeded. Not the underclass. Descended from slaves, rescued by the industrial age and then cast aside when that age ended, these people are the victims of an economic and historical catastrophe.

All this is the creation of the industrial age. But we're in a new economic and historical era now. The industrial era produced welfare. The global era produced "the end of welfare as we know it." This "end of welfare" may or may not have been a good idea. But what it symbolized was society in global cities wiping its hands of the urban poor.

Globalization may be the most egalitarian force in history. It offers rich rewards to the most highly skilled, educated, mobile, entrepreneurial—and it doesn't much care what color or gender these winners might be. White males, Europeans and their descendants, ran the industrial era. Some leaders of the global era are white males—but others are Indian and Chinese, Latino and Korean. More and more of them are women. Black Americans are CEOs, surgeons, and college presidents. If you're good, you've got a chance. If you've got the education and the skills, the door is open.

But if you don't have the education and the skills, you're out of luck. And that description—uneducated and unskilled—describes most of the underclass, particularly its men, in the ghettos of Mid-western cities. If the Midwest's future contains manufacturing, it will be high-end, high-tech manufacturing, demanding two-year degrees at the least. Biosciences will hire no dropouts. There will be jobs at lower levels, of course—in restaurants, on landscaping crews, in basic construction—but immigrants are already seizing most of these opportunities.

There was a nostalgic weekend in Chicago in the summer of 2006, when about two dozen aging civil rights activists—the kind of people who marched with Martin Luther King—gathered to celebrate the fortieth anniversary of the Chicago Freedom Movement, which aimed to end the misery of the inner-city slums. Their goal now, they said, is to finish this work, by ending segregation and poverty.

One of the activists, eighty-year-old Kale Williams, admitted, "Some say these are the conditions we addressed forty years ago, but we haven't been fully successful. My sleeves are still rolled up." Another old activist, seventy-four-year-old John Porter, said the conference "makes you want to get out there and start marching again."

This was rather pathetic—a reunion for old folks whose greatest moment was fighting legal segregation, faced now with an economic segregation that no amount of marching will dent. This segregation separates the rich from the poor, the employed from the unemployed, and the global from the ghetto-bound. It's also self-segregation. Everyone knows how to beat the system now, and it's through education. Those who don't have it are going to lose the global race. Marches and picketing won't work in an era when lives are limited not by the Klan but by the impersonal demands of global corporations.

African-American history is defined by economics. The slaves were brought to America because they were needed on cotton plantations. They came North during and after World War II because they were needed in the factories. Today, a black high school dropout isn't needed anywhere for any but the most menial jobs.

"The history of racism is real," Ned Hill, a Cleveland economist, told me, "but in a global economy, you have to say, 'I understand that, but the solution depends on me.' Manufacturing today is not a refuge for the undereducated and the stupid. It's going to be very highly skilled. Instead, we've got an entitlement mentality at work, and the global economy does a terrible job of supporting people's self-esteem." If the elderly Chicago activists understood this, they gave little sign of it. Their children got it. Few young people attended this conference.

The future Midwestern landscape will be dotted by rotting neighborhoods housing people for whom the global economy holds no meaning. This economy won't discriminate against these people; worse, it will ignore them. The industrial era at least took some responsibility for them, through welfare and social programs; the global era, accepting no blame for their plight, may not even do this.

Senator Barack Obama, who knows the inner city better than most politicians, has written with cautious optimism about things that might work. He wants more early-childhood education, better policing, programs aimed at helping young single mothers raise productive children, affordable child care, programs to help ex-felons find work.

Cities themselves can do much just by making sure that everyday civic planning includes the whole city, not just the neighborhoods where the global citizens live and work. Most Midwestern cities need to update and rationalize their public transit systems: when this is done, the new bus lines must serve all neighborhoods, not just speed traders and bankers to their jobs. Fiber-optic cable is the communications network of the future, and global cities have to have it; but when it is laid, it must extend not just to downtown businesses but to every school, library, police station, and fire station in the city—in other words, to all neighborhoods. A grid like this is as crucial to investment in the twenty-first century as streets and telephone lines were in the twentieth century. A neighborhood that has it will be plugged into the global economy. A neighborhood that doesn't, won't.

"What would that be worth to all of us—an America in which crime has fallen, more children are cared for, cities are reborn, and the biases, fear, and discord that black poverty feeds are slowly drained away?" Obama has written. "Would it be worth what we've spent in the past year in Iraq? Would it be worth relinquishing demands for estate tax repeal? It's hard to quantify the benefits of such changes—precisely because the benefits would be immeasurable."

The inner cities are America's great failure. The solution, as so often in this country, is an economic one—jobs, which depend on education, which depends on the willingness of society to make this transformation happen; only then will the promise of Obama's title—*The Audacity of Hope*—be more than a pipe dream.

But how far we have to go! There are children in the Chicago neighborhoods of North Lawndale and Garfield Park, five miles west of the city's Loop and lakefront, who have never seen that lake. I know grown men, living within easy eyesight of the Loop skyscrapers, who have no idea at all how to apply for a job. I've talked with teenage dropouts who say their life's ambition is to be a doctor or a lawyer, but don't understand that, first, they need an education. These people aren't ex-cons or drug addicts or gang-bangers. They want the same things we do, but they might as well live on a different planet for all the chance they have of getting it.

What will happen to them? The worst scenario is—nothing. In a fast-moving global society, the people who run Midwestern cities will care more for relations with Shanghai and São Paulo, ten thousand miles away, than they will for the people in their own city, tucked into no-go neighborhoods, like the Bantustans of apartheid, out of sight and out of mind, not persecuted, just ignored.

CHAPTER 11

Flunking Out

The Midwest has always boasted superior education. The earliest settlements clustered around a church and a one-room schoolhouse. Midwestern states such as Iowa and Minnesota claim some of the nation's highest literacy rates. The land-grant colleges grew into great universities that became not only the pride but the very identity of their states: a recent survey of the world's twenty greatest universities listed six Ivies, five in California (four of them in the mighty California State university system), and three—Chicago, Wisconsin, and Michigan—in the Midwest. No other nation and no other American region came close.

Which makes it odd that, of all the problems facing the Midwest today, education may be the biggest and most intractable. Education is central to the Midwest's ability to cope in an age of globalism. The industrial economy is ended. The knowledge economy is here. The best jobs will go to the best-prepared students. The best cities will have the most college graduates. But at every level, from the earliest years to the postgraduate heights, the Midwest is shortchanging its schools and its children.

The dropout rate in city schools is simply stupendous, 50 percent or more. Those who do graduate from high school, in cities or small towns, emerge unprepared to compete in a global economy. Two-year community colleges, teaching hands-on marketable skills, have emerged as perhaps the key institutions in local economies, but they are stretched tight, between the need to repair the damage done to those ill-prepared students and the demands of the rapidly changing economy. The universities themselves are caught in a financial vise. With public support vanishing, many are asking themselves just what they owe, if anything, to the states whose names they bear. Midwesterners simply may not value education as they once did. Or, more likely, they don't understand what education means to the region's future in the global era.

When I was in Michigan, everyone I met who cared about the state's future wanted to talk about a recent poll on the state's attitude toward education. Basically, the poll said that if Michigan's future depends on education, there is no future.

The poll, sponsored by the *Detroit News* and carried out by a Michigan-based pollster called EPIC/MRA, showed that only 27 percent of parents in Michigan felt that a good education is "essential for getting ahead in life." Put another way: three fourths of the state's parents—the people most responsible for the state's children—don't think that those children need to go to college to succeed.

It wasn't that they were hostile to higher education. Just indifferent. Most felt it was "important." But "essential"? No. By a two-to-one margin, the parents felt it was more important that a child "be happy" than that he or she had a good education.

"There's a big difference between 'essential' and 'very important,'" Ed Sarpolus, who carried out the poll, told me. "'Very important' means 'not mandatory.' I was a first-generation immigrant, so I had to go to college. There was no question. We've lost that immigrant attitude since then."

Other voices are even more alarmed. "We're doomed," Nolan Finley, the editorial-page editor of the *Detroit News*, wrote on the day the poll appeared. "Doomed to a perpetually shrinking economy. Doomed to an ever diminishing quality of life. Doomed to flipping the hamburgers, shining the shoes and sweeping the floors of the states that will prosper as the national economy shifts from rewarding muscle and sweat to valuing brains and knowledge. Michigan is doomed to be the new Mississippi. A backward state locked to a last-century industry, awash in ignorance and unprepared to seize the opportunities presented by new technologies and scientific advancements."

In more measured tones, the governor, Jennifer Granholm,

agreed: "In the last century, people came to Michigan because they didn't have to have a college degree to get a good job with good benefits. They could go right from a high school graduation line to a factory line. That opportunity in the last century is our challenge today. As the last few years have made painfully clear, globalization has cannibalized those jobs. They are not coming back. So Michigan now must adjust to survive and thrive."

Not that Granholm's government is doing much to help. As we shall see, the state of Michigan, like most Midwestern states, is shortchanging education at the moment in history when it's most important.

It's easy to conclude that the poll numbers were dragged down by Michigan's black population, much of it locked in an urban underclass. But of the African-Americans polled, nearly 40 percent considered college essential—less than half, to be sure, but a lot better than the 25 percent of whites who saw the real point to education. Sixty-three percent of blacks and 76 percent of Hispanics felt that "everyone should get a college education." Only 48 percent of all whites did.

"It's not the color of your skin that determines this," Sarpolus said. "It's economics."

It's class, too. Michigan—and, in fact, much of the Midwest—is still gripped by a blue-collar mentality that values a strong back over a quick mind. Sarpolus pointed out that most upper-class and educated parents see college as essential for their kids. But the vast majority of Michigan parents worked at jobs connected to the auto industry, mostly on assembly lines or other positions in which a high school education was good enough. Everyone in Michigan should know that, as Granholm said, those jobs are gone forever. But these parents feel they made a good living on the line, without education, and what was good enough for them is good enough for their kids.

I cited these Michigan figures when I talked with people in other Midwestern states. At first, they were shocked. Then they said that, if a similar poll was taken in their states, it would reveal about the same attitudes. This is especially true in Ohio and Indiana, states where the auto-based economy, as in Michigan, provided solid incomes to generations of assembly-line workers who never went beyond high school. Most people in Iowa and Minnesota expected that their states, traditionally devoted to education, would score better, even though they're experiencing an antieducation backlash of their own.

(States differ on results as well as attitude. Minnesota has the highest percentage of adults with a high school diploma, about 88 percent; Illinois has the lowest, only 81 percent; Michigan is about in the middle. In percentage of adults with a bachelor's degree, Minnesota is also at the top, with nearly 28 percent; Indiana is last with 19 percent; and Michigan is in the middle, with 22 percent. There are differences within states, too: in Minnesota, only 17 percent of residents outside the Twin Cities have college degrees; in Minneapolis and St. Paul, it's nearly double, 33 percent.)

From kindergarten to the most ivy-bound university, Midwestern education is in a quiet crisis. Across the region, educators and officials try to reform, or at least control, systems that have slipped from their grasp. In a globalizing world, how do schools, chartered by and responsible to their communities and their citizens, fulfill a global mission?

The Midwest holds no monopoly on any of these educational challenges. All across the United States, the test scores of elementary and high school students are a national scandal. State universities nationwide face declining state support, while rising tuitions squeeze poor and middle-income students out of student bodies.

But if education is a national problem, the impact is being felt most sharply in the heartland, which, more than any other region, relied on heavy basic industries that rewarded strength and hard work more than education. Between the big corporations and the big unions, men and women who carried lunch pails and spent their days on assembly lines could earn good wages, own their own homes, feed their families, and keep a cottage by the lake. It was a safe, solid way of life, and it didn't require much book learning.

One step up the ladder stood the trades, the jobs in construction and nursing and repair. The junior colleges and vocational schools taught these trades and taught them well. If they didn't teach

much science or math, that was all right, because only students going to universities needed that knowledge.

The colleges and universities turned out the managers of this
Midwestern economy. The mills and factories needed to be run,
and students needed to know how to run them. What they didn't
need was a grounding in innovation or entrepreneurialism. The industrial economy of the Midwest rewarded managerial skills but
not necessarily imagination. If innovation had created this economy a hundred years ago, it was steady, solid management that
kept it going.

Now that way of life is gone. More than any other part of
America, the Midwest has lost the knack to compete in the new
economy, and the schools have lost their ability to teach it.

The failure of America's K–12 system to prepare its students for
life in a globalizing world is so well-known that it needs little
stressing here. It poses a crisis for the nation, not just the Midwest.
But as noted above, the Midwest has more at stake. It is also doing
a worse job. The U.S. Department of Education recently issued a
"Nation's Report Card," rating fourth- and eighth-grade students
in ten cities, from Boston to San Diego, on scientific knowledge.

None did very well, but even by these standards the Midwest's
cities lagged. Chicago and Cleveland ranked at the bottom, along-
side New York and Los Angeles. In both cities, white students
scored well below the national average. And in each, black and
Hispanic students scored below white students. Cleveland's school
population is overwhelmingly black. Chicago's is overwhelmingly
black and Hispanic.

A report by the Schott Foundation showed that, at all levels,
black students—especially males—are falling hopelessly behind.
The report charted the percentage of black and white boys who
graduated with their age group. In Chicago, the black rate was only
30 percent, in Detroit 35 percent, in Indianapolis 33 percent, in St.
Louis 28 percent, in Milwaukee only 24 percent, and in Cleveland
an astounding 19 percent. The rate for white boys was better, but
still astonishingly poor—53 percent in Chicago, only 26 percent
in Detroit, 43 percent in St. Louis, 46 percent in Milwaukee, and 23

percent in Cleveland; in Indianapolis and Detroit the white graduation rate was below the black rate. Even in supposedly superior
Minneapolis, only 35 percent of black males graduated with their
age group (against 76 percent of white males). The report did not
say how many of these boys graduated at all, but students who fall
behind their age group are more likely to drop out altogether.

Each city has a handful of bright spots, charter schools or
schools where middle-class parents demand higher standards. But
there is no conclusion except the obvious: the Midwest is failing its
children. The debate to assign the fault for this goes on and on, with
no result. Parents blame the schools. Schools say they get no support from parents. Everybody blames television, or poverty, or a
youth culture that devalues education, or drugs. And year after year,
more Midwestern children enter the real world unequipped to cope.

Perhaps Chicago can wink at this, if it is cynical enough to con-
demn most of its students to part-time minimum-wage employment: it is one of those global cities that lure enough high-powered
graduates to make up for its failure to educate its own children.
Cleveland has no such comfort. Basically, no one is moving to
Cleveland—or to Detroit or St. Louis or Milwaukee.

"We're sleepwalking," Stephanie Pace Marshall, the dynamic
president of the Illinois Mathematics and Science Academy, says.
The academy, in suburban Chicago, is a free boarding school for
talented Illinois high school students. With its selective admissions
and innovative teaching, it produces topflight graduates that go on
to the best universities. But it can afford only 650 students at a
time, a drop in the ocean of the state's scientific needs. If the Midwest is to meet these needs, it must import its scientists from India
or China, because it sure isn't going to find them at home.

"It's not the gene pool, it's the social priorities," Marshall insists. "The world has changed and education has not." Echoing
the National Academy of Sciences report on science education, she
thinks this country should recruit ten thousand science and mathematics teachers each year by giving them full four-year scholarships. She wants to expand her current program to train existing
teachers, many of whom are unqualified to teach the science and
math courses for which they're paid. And she wants to break

down the balkanization of science and math teaching by setting a national curriculum and national standards. At the moment, each state sets its own standards, "and physics doesn't change if you're in Michigan or in Iowa."

This means that, as in so much else, state legislators must loosen their grips on budgets and standards. "One legislator wanted our kids to take the Illinois science tests," Marshall said. "I pointed out that they already take international tests and score at the top. But he still insisted that they test in Illinois, too. What he was saying was, 'You're the best in the world, but are you the best in Illinois?' "

Nor does traditional Midwestern education in small towns necessarily produce better results. In my Iowa hometown, I spent time with Randy Fitzgerald, the operations director at Proliant Biologicals, a global corporation that makes high-purity proteins from animal plasma. He told me his company opened its twenty-four-thousand-square-foot production plant in Boone for lots of reasons—good tax breaks, a nice town, a four-lane highway nearby, smart people at Iowa State University in Ames, thirteen miles to the east. But he didn't think he'd be hiring many people from my alma mater, Boone High School.

"Boone tries to take education seriously, but they've got the same mentality as Michigan," Fitzgerald said when I told him about that parents' poll. "It's a blue-collar town here. Farm communities are the same. People say, 'What we've got is good enough for me.' It's a cultural thing. You've got mind-sets that are opposed to change."

Faced with this K–12 crisis, educators are considering drastic reforms. One recent national commission issued a report that called for funding high-quality early-childhood education starting at age three. School weeks could be lengthened, from five days to six. So could school years: three-month summer vacations are a quaint hangover from the agricultural days when the kids were needed in the fields. Most students could be graduated from high school after the tenth grade. Those who pass "rigorous" exams could go directly to state technical schools and colleges. Only students who want to go to top universities would stay on in high schools for more precollege education.

At the university level, the Midwest should be doing fine. Each state has one or two flagship universities, major institutions with rich traditions of education and research. Many of these state schools—Wisconsin, Michigan, Illinois, Minnesota—rank among the best in the nation. Nestled among them are world-class private universities such as Chicago, Northwestern, and Notre Dame. All together, they command a wealth of brainpower probably unexcelled anywhere else in the world, including the Ivy League.

But they never work together. Instead, they compete for students, grants, professors, and eminence as fiercely as their football teams compete on autumn Saturdays. Throughout their history, they have been less than the sum of their parts, imprisoned within state lines, cut off from their natural Midwestern collaborators by state legislatures and state spending.

Now, even that state identity is in question. The Midwestern states, crippled by a declining economy, are taking money away from these great universities. Instead of using it to prepare for the future, they are diverting it to prop up rusting industries of the past, or to build prisons. In most Midwestern states, the state governments provide less than 25 or 30 percent of the money for the operating budgets of their state universities. In Michigan, the state pays only 7 percent of that budget. (Michigan, like other Midwestern states, spends more per prisoner than it does for each college student. The University of Minnesota, in a spasm of cost-cutting, even converted one of its branches, in Waseca south of Minneapolis, into a prison; perhaps its best-known enrollee is former Enron president Jeffrey Skilling.)

University administrators now talk about the coming privatization of public universities. If the state isn't willing to pay for the universities, they ask, then what do the universities owe to their states? Can the great state universities do more for their states and the Midwest by abandoning education and focusing on research, often in collaboration with private corporations? Is it foolish to educate the children of a state when those children grab their diplomas and move to California? What should be the goal of a state university in a globalizing world?

These questions go to the core of the universities' structure. At these big, traditional universities, the professor, not the student, is king. Research comes before teaching, and course offerings depend on the faculty's expertise, whether or not it has anything to do with the world the student will occupy after graduation.

Once this made no difference. The big Midwestern state schools are land-grant universities, established 145 years ageo by an act of Congress, which gave them land in exchange for a mandate to teach both the practical arts, such as farming, and the classics. Their charter contained a double commitment, to the minority who wanted a higher education and to the states that supported them. Teaching and research went hand in hand. These land-grant schools and their smaller public and private brethren monopolized higher education. Anyone who wanted an education went to these schools, because that was all there was. Anyone who didn't want an education went into the local Ford or Delphi factory and took a job for life.

Now these universities find themselves squarely in the path of change. In the new economy, the majority of people—not the minority—will need higher education. But these people don't necessarily want to learn the classics. Instead, they need skills that universities have forgotten how to teach. Great Gothic institutions rooted in proud histories, these universities cannot be nimble enough to function in a fast-changing economy. Suddenly, they find themselves in competition with both community colleges and the for-profit schools, such as the University of Phoenix, for the students and tuition dollars of the global generation.

As the *Economist* magazine said, universities have always been places devoted not only to "transmitting a body of facts, which the internet does pretty well, [but] about learning to argue and reason, which is best done in a community of scholars." This remains true and justifies universities as elite institutions. But in the new knowledge age, most students seek no more than "a body of facts." The higher scholarship, the argument and reasoning, is becoming the province of the minority; so is the research that draws in tomorrow's innovators and entrepreneurs. When only a minority sought higher education, this structure met the need. In an era in which the majority will seek postsecondary education, the structure must change.

This, then, is the dilemma facing the great Midwestern universities—the Big Ten universities mostly. Once they held a monopoly on higher education, but the community colleges and for-profit universities are chipping away at this edge. The big state schools still dominate research, particularly basic research. But unlike MIT in the East or Stanford in the West, they have not yet become the engines of innovation that the new economy will demand. Can they do both—provide a broad education while inventing the new Midwestern economy?

James Duderstadt, the former president of the University of Michigan, has stated it more clearly than anyone else: "Regions must create and sustain a highly educated and innovative workforce and the capacity to generate and apply new knowledge, supported through policies and investments in developing human capital, technological innovation and entrepreneurial skill."

But Michigan as a state, and the Midwest as a region, isn't doing this, Duderstadt said: "For the past two decades Michigan has been shifting public funds and private capital away from investing in the future through education, research and innovation to fund instead short-term priorities such as building prisons, gimmicks such as casino gambling and professional sports stadiums, and ill-advised tax cuts, including tax abatements to prop up dying industries and tax exemptions for politically influential businesses."

Even though the University of Michigan is a state school, answerable to the state legislature and a political governing board, the state has virtually stopped supporting it. Duderstadt expects the percentage of state support, now 7 percent, to be around 3 percent by the end of the decade.

As Duderstadt put it, Michigan—perhaps the best state university in the Midwest—"has evolved from a state-supported to a state-assisted to a state-related to a state-located university . . . As a consequence of inadequate state support, several of Michigan's public universities are rapidly becoming 'privately-financed public universities,' facing the challenge of sustaining their public purpose and service to Michigan citizens through competing in the marketplace rather than depending primarily upon adequate state support."

If they're doing their job, universities train students to compete in a global economy, often working for corporations that operate globally. It is anachronistic, even ridiculous, to give parochial politicians, with worldviews blocked by state lines, a voice in how these universities are run.

Other Midwestern states give more generous support to state universities, but not much, 20 percent or less. It's falling in every state, part of a national trend. Iowa, for instance, provided 35 percent of the operating budget at its flagship University of Iowa in 2001; in 2007, it will provide only 20 percent.

This has several results. One is rising tuition, as universities try to balance budgets; in turn, low- and middle-income students find themselves squeezed out of an education at universities that are chartered to educate everyone. Another is closer ties with corporations that sponsor research. A third is a complete rethinking of the universities' relation to their states and society.

Duderstadt is an angry and passionate man, frustrated by his eight years of running the state university against the headwinds of Michigan politics. He now directs the university's Millennium Project, which describes itself as "a laboratory where new paradigms of learning institutions can be designed, constructed and studied." In other words, he's trying to imagine the future of Midwestern universities.

Duderstadt feels these universities should concentrate more on research and less on teaching, at least at the undergraduate level. These universities can benefit their states and regions most by stressing research in new, global, twenty-first-century industries that will power the economies of the future. If their research helps existing corporations spin off new businesses, all the better. This is what happened around MIT and Stanford. It's what's happening now around San Diego. The evidence lies along Boston's Route

128, in Silicon Valley, and, most recently, in the biotech cluster in San Diego. But it's not happening much in the Midwest, and according to Duderstadt, it should.

These universities can't abandon undergraduate education altogether, Duderstadt says. But it can lop off the freshman and sophomore years. These are the "socialization years," when students, away from home for the first time, plunge into clubs, residence dorms, intramural athletics, and the other activities that make college so much fun—and so expensive. Most of these students are in-state and pay in-state tuition, typically one third or less of a university's true cost to out-of-staters. "We provide a $25,000-to-$30,000-a-year education for about $8,000," B. Joseph White, the University of Illinois president, says.

It would make more sense for these young students to spend their first two years at community colleges, which are moving more and more into general education, or into the other, smaller state colleges that see their mandate as education, not research, or at the small, excellent private liberal arts colleges that dot the Midwest, or simply learning online. The major universities would take them as juniors or seniors, although it would prefer to get them as graduate students.

The smaller colleges, especially state colleges, will oppose this idea. All these schools also see themselves as centers of research and will resist any attempt to confine themselves to teaching. Every college wants to recruit top professors who bring in research grants. These professors are hired to spend their time in the lab, not the classroom, which means their students get shortchanged. But without the money they bring in, colleges must raise tuition, forcing out the poorer students whom these second-rank state schools were created to serve.

Duderstadt and others argue that state funds should help these lesser schools teach undergraduates. This would free the big universities to do what they do better, which is research, often with corporate funding. As Duderstadt says, the Midwest has "the strongest concentration of flagship research universities in the world"—the Big Ten schools plus the University of Chicago. "These twelve universities conduct more research, produce more scientists and engineers, doctors and lawyers, business executives and teachers, than any collection of universities in the world, including the University of California, the Ivy League, Oxford and Cambridge and the other leading universities in Europe and Asia. More specifically, they conduct over $6 billion per year of research and development, award roughly one-fifth of the nation's doctorates in fields such as engineering, chemistry, mathematics and computer science." The Midwest has brainpower aplenty.

But these universities compete. Theoretically, this competition should be a good thing. But when the Midwest itself is competing for a place in the world, cooperation between universities could harness all this brainpower into an intellectual powerhouse. At the moment, all these schools teach engineering, medicine, chemistry, and biomedical science, but they don't all do it equally well. Illinois stars in computer technology, Minnesota in chemistry, Ohio State in materials science, Michigan State in agricultural technology, Wisconsin and Michigan in engineering, and so on. There are glimmers—no more than that—of real cooperation, of a true Midwestern research consortium.

Midwestern universities already share library resources and cooperate in other areas. But true collaboration has just begun. As Michigan's John Austin has suggested, these state schools could offer in-state tuition rates to all Midwestern students, not just those from their own states. Weaker graduate schools could be closed and consolidated into those with real eminence. Online learning will permit students to "attend" many universities at once, a process that should be recognized and encouraged. Fiber-optic networks will enable university researchers to collaborate across the miles that now separate them.

There's a model for this—the state university system in California. In 1960, with the baby boom generation nearing enrollment age, California developed its Master Plan for Higher Education. Most research and doctoral training was assigned to the big universities, such as Berkeley, within the University of California system. The schools, such as San Francisco State, in the California State University system focused on undergraduate education and teacher training. Community colleges concentrated on two-year and vocational education. Despite modifications over the decades, the system remains intact. It not only produced an efficient framework, avoiding the duplication that plagues Midwestern schools, it is credited with creating the most powerful system of public higher education in the world and, in the process, with powering the California economy.

As in everything else, California is a special case. Political reality means the Midwest is unlikely to adopt any of these revolutionary ideas tomorrow. But they, and others, should be the goal for educational leaders trying to emerge from behind state boundaries into the world.

Within university circles, Duderstadt is a radical thinker but not necessarily a lonely one. Katharine C. Lyall used to be president of another Big Ten school, the University of Wisconsin, and she argues, "America is privatizing her public higher education institutions. Largely without serious public policy analysis or debate, a series of individual state budget and revenue decisions over the past decade have made states increasingly smaller shareholders in their public colleges and universities. At the same time, the influence of other shareholders—parents, donors, alumni and corporations—is growing."

In short, these big universities, lacking state support, have to figure out how to support themselves, and they'll do it. Lyall, like Duderstadt, sees the big state universities focusing on research, and delegating the teaching to other state schools. "Flagship institutions will rebalance their roles between research and instruction to focus on those portions of their mission that can be self-sustaining, resulting in fewer and smaller first-quality public research universities," she said. "Meanwhile, two- and four-year comprehensive state universities that largely confine themselves to undergraduate instruction and have fewer, less affluent alumni will experience intensified enrollment pressures and quality erosion."

As in so many other areas of life, this result of globalization will increase the gap between the rich and the poor or, in this case, between the topflight and the second-rate. It's a Darwinian process, Lyall says, in which the best minds will flock to a few top universities, grown rich—like Stanford or MIT—on their research ties to global corporations, while the rest of the nation's colleges will become more and more crowded with students getting a lesser education.

In the middle, between K–12 and the universities, are the community colleges. Everywhere I went in the Midwest, I found community colleges emerging as the engine of local economies.

In Newton, the local Des Moines Area Community College (DMACC) campus retrains Maytag workers who thought they would be making refrigerators for the rest of their lives. Indian Hills Community College, which services southeast Iowa, has set up its Iowa BioDevelopment campus near the little town of Eddyville, across the road from the giant plants where Cargill makes ethanol and high-fructose corn syrup. Its students spend twenty-one months learning to be either bioprocess technicians or ethanol-plant technicians, specializing in such processes as fermentation or growing tissue cultures. Thirty students are in the two programs, and Cargill hires almost all of them, at a starting pay of $36,000 a year—good money in that area. In Warsaw, Indiana, Ivy Tech trains the workers who polish artificial joints at the companies that have made the town the orthopedics capital of the world. The same campus is trying to retrain laid-off General Motors workers who drive over from Fort Wayne to try to put their lives back together.

In short, community colleges are stretched—between younger students training for the twenty-first century and older casualties of the last century's economy, between spot-welding and biosciences, between a culture that never valued education and a new economy that demands a lot of it.

The community colleges also are caught in an identity crisis. Most were born as two-year junior colleges, stressing vocational training for students who never planned to go on to a four-year college. In the Rust Belt era, they became the focus of local economic development, not only training workers but helping small-business owners make the jump into the digital age.

Then came the global age, decreeing that only workers with a two-year diploma would be employable. At the same time, tuition at the state universities went up and up, so many students began spending their first two years at the community colleges, at $3,000 per year, then transferring to the university for their last two years. As the community colleges became stepping-stones to universities for these students, the universities began demanding that the community colleges adhere to university standards. For schools that prided themselves on their ability to set up midnight classes in factories, this new rigidity came as a shock.

Most community college officials view the university accreditation process as a cartel run by professors for professors. Community colleges keep their costs down by hiring cheap adjunct professors, tailoring courses to students' needs, cooperating with local companies, stinting on facilities, and going for quick results. It isn't plush but it works. Universities, on the other hand, hire expensive professors, stress research, pride themselves on their facilities, and march to the four-year beat of a traditional degree.

"Universities are still deeply embedded in four-year programs, and that's too long for a lot of our students," a local college dean told me. "These people got families to support. We can give them what they need for a teacher's certificate in a year."

I talked with Carol D'Amico shortly before her retirement as the executive vice president of Ivy Tech, which has twenty-three campuses all over Indiana. In a state that has not yet come to terms with the global economy, she felt this schizophrenic pull acutely. Ivy Tech, once strictly a vocational college, finally became a community college in 2005 just so its students could take courses that the state universities would recognize. "Now we're under pressure to look like junior universities, with a tenured faculty, grand facilities, traditional semesters," she said. "Before, we could be more agile, because we didn't depend on a full-time tenured faculty. We could put our facilities in the neighborhoods and strip malls, where the people are. We could develop technology quickly, because we didn't have to go through the bureaucracy.

"Look at their [the accreditors'] criteria. How much square footage you have. How big are your classrooms. Having tenured faculty. Our arrangements fly in the face of their core values—that facilities matter, that there has to be core courses. This doesn't fit our model, which is that we have to reengineer a big bulk of a workforce very quickly."

Ten years ago, she said, there was no such occupation as "webmaster." Now community colleges have to train webmasters, and it's unreasonable to require them to hire a Ph.D. in webmastery to teach the course. When the FedEx terminal in Indiana announced layoffs, Ivy Tech set up nighttime classes inside the terminal to retrain the workers. It's hard to imagine Indiana University doing this. Similarly, it's hard to imagine an Ivy Tech teacher winning a Nobel Prize.

"It doesn't have to be either/or," Carol D'Amico told me. But the dividing line, between the competing demands of vocational and university educations, is getting awfully thin.

I was impressed by how thin it is when I visited John Erwin, who is the president of Illinois Central College (ICC), a two-year campus set prettily in the East Peoria hills above the Illinois River. Dr. Erwin was slightly jet-lagged, having just returned from China. It was his second trip—on business. ICC has programs in two Chinese colleges, with a third in the works, teaching things that no Harvard professor could handle.

ICC's Caterpillar program is a prime example. Caterpillar, the global heavy-equipment manufacturer, is headquartered in Peoria and still dominates the city's economy. In 1998, Caterpillar wanted to set up a training center for its dealers and technicians, to make sure that anyone who sold Caterpillar equipment could also repair it. ICC agreed to house the center and help with the teaching. Under the program, students spend eight weeks studying practical physics and other courses at the facility at ICC, then another eight weeks interning at a Caterpillar dealership. So far, 90 percent of graduates have gone to a Cat dealership, at an average starting salary of $40,000.

To do this, ICC had to figure out how to cram its normal sixteen-week term into the eight weeks that Caterpillar wanted. It was a joint college-corporate deal, set up to serve one powerful local corporation, which paid the bills. It worked. The program has become a fixture at ICC, and over the years the program has expanded to other countries where Caterpillar makes and sells equipment, including China.

Since 2001, when a delegation from the Shenzhen Polytechnic University visited Peoria, ICC has set up two programs with Chinese schools, in Shenzhen and Xiamen, involving both exchange students and Caterpillar. Basically, a program developed in Illinois is being used to train Caterpillar's Chinese dealers, who take the same test as graduates in Peru or Peoria.

"A worker who graduates from ICC as a dealer technician can also work in China," Erwin told me. "The point is that this is a program between a business and a college. The business is designing a curriculum for a college that is acceptable, both to the business and academically." But while some of Erwin's students end up selling Cats, about 50 percent go on to four-year schools. In the process, another thin line is vanishing.

Universities award degrees in English or sociology that are fine for students who plan to go to graduate schools to prepare for a job. But few universities teach the technical skills that many students need today to survive. Either universities must start teaching these skills or, more likely, turn over an important part of modern education to community colleges.

Erwin thinks that the fast changes and new skills demanded by the modern Midwestern economy have devalued the traditional four-year college degree, which comes out of ivied institutions unprepared to move so quickly. "If you understand the global situation, it's going to be a skill set that carries the day, not the degree. We have students with a BA who are coming back here to learn new skills. This is happening because universities won't change, they won't teach these technical skills."

At the same time, community colleges are under pressure to offer more than an associate's degree—possibly a three-year degree teaching skills that can't be learned in two years but don't require four years to learn.

From the fringes of academia come more pressures. In suburban Chicago, both Motorola and McDonald's have set up their own training centers and called them universities. In Warsaw, Indiana, the orthopedics companies do some of their training in-house and other training through Ivy Tech. Online teaching has yet to achieve its early potential, but it is expanding slowly.

Erwin said that ICC offers a full associate's degree online and has one thousand students enrolled in the program, out of its total thirteen thousand student body. Then there are hybrid courses, which meet a few times on campus and do the rest of the work on-line. The student body makes this flexibility necessary. The average ICC student is no longer an eighteen-year-old just out of high school but a twenty-six-year-old woman who lives somewhere in a ten-county area, holds a job, and has to commute to campus for the education she needs just to stay employed.

At the turn of the century, Erwin got one third of his money from the state, one third from tuition, and one third from local property taxes. Now the state's share is 19 percent and Erwin wants to get it down to zero. This means more deals with corporations like Caterpillar, more fund-raising, more overseas operations.

It's the wave of the future. All schools—both community colleges and state universities—are looking over their shoulders at private for-profit universities such as the University of Phoenix, which has 239 campuses around the world and, with 280,000 students, is America's largest university.

Phoenix isn't alone. There are for-profit business schools, communications schools, even law schools. They cater to working adults, often low-income workers who had trouble in more traditional universities. If they offer few degrees in medieval literature, they produce plenty of graduates in business administration, computer technology, cooking, and office management. Campuses are office buildings, not quadrangles. What they lack in activities and school spirit they more than make up for in parking places. Phoenix fields no athletic teams but, like a major corporation, has paid $154.5 million to put its name on the home stadium of the local pro football team, the Arizona Cardinals. Many students take online courses. Teachers are no more than employees, hired not to do research but to deliver practical information as efficiently as possible.

The schools know their customer base and excel in marketing: financial aid administrators occupy plush suites, while teachers work from cubicles.

There are many competing demands for state money and, no doubt, many reasons why the states are shortchanging their universities. But one reason, Lyall thinks, is political, a conservative backlash, "a growing ideological undertone, with universities being criticized for having a 'liberal' agenda, championing racial diversity and trying to keep American universities open to international students."

This may be a Lake Wobegon backlash. In Minnesota, a state representative named Bud Heidgerken, hearing that some university students were having trouble understanding their foreign-born instructors, introduced a bill in the state legislature insisting that all teachers of undergrads use "clear English pronunciation." The bill went nowhere. Heidgerken, a Republican, represents Freeport, Garrison Keillor's inspiration for Lake Wobegon, and even used to own Charlie's, the model for the Chatterbox Café.

All universities know they can cope in a global world only by increasing their global ties, which means bringing in more and more foreign students. These students not only open universities to global thought, but as foreign governments and foreign companies send their students to Midwestern universities, their research grants might follow. With luck, many of these foreign students—often the best and brightest of their home countries—will stay on after graduation and enrich the Midwestern economy. Some, even those with funny accents, may try to teach Midwestern students.

If universities know this, voters don't. Any attempt to increase foreign enrollment, especially at the undergraduate level, faces hostility from residents who resent paying taxes to educate foreigners. The University of Illinois's White learned this in 2006 when he announced plans to increase out-of-state enrollment from a measly 10 percent to 15 percent over the next five years. This wasn't all about foreign students: some of these students would have come from Indiana, not India. But to many Illinois parents and taxpayers, any outsider is an alien; they howled, the legislature threatened hearings, and the university backed down.

On the surface, this is a debate over the connection between a university and its state or, possibly, the academic fallout from the urban-rural split. Underneath are more fundamental debates.

Alan S. Blinder is a Princeton economist and former Federal Reserve Bank governor. In an influential article in *Foreign Affairs*, he argued that education is good but not enough. A lot of well-educated people—real estate lawyers, radiologists, stockbrokers—are going to find their jobs outsourced to Third World countries. Others—divorce lawyers, internists, lobbyists—deliver "personal services" that are harder to outsource. Schools must educate their students to do the jobs that will stay here. No one—least of all the schools themselves—has begun to think about this.

Beyond that is a growing debate over whether education is a public good or a private good. Does education benefit society as a whole, and should society pay for it? Or does it benefit only those who get it and who should pay for it themselves? Should Americans pay taxes to support universities? Or should the government, at most, provide loans to individual students, who will use their education to make enough money to pay them back?

Like most educational issues, this one isn't confined to the Midwest. But it has special resonance for the Midwest, which needs all the education it can get to make the transition to globalization and the knowledge economy.

Traditionally, Americans agreed that education is a public good. That belief underlay the Land Grant Act, the GI Bill, and the other great government programs that created and paid for public universities. Now, Midwesterners seem to have changed their mind. Clearly, they aren't willing to support universities with taxes.

"The Land Grant Act was terrific," Joe White at the University of Illinois told me. "The idea behind it was that you can't build a democracy or an economy without educated people. But now states are backing away. They're backing away from public universities. We don't believe in public goods in America anymore. We believe in user fees."

James Duderstadt has a thought on this: "There is an increasing sense that the growth of higher education in the 21st century will be fueled by private dollars. Public policy will be replaced increasingly by market pressures. Hence the key question: Will the leaders of government and higher education attempt to use public policy and public investment to shape global knowledge and the learning marketplace to preserve the important values, traditions, missions and purpose of the university? Or will they continue to burden these institutions with archaic, politically motivated, and cumbersome policies and regulations, crippling higher education's capacity to adapt to the realities of the marketplace and serve society in the dramatically different circumstances of an age of knowledge?"

Education has gone global. Universities, like farms and factories, compete globally with others all over the world. We are seeing a new hierarchy of "global universities," competing for the best professors, the best researchers, and the best students. This means consolidation because, as in everything else, size will count. Increasingly, the best minds will belong to one global pool and will be able to go anywhere. Only the biggest, richest, strongest universities will be able to afford the research and the facilities that will draw this global intellectual elite. These "megaversities" will in turn be linked electronically with other academic powerhouses into a global campus.

It's no longer possible for a state university—even the huge state universities that have been the pride and lodestars of Midwestern education—to stay locked up inside their state lines, teaching only the state's children and surviving only on the state's taxpayers. Similarly, it's no longer possible for those children—and their parents—to pretend that a high school diploma is a passport to a good job in the new economy. And it's time that those taxpayers realize that unless they pay the fare, the global train won't stop in the Midwest anymore.

CHAPTER 12

Betting the Farm

All day the trucks drive in, five or six hundred of them, each one loaded with corn. Once they pounded through the center of Eddyville, a little town in southeast Iowa, but now the state has built a bypass highway, to accommodate the owner of the trucks' destination, which is the big Cargill plant on the edge of town. Most of the corn grown for a hundred miles around ends up in these trucks and, eventually, at Cargill, where it is transformed into ethanol and other products. What Cargill doesn't ship back out goes across the road to two factories—one Japanese, the other German—which make MSG and clothes softeners. Eddyville, a dot in the Iowa countryside, halfway between Ottumwa and Oskaloosa, is indisputably global.

The Cargill plant probably saved Eddyville, a former farm town, from extinction. More important, it may symbolize the salvation of the Midwestern economy. Or it may not. Much of the Midwest is betting on it, and no one knows whether that bet will pay off.

What Cargill does in Eddyville is biotech, which is the buzzword du jour across the Midwest these days. The plant is an old power station that Cargill converted in 1985 to make high-fructose corn syrup, which substitutes for sugar in a vast range of foods, from soda pop to cereals. In 1991, it became the first Cargill plant to make ethanol, the corn-based gasoline supplement.

More than one hundred ethanol plants operate in the United States today, most of them in the Midwestern corn belt. More are being built, although the pace is slowing. Some are locally owned by Midwestern investors or, more often, farmers' co-ops. Many are owned by big agribusiness corporations, such as Cargill or, especially, Archer Daniels Midland (ADM), the giant of the industry. Bill Gates is an investor. So are Sir Richard Branson, chairman of Virgin Airlines, and Vinod Khosla, a founder of Sun Microsystems (but, notably, not Warren Buffett, the Midwestern investment sage, who thinks it's a fad). Even Australian investors are buying up Iowa ethanol mills. These plants now turn out about six billion gallons per year; the government is pushing for more.

For the government, which subsidizes production while keeping out foreign competition, ethanol could help reduce dependence on oil from the Mideast. For investors, it's been a get-rich-quick formula—so far—to double their money in about two years, though these bonanza days seem to be ending. For corn farmers, it's been a windfall, driving corn prices to record heights. For farm-state politicians, it's a no-lose issue.

In other words, it looks too good to be true. Maybe it is. Its critics, such as Buffett, call it a boondoggle propped up by government subsidies, sucking in desperate farmers and farm towns who see it as an escape route from global extinction.

Ethanol is the most familiar face of the larger issue of biotech and biosciences, the industry of turning plants and animals into products that go far beyond food. The potential product lines are endless—drugs, medical devices, biofuels, chemicals, agricultural feedstocks, fertilizers, food additives, vaccines, diagnostic substances, packaging, plastics, new fibers, paints, cleansers, inks.

Beyond these products is a big and growing economy, based mostly on the use of bioscience in health care—the use of biotechniques in diagnosing and treating disease. This means research, which is going on in universities, hospitals, and private companies. It means new products to sell and new techniques to use: in the past two years alone, the government approved more than fifty biotechnology drugs, treating everything from breast cancer (Abraxane) to HIV infection (ATRIPLA) to diabetes (Byetta) to rheumatoid arthritis (Enbrel and HUMIRA) to macular degeneration (LUCENTIS) to alcoholism (Vivitrol). All this promises new laboratories and hospitals, with jobs for doctors, nurses, researchers, orderlies, technicians.

Without question, bioscience and biotech, by offering cures to previously untreatable diseases, will drive the future of the American
health industry, which in turn is expected to help drive the nation's
economy for years to come.

None of this is pie-in-the-sky. It's already happening. If it
should happen anywhere, it should happen in the Midwest. Bio,
after all, is based on plant and animal sciences. Plants and animals
are what the Midwest does for a living. If the future will be built
on the past, the Midwest's future clearly lies in bio.

But as with ethanol, there are two schools of thought. One
holds that the Midwest's bio future is bright, if it can grasp the opportunity. The other says this future has already passed it by.

Ethanol, hailed by many as the magic liquid that will save our
economy and our foreign policy, is grain alcohol. In fact, some
Midwestern ethanol is used to make vodka. In a sense, a good
vodka martini is three parts ethanol to one part vermouth.

Ethanol is relatively easy to make, which is one reason why so
many people make it. Another reason is that ethanol plants, while
not big employers, do create jobs and bring in tax revenues to
farm towns that have lost their other industries. In the Midwest,
where tired old factory cities court casinos, tired old farm towns
court ethanol plants.

Certainly, Cargill and its bio/ethanol plant have been good for
Eddyville. In a town of eleven hundred, Cargill employs four hundred workers. The plant produces ethanol, high-fructose corn
syrup, citric acid, and other corn bioproducts. Much of it is
shipped out by rail or in huge container trucks. Some of it is piped
to two plants next door. One, the Wacker Biochem Corporation, is
German-owned and makes a product, called cyclodextrin, that removes odors and softens fabrics. The other, Ajinomoto Heartland
Inc., is Japanese-owned and is the only MSG plant in America; the
next time you dine in a Chinese restaurant, part of your food will
come from Eddyville.

"This used to be farming and coal mining," recalls John Johnston, a retired electrician who is the mayor of Eddyville and has
lived there all his seventy years. "All the other little towns around

here are dying out. We would've died out, too, if these plants hadn't come. Now we've got new houses being built. We've kept the high school. Of course, the big shots, the executives, they want to go to Oskaloosa or somewhere where the country clubs are. But we're about one hundred and sixty years old, like most of the towns in the area, and we're still here."

Across the Midwest, other little towns are paying attention to what's going on in places like Eddyville. A few ethanol plants are in Oregon, Georgia, and California, but the vast majority sit in Iowa, Minnesota, Illinois, Wisconsin, Indiana, Nebraska, and the Dakotas, with more being built. The last Midwestern industrial boom took place in big cities like Chicago and Detroit. This one is happening in tiny places like Friesland, Wisconsin; Nevada, Iowa; Galva, Illinois; and Malta Bend, Missouri. About half of them are locally owned, but that will change if the business grows and demands the kind of capital investment that only an ADM or Cargill can provide. In 2003, about half of all ethanol plants were small ones, turning out forty million gallons per year, and they were owned by farmers; new plants produce one hundred million gallons or more, and 80 percent are owned by corporations or other absentee owners.

The economics of ethanol is complex. So is the politics. Both are based on two of the world's most volatile markets, for corn and for oil. Fans of ethanol say it brings much-needed investment into dying farm towns, creates good jobs, reduces air pollution, and provides a huge market for corn in an increasingly competitive world. So far, the United States uses 4.4 billion gallons of ethanol annually, or about 3 percent of the 140 billion gallons of fuel that Americans burn each year. Federal law says this has to go to 5 percent, or some 7.5 billion gallons, by 2012. (Actually, plants now operating or under construction will boost capacity to nearly 8 billion gallons long before that 2012 deadline arrives.)

Already, about one quarter of the Midwest's corn crop goes for ethanol production. If plans for future production pan out, this could go to half or more. Naturally, this has created a huge demand for corn. Prices doubled between 2005 and 2007, to more than $4 per bushel; in the past, any price over $3 was rare.

This means money for farmers. A big farmer with, say, one thousand acres in corn saw his income double in a year, from some $350,000 to $700,000 or more. Not surprisingly, this raised the value of farmland in the same year, by 9 percent in the Midwest as a whole and 13 percent in Iowa. Many big farmers rent out part of their lands, and the rents they charge are going up, too.

But this isn't all money in the bank. Both the profitability of ethanol and the net income of corn farmers are tied directly to the price of oil. The farmers feeding that Eddyville plant have a huge stake in what happens in the oil nations of the Middle East.

In mid-2006, oil prices were sky-high, at $70 per barrel or more, three times the price when the Iraq War started in 2003. Gas prices at American pumps also rose to record heights. Since ethanol is added to gas, it was worth about $3.45 per gallon. The price of corn makes up about 70 percent of the cost of a gallon of ethanol, and corn prices then were relatively low, about $2.40 per bushel. The result: ethanol plants were wildly profitable. Some investors recouped their money in a year. Towns, companies, and co-ops raced to build more plants. The boom was on.

The economics change almost daily. While I was writing this, oil prices fell to about $56 per barrel. This drove down the price of gas and, hence, the price of ethanol, to some $2 per gallon. But corn prices, responding to the demand from all those ethanol prices, were more than $4 per bushel. The result: ethanol plants barely broke even. Soon after, oil prices were back to $65 per barrel and gas prices were nudging $4 per gallon at the pump.

Wallace Tyner, an ethanol expert at Purdue, figures that if Middle Eastern crude oil costs $60 per barrel, then ethanol plants can pay up to $4.82 per bushel for corn and break even. But if oil falls to $40, then the ethanol plants can only afford to pay $2.40 for corn. At $50 per barrel, the breakeven price is $3 per bushel.

That means that the value of Midwestern corn depends on what happens in the Middle East. What's going to happen in the Middle East? Who knows? Maybe war will break out throughout the region and oil will go to $100 per barrel, at which point Midwesterners will start plowing up cities to plant corn. Or maybe Saudi Arabia will tap its huge oil reserves to drive down the price of oil to cripple its hated rival, Iran. If this happens, the collateral damage will be felt everywhere from Russia to Iowa.

Even if corn prices stay high, farmers don't get to keep all the money. Many of the things that farmers buy, such as fuel and fertilizer, are oil-based. High oil prices may raise the price of corn, but they also raise the price of raising that corn. There are no firm figures on net farm profitability, but most experts think the ethanol boom is making farmers richer, though certainly not doubling their net income.

This happens only with a lot of help from Washington. The government gives a fifty-one-cents-per-gallon tax credit for ethanol producers. Fourteen states add subsidies of their own. But there's more. The largest ethanol producer in the world, Brazil, distills it from sugarcane, not corn, and sells its ethanol for about half the American price; to keep out this low-cost competition, the United States levies a fifty-four-cents-per-gallon tariff on all Brazilian ethanol. Much of this is the result of lobbying by ADM, which controls nearly one fourth of the U.S. ethanol market, about five times as much as its nearest competitor.

For the Bush administration, these subsidies produce an alternative fuel that postpones the day when it has to impose carbon caps, higher fuel-economy standards, or other conservation measures. But without these subsidies, ethanol would cost a lot more. The subsidies make the difference between profit and loss for ethanol makers, and without them, the fuel would probably become uneconomical to produce. If a future administration or Congress removes the subsidies, the ethanol industry will collapse. Already, it is slowing. Some new plants are being built, but ones that were only in the planning stage when oil prices began to fall may never appear.

In the Midwest, it seems cruel to look skeptically at ethanol. There is a terrific emotional push behind it, a last roll of the dice for rural areas where nothing much good has happened for decades. The ethanol boom—the investments, the hype, the subsidies—can be defended socially, if not economically, much as other farm subsidies are justified as a vital prop for farmers and their dying towns.

But sentiment only goes so far. Ethanol is controversial even in farm territory. "It's a politically protected industry," Roger Mc-Eowen, a professor of agricultural law at Iowa State University, told me in his office in Ames. "Warren Buffett says it's not economically efficient to produce, and he's right. I know the whole Midwest is counting on this, but we're telling farmers who've invested in these plants to get out."

As Buffett argues, an end to that fifty-four-cents tariff on Brazilian ethanol would wipe out the American ethanol industry. So would an end to that fifty-one-cents subsidy. That means that ethanol producers and corn farmers are gambling on the government supporting them forever. If they lose the gamble, they lose their businesses.

Beyond that, McEowen said, ethanol doesn't save the small family farm or the small rural town. Instead, it only speeds up the process that is wiping out both of them. The subsidies reward bigness, because the more you produce, the more the government gives you—the same reason the overall farm-subsidy program has led to consolidation. If the ethanol industry grows, it will be dominated—just as the rest of farming already is—by the big corporations, such as ADM.

"Will this keep farmers in business?" McEowen's colleague Paul Lasley asked. "A lot of farmers are mortgaging their assets, going into debt. I sure hope they're right. Already, two or three ethanol plants have been bought by foreigners. That's part of globalization. Maybe Iowans can retain ownership of this industry. And maybe we'll find ourselves like ranchers in Oklahoma, who may own the land above the oil, but all the pumping and processing is owned by external folks."

Midwestern livestock farmers worry about the ethanol boom, because it uses corn that would otherwise be eaten by hogs and cattle. It also uses corn that could have earned money on the export market: in 2000, the United States exported four times as much corn as it used for ethanol; now those figures are even, and ethanol is expected to consume twice as much corn as exports before the decade is out.

Long before we produce enough ethanol to make a real dent in oil imports, we're going to run out of corn. The Eddyville plant already consumes most of southeastern Iowa's crop. By the time federal mandates are met, the ethanol boom may achieve the impossible. It could cause a shortage of corn in the Midwest.

(It's important to stress that all the above is true as it's being written. This whole ethanol market is so volatile that, by the time you read it, the picture will have changed. Farming swings between booms and busts. One or the other is coming, but no one knows which.)

Finally, ethanol seems the wrong answer to the global challenge. In the old, pre-global world, the Midwest survived on commodities—corn and soybeans, coal, mass-produced goods from big factories. Back then, before anyone had ever seen a Japanese TV set, the rest of the world presented no threat to what the Midwest did. Midwestern crops and Midwestern products supplied the world, but it was a one-way trade.

Now Midwestern crops, like Midwestern refrigerators and washing machines, compete with crops around the world, including those from Brazil, where land and labor, like workers in China, are unimaginably cheap. If the government protected the Midwest's refrigerators and washing machines with the same subsidies that it gives to ethanol, neither Newton nor Galesburg would have the problems they do. Corn-based ethanol, the last best hope for much of the rural Midwest, may be a pipe dream.

If there's a rescuer on the horizon, it's called biomass. With luck, biomass will ride in before the Midwest runs out of corn and could turn ethanol into a realistic and economical alternative to foreign oil.

Biomass is animal and plant matter that basically isn't good for anything else. This includes switchgrass and other prairie grasses, and also cornstalks, wood chips, sawdust, animal waste, old stems, and leaves. If it burns, it has calories. If it has calories, it can be turned into fuel.

Unlike corn-based ethanol, biomass is the only natural, renewable carbon resource plentiful enough to really substitute for fossil fuels. We can only produce enough corn-based ethanol to replace about 10 percent of imports before we run out of corn; not bad, but not exactly a solution. Biomass by contrast, can replace about three times this much.

There is an awful lot of biomass around, much of it in the Midwest. As one Chicago scientist said, "We are to biomass as Saudi Arabia is to oil." Because much of it is waste, it's not being used for anything else. It doesn't need to be cultivated—most prairie grasses grow wild, and if farmers pay any attention to them at all, it's only to burn them off—so it doesn't need fertilizers, pesticides, or other chemical products.

Ethanol produced from this biomass is called cellulosic ethanol, because it is made by breaking down the cells that form the raw material. Scientists know how to do this. But they don't know how to do it fast or efficiently or cheaply, because the biomass cells are tough and resilient. Kernels of corn, protected inside their husks, are soft and tender. But the husks themselves, exposed to the elements, have to be tough. So do the cornstalks, which quickly grow as high as an elephant's eye in all sorts of weather. So do the prairie grasses, which bend to the ground before the winds, then snap back up and keep growing. Switchgrass grows in thick tangles eight feet high, with roots just as deep. Giant miscanthus, an Asian grass now under study at the University of Illinois, has bamboolike stems that grow up to thirteen feet. If scientists are going to get at the sugar locked inside these cells, they have to learn how to break through the cell walls.

Right now, it's cheaper to import a gallon of gasoline than to make a gallon of cellulosic ethanol. So far, the day is not in sight when biomass will light a flame under the Midwestern economy. But a breakthrough at one of the Midwest's big research universities would transform the nation's economy and, probably, its foreign policy.

Beyond ethanol and biomass, much of the Midwest talks about betting its future on bioscience, which studies living organisms, both plants and animals, and biotechnology, which applies that knowledge to making things. Bioscience is research. Biotechnology is industry. The Midwest is flush with big research universities, and it's always been good at making things. Can there be any doubt that bio is where the Midwest has to be?

The answer depends on who you talk to. Walt Plosila and Joe Cortright aren't exactly household names, but they're leading the debate on bio. The Midwest has a crucial stake in who's right.

Walter Plosila is a vice president for Battelle, the big nonprofit consultancy specializing in technology and its commercialization. Battelle is headquartered in Columbus, but Plosila works out of a small office outside Cleveland, where I visited him. He has no patience with people who think bio has a small future because it hasn't yet transformed our present. He sees an infant industry, just dipping its toe into the wealth of new drugs, new diagnostic measures, new ways of treating and curing people, that bio, and especially its manipulation of human genes and proteins, will create.

"Look," he said, "this is the bio century. Look at the impact that the personal computer has had in the last thirty years. At the start, we thought its main impact would be to put secretaries out of work. Now computers are a mature industry.

"Bio is where the PC revolution was thirty years ago. It can't be narrowly prescribed—just putting metal in people's bodies, for instance. It's regenerative medicine. It's drugs and pharmaceuticals and genomics. It's personalized medicine and predictive medicine. It's going to change the health-delivery system, which is becoming the biggest employer in most counties. It's going to be like autos were in their day—a big spin-off of jobs.

"When will this happen? When will bio grow? Nobody knows. It's going to be ten or twenty years before there's a big impact.

"In different regions, this is going to vary. In the Midwest, we've got this manufacturing heritage. We can use that to move into devices that we can make, and we can use our academic centers for biologics, research, testing, all that. It could have a major impact."

On the other side is Joseph Cortright, an economist who did a study called "Signs of Life" for the Brookings Institution that presented the opposing case. Cortright focused on biotechnology, which is, after all, the business end of the bio boom. He doesn't dispute that bio is going to grow, nor that it's important. But he implies that it's wishful thinking for the Midwest to imagine that bio is the solution to its economic malaise.

According to Cortright's study, only nine cities account for three fourths of the biggest and the newest biotech firms. They are Boston, San Francisco, New York, Philadelphia, San Diego, Seattle, Washington, Los Angeles, and Raleigh-Durham. Not a Midwestern city on the list.

It's not that the Midwest lacks resources. A recent Battelle report identified the states that are active in biosciences. In agricultural feedstocks and chemicals, Iowa, Illinois, and Ohio were three of the four biggest. In drugs, Illinois and Indiana ranked in the top six. In medical devices, Indiana and Minnesota are big: nine of the top twenty firms in the world are in the Midwest.

As we saw in the chapter on education, the Midwest owns some of the world's leading research universities—mostly state universities such as Michigan, Wisconsin, and Illinois, but also the University of Chicago and Washington University in St. Louis. It has a stupendous lineup of bio firms—agribusiness and chemical companies like ADM, Cargill, Dow AgroSciences, Monsanto, Pioneer Hybrid; drug companies like Abbott, Baxter, and Eli Lilly; medical-device giants like GE Healthcare, Medtronic, Stryker, and Zimmer. It has giant medical complexes, led by the celebrated Mayo Clinic in Rochester, Minnesota. In moribund Cleveland, the Cleveland Clinic, a major academic medical center and hospital, is an economic power.

Cortright concedes that Chicago, St. Louis, and the Detroit–Ann Arbor region are all hotbeds of research. But the problem is that they haven't been able to turn that research into business. Between them, they produce as much research as Seattle, San Diego, and Raleigh-Durham, but only about one sixth as much commercial activity. Other Midwestern cities—Cleveland, Columbus, Indianapolis, Milwaukee, Kansas City, and Minneapolis–St. Paul—also create substantial research but, again, little production.

The problem is money. Any biosciences boom in the Midwest will have to be a financial and scientific collaboration between universities and companies. Bioscience backers assume that the industry will grow much as the computer and information industries did, with companies funding university research or with university researchers taking their ideas and setting up their own companies. But this takes money, and as we shall see, the Midwest so far is short of the kind of red-blooded venture capitalists who finance new ideas and new companies.

Cortright also argues that, if bio is growing, it's growing slowly, and not creating many jobs. He counts about two hundred thousand persons working for biotech firms across the country. Even in the nine big centers, he says, biotech accounts for only about 3.5 percent of all manufacturing jobs. Only forty-four biotech companies have more than one thousand employees. Even in Boston and San Francisco, no biotech firm ranks among the twenty-five major private employers.

Plosila says Cortright defines this universe too narrowly, limiting it to about two thousand firms. If the definition is broadened to include bioagricultural plants like the Cargill operation in Eddyville, the total grows to some forty thousand firms and 1.2 million jobs.

Even so, Cortright says, it's a mistake to think that the bio revolution will blossom into the economic force that the computer revolution became. "Many assume that the new insights about the human genome will produce changes as sweeping as those induced by the personal computer and the Internet," he wrote. "It is of course impossible to predict, but there are indications that the implications of biotechnology may be far less sweeping." Computers became steadily cheaper and steadily more powerful: Moore's law decrees that each computer chip doubled in power every eighteen months while falling in price. So far, there's no Moore's law for biotech.

In fact, both Plosila and Cortright are right. A terrific amount of bioscience and biotechnology is going on around the Midwest, with more to come. Plant and animal science, and the drugs and other products that it produces, will play a major role in Midwestern economies. But all this activity so far is still much less than it could be. The Midwest lags behind the coasts in exploiting a business that it should dominate. And no one really knows if bio can

replace heavy industry as the locomotive of the Midwestern economy or make up for the jobs being shed by the region's factories.

Across the region, states and cities are trying to jump-start a
bio boom. Ohio's Third Frontier program will give $1.6 billion in
grants to science projects, including bioscience, around the state.
Michigan used the money it got from the state lawsuits against to-
bacco companies to set up a $50-million-per-year bio program
(but later downgraded it to $10 million per year, effectively gut-
ting it). Iowa created an Iowa Values Fund and used part of the
money to fund bio research.

Although the Midwest lags behind the two coasts, it is still very
much in the international running. Asian nations such as China
and Korea, which hope to do in biosciences what Japan did in
electronics, are just getting started. European public antagonism
to genetically modified organisms (GMOs) has held back the bio
industry there. The United States remains the world leader.

But the field is getting crowded. According to Battelle, at least
forty-one states have programs specifically targeting bio for development. Midwestern states such as Iowa and Missouri have commissioned huge reports from Battelle on turning bio into a major
industry. For every Cortright warning that there isn't enough bio
to go around, there's a governor betting his state's future on turning plants and animals into products.

In an office park outside Des Moines, I talked with Ted Crosbie, a vice president for global plant breeding for Monsanto and,
at the time, a science adviser to Tom Vilsack, then the governor of
Iowa. Crosbie had chaired the Bio Science Alliance of Iowa, which
tries to link the state's research universities to industry.

Crosbie said he'd like to turn Iowa into a bio replica of Silicon
Valley—not so far-fetched, he says, when you consider the number
of Midwesterners, including Iowans, who went to California to
turn their good ideas into products. "Now," he says, "we have to
recruit people from outside—people who are tired of California,
tired of housing prices, tired of bad schools."

The future lies in making things out of plants, and Iowa already
has the plants, Crosbie told me. Now it needs to specialize, to get

ideas from its universities into companies that can establish an Iowa niche in a bio world.

"Anything you can make with petroleum, you can make with soybeans or corn, from diesel to high-tech manufacturing. Iowa shouldn't concentrate on making the final product. We're not that competitive with China or India. Instead, we can make the components. We have technology. We've got a long history of genetics and computers. We can do testing here. Iowa might be a low-cost, high-quality pharmaceutical-trial network. There's a lower cost of living here, so it costs less to run trials here. And let's face it, anything that involves aging or obesity, we've got the population for it."

I talked with another executive of a big agribusiness firm in Iowa who frankly doubted his state's ability to compete in the global bio league. It's not only that Boston and Berkeley have a head start on Des Moines, he said. Indianapolis and St. Louis do, too. As Crosbie noted, the Midwest needs to lure back its prodigal graduates or poach scientists from California or India, and at the moment these footloose bio-nerds are unlikely to go to Iowa.

Like every Midwesterner who's thought about the region's economic future, Crosbie sees each state scrapping on its own to grab a project or a product from the state next door, instead of cooperating to take on the world. Iowa has three state research universities; the Bio-Science Alliance, a program to bring university researchers and companies together, was partly aimed at keeping the universities from duplicating each other in fruitless competition. But the Midwest as a whole has at least fifteen world-class research universities, plus some major research institutions such as Mayo or the Cleveland Clinic. Each operates alone. No one tries to link their research, set up cooperative programs, persuade each to do what it does best, then promote their results to the huge Midwestern biotech companies that actually make the products.

Not surprisingly, the most interesting projects are being driven by cities, not states, because cities are where the companies, researchers, and money are. Many of these projects are spearheaded by wealthy and focused donors, not city or state governments.

This is the "sugar-daddy phenomenon" that is beginning to rescue cities lucky enough to have a sugar daddy. Once families like the Maytags and the Balls dominated their Midwestern cities. They're gone now, but they've been succeeded by families—the Danforths in St. Louis, the Van Andels in Grand Rapids, the Stowers in Kansas City—all with ambitions to turn their cities into centers of medical or bio research.

In Kansas City, Jim and Virginia Stowers, both cancer survivors who made their money from a mutual fund, set up the Stowers Institute in 1994 with gifts that have grown into a $2 billion endowment. The institute's goal is to turn Kansas City into a cancer-fighting center, through genetic and bioscientific research aimed at understanding and defeating disease. The institute is in Kansas City not because it has any bioscience tradition, but because that's where the Stowers are. The city, in fact, has no research university—usually a prerequisite for bio research—so the Stowers are importing top scientists from Harvard, Berkeley, and other centers, hoping to build a research titan from scratch.

In Grand Rapids, the Van Andel and DeVos families, who co-founded Amway, hope that medical research and treatment will replace the shrinking furniture industry as the anchor of what was a decaying city. The Van Andels created the Van Andel Institute to carry out research, especially into cancer and Parkinson's disease. The DeVos family are major contributors to Spectrum Health, a hospital complex. As local factories close, the research boom—not only the institute and hospitals but medical companies that they have drawn to town—have added fourteen hundred jobs to a city that needs every new job it can get.

Grand Rapids also lacked a research university, but instead of just importing scientists, it imported a whole university, or at least a branch of it—a new department of Michigan State's medical school, which will specialize in molecular medicine and on training scientists.

If any Midwestern city turns itself into a center of bio research and technology, it will probably be St. Louis. Once a major river port that aspired to be the capital of the Midwest, St. Louis today is a dreary, empty city that has lost more than half its population, is saddled with an ineffectual city government, and comes to life only on the nights that the Cardinals play downtown. Not exactly fertile soil for a twenty-first-century industry.

But St. Louis owns some enviable assets. One is a cluster of bio and agribusiness firms, such as Monsanto, that live and die by research. Another is that, unlike Kansas City or Grand Rapids, it already is home to a first-rate research school and one of the nation's best medical schools, Washington University in St. Louis (often confused by outsiders with the University of Washington, out in Seattle). A third asset, and the one that really makes St. Louis different, is the Danforth Plant Science Center, the creation of the Danforth family, which made its money from Ralston Purina, the big animal-feed and cereals company. The best-known Danforth is John, a former senator, but the center owes more to his brother, William, a doctor and former chancellor at Washington University.

I spent an afternoon at the center talking with Roger Beachy, its dynamic and fast-talking director, about his plans. "We're not a university," he said. "We don't teach. Our role is strictly research. Our idea is to brand the St. Louis region as the Bio Belt. Our goal is economic development."

Beachy's model is not the major research university, such as MIT or Stanford, but the independent research center, like the Salk Institute for Biological Studies in California, which calls itself "a crucible for creativity." Salk, along with the Scripps Institute and the University of California at San Diego, led the San Diego boom, Beachy says, which restored an economy crippled by the collapse of the local defense industry. St. Louis also lost much of its defense industry, and Beachy, like other local leaders, sees biosciences, anchored by the Danforth Center, as the city's savior.

In 2000, St. Louis commissioned Battelle to tell it what to do next. Battelle recommended that the city set up a network of "angel investors"—independent investors who put money into companies before they're ready to attract venture capital—to create incubator buildings for fledgling companies, and create a workforce. Since then, a network has been set up and two incubators opened.

But building an educated workforce could be trickiest. St. Louis officials claim that the city is beginning to attract educated young people from outside. But biotech needs both Ph.D. scientists and a pool of two-year and four-year graduates—the community-college products—who know how to run robots and do the other chores that this new industry requires. So far, St. Louis has laid the foundation of its new economy but still has a lot of building to do.

St. Louis, Grand Rapids, and Kansas City have many things in common, including committed families with deep pockets. One other thing they have in common is a regional scope and a willingness to ignore state lines.

St. Louis is the hub of a twelve-county economic region, with half the counties across the Mississippi River in Illinois. Kansas City is the Missouri base of a two-state, two-city region stretching in Kansas. In Grand Rapids, leaders see themselves linked less to the state of Michigan than to the city of Chicago. Detroit is closer than Chicago is, but the Illinois metropolis is more of a magnet, culturally and economically, than the dying Motor City to the east.

Most people, if they think of Peoria at all, see it as the epitome of Middle America, an unimaginative place with such normal tastes that it is the nation's focus group, the proving ground for every new product or program ("if it plays in Peoria . . ."). If fact, Peoria, an unexpectedly beautiful little city in central Illinois, tucked into a valley along the Illinois River, may have imagined the Midwest's future.

Peoria hit bottom about fifteen years ago and is reviving now, largely on the basis of bio. This is less surprising than it appears. Peoria is the headquarters of Caterpillar, which has been important to its revival, but also used to be one of America's whiskey capitals, the home of Hiram Walker. ADM owns the old Hiram Walker distillery now and uses it to make ethanol, which it exports to Russia for vodka. As one city father told me, "We know fermentation."

Peoria is an interesting place. Like many Midwestern cities, it has been dominated for years by one big company, Caterpillar, but that company isn't Maytag or Delphi: it didn't bail out. The city went through crisis in the late 1980s and early 1990s; unlike many other Midwestern cities, it recognized that crisis as the end of an era and retooled itself for the future. It managed to become global without destroying itself locally. It had strengths, especially in bioscience, and learned how to use them. It had useful institutions that had never had much to do with each other and persuaded them to start pulling together.

Caterpillar once employed forty thousand people in Peoria, most of them on assembly lines making Cat's farm machinery and huge construction equipment. Then the Japanese came: Komatsu challenged Caterpillar as much as Toyota challenged GM. Cat, like the auto companies, had old factories, high wages, strong unions, expensive benefits. Like the auto companies, it faced a new world in which it couldn't compete.

Caterpillar did many of the things the auto companies did, such as cut back employment in Northern cities like Peoria and open plants in nonunion Southern states. The United Auto Workers fought back with two strikes. By all accounts, they were horrible.

"The strike in '91 was the most devastating," recalled Dave Koehler, a local Democratic politician and leader of a labor-management coalition. "It split families. All the big issues, like seniority, were at stake. In the end, people crossed the line and the strike was broken. UAW lost big.

"And then reality set in. People realized that it wasn't the good old days anymore. They learned that this is a different world. There were courageous labor leaders who realized they didn't want to give Cat any reason to move out of town."

It worked. While much of the basic manufacturing went South or went overseas, Cat kept its headquarters and many of its white-collar jobs in Peoria. Cat's payroll, once down to seventeen thousand, is back up to twenty-five thousand now, "but three quarters of them are global administrators," according to Jim McConoughey, who is president of the Heartland Partnership, a local economic development agency.

Cat not only stayed in Peoria but helped in other ways. Like many companies, it had come up with good ideas that it never used but refused to give to anyone else. Now, it has released some of these patents, which have become separate companies, such as Firefly Energy, which makes lightweight batteries.

These companies have stayed in Peoria because the local

community college, Illinois Central College, set up an incubator for new businesses. Now the city is setting up Renaissance Park, a bigger incubator, sponsored by Cat and other institutions, including Bradley University and local hospitals. Bradley, until now a lesser player in the local economy, is expanding its business program to train management for the kind of small companies that the new economy will create.

Peoria always had good hospitals, partly because the health benefits at Caterpillar were so generous. Those benefits have been cut back since the strikes, but the city is looking outward, trying to become the big medical center between Chicago and St. Louis. Four major local hospitals employ thirty-one thousand people, more than Caterpillar.

Perhaps the most important institution is the National Center for Agricultural Utilization Research, a U.S. Department of Agriculture laboratory, which, like similar labs around the country, exists to find ways to commercialize local farm produce. The Peoria lab opened in 1940, helped develop penicillin, brings in $30 million in federal grants, employs 120 Ph.D.'s—and never did much for Peoria.

"We produced hundreds of products with big success, but never made them in Peoria," Peter Johnsen, the lab's director, told me in his office, a few weeks before he left, after twelve years, to become provost at Bradley. "Not one Peoria company had spun off an Ag Lab idea." Working with local leaders, Johnsen changed that policy. The result is two new companies, zuChem, which produces sugars for pharmaceuticals, and iSoy, which makes a cosmetic sunscreen. ZuChem, especially, plays on Peoria's fermentation expertise as a onetime whiskey town.

Ethanol, not surprisingly, is part of this. Some $700 million is going into new ethanol and biodiesel plants in the region. An equal amount is being invested in a wind farm going up in Woodford County, across the Illinois River.

"We were founded as an agricultural community," Johnsen said. "Then we got into ag processing—that's the whiskey. Then we got into ag manufacturing, Caterpillar. Now we're adding commodity transformation. This region is trying to diversify its economy on the basis of its strengths, but also on the realities of globalization."

In all this, the city government is a passive partner but isn't a leader. Neither is the state government. Instead, Peoria, in the heart of Illinois, looks across state lines for its future, like the other bioscience success stories in this chapter. For its part, Peoria is touting something called the Discovery Corridor, trying to hook together a tristate region based on bioscience. The corridor starts in St. Louis and runs up to Peoria, then through the university towns of Bloomington, Champaign-Urbana, and West Lafayette to Indianapolis. So far this seems to be more ambition than accomplishment. But unlike so much of the Midwest, Peoria is asking the right questions.

It's also going to a lot of the right places for answers. It sponsored its own Battelle report. It brought in the urban guru Richard Florida to find out how to become a "creative city." (This was less successful. Peoria, as Jim McConoughey told me, "is a classic prototypical Midwestern town—nothing good, nothing bad. We're not very bohemian.")

In that sense, then, the national image of Peoria—a little bland and bourgeois—is accurate enough. But the town, having gone through deep decline, has picked itself up, counted its strengths, put them together, and used them to build a new city that doesn't look much like the old, twentieth-century Peoria but may be a model for the new century.

As this chapter makes clear, a sunburst of bioscience and other twenty-first-century innovation is going on around the Midwest. Major universities, companies, cities, and independent institutes do it. States want bioscience and devote millions of dollars to it. Everybody, from farmers to college presidents, favors it.

Why, then, doesn't it add up to more? The Midwest is the ag capital of the universe. It should be the ag-bio capital, and it isn't: the ag-bio capitals, as Cortright says, are all on the coasts, far from the farm belt. In the Midwest, any bio activity is less, much less, than the sum of its parts. There have to be reasons, and there are.

There are places where the seeds of bio bloom lustily. Boston and San Francisco are examples. So is San Diego, which is held up as the epitome of "cluster" development, where companies and scientists come together in a critical mass. St. Louis shows this kind of life, and so does Peoria.

These places have several things in common. A first-rate research university is often at the core. These universities make it easy for their scientists to spin off their ideas into companies. There's a strong support network—civic leaders, community colleges, a tight-knit civic life, lawyers and accountants who understand bio, a local government that is willing to help without taking the lead. Mostly, there's money—a big pool of venture capital ready to invest in unproven ideas, most of which will probably fail.

The Midwest lacks much of this. In the century since a constellation of Midwestern dreamers ignited the industrial economy, the region lost the knack of inventing, innovating, and taking risks. The Midwest's virtue of safety and security has become its curse. Government, universities, businesses, lawyers, and bankers—all understand heavy industry, not computer nerds with a new idea.

Mostly, though, there is no money. The true bio hotbeds on Cortright's list not only have research capacity but the ability to convert that research into products. Venture capital concentrates in Boston and San Francisco. San Diego has its own venture capital industry. Washington has government funds and New York has the big investment houses.

Midwestern universities and other research centers get their share—about 20 percent—of grants from the National Institutes of Health. This finances a lot of research. But only 4 percent of the venture capital spent in the United States—the money that turns this research into jobs—is spent in the Midwest. By contrast, 47 percent is spent in California. The moral: if you have a good idea, you can develop it in a Midwestern university. But if you want to set up a company, you better go to California, where the money is.

One of the few lonely venture capitalists in the Midwest is Dan Broderick, who plies his trade from his base in Milwaukee. According to Broderick, the Midwest has most of what it needs, except money. It has more people than the West Coast. It has plenty of graduate students in the biosciences: Iowa ranks sixth in the nation, Minnesota seventh, all the other Midwestern states above average. Its big companies—Baxter, Abbott, Lilly, Monsanto—provide a research base. Most important, it has all those big research universities.

But Midwestern ideas get developed elsewhere. Netscape was dreamed up at the University of Illinois but developed in California. Amgen, the world's biggest bioscience company, was founded in Chicago but grew in California. Why?

"Maybe it's tradition," Broderick told me. "Venture capital was invented in California. So entrepreneurs started there, and then they split and begot other companies, and this money drew in other entrepreneurs. The Midwest, by contrast, has a cultural problem. People who go to California go to seek their fortune. They're risk-takers. But Midwesterners aren't risk-takers. There's a fear of failure here."

In fairness, it's easy when everyone is close to everyone else. Boston has a dense network of universities and medical centers. San Francisco, Stanford, Berkeley, and Silicon Valley huddle together; so does the bio cluster in San Diego.

As we've seen, the Midwest has brainpower to meet this challenge. Medical schools in Ann Arbor, Madison, St. Louis, and Chicago are among the nation's best. Illinois sparkles in computer science, Ohio State in materials sciences, Wisconsin in engineering, Minnesota in chemistry, Iowa State in agricultural sciences. But they are a long way from each other, two hundred miles or more. Venture capitalists say they like to be near their money. It is hard to get a venture capitalist to invest in a company that is going to be a couple of hours away. William Testa, a Chicago economist, calls this "the tyranny of distance." It is, at the least, history's revenge: the original location of land-grant universities far from each other, with a mandate to educate and develop their own states, now keeps them from working together in the kind of regional cooperation that the states need.

"We're going to have to get over this," Broderick said. "We have to accept that, instead of driving three hours in Boston traffic, we have to take ninety-minute flights around the Midwest."

In fact, it's going to take an attitude transplant by everyone involved. Big companies need to spin off ideas into smaller companies, as Caterpillar has. Big universities not only need to encourage researchers to commercialize ideas, but need to help them: most Midwestern universities have offices to do this, but only some of them, such as the University of Wisconsin, do a good job. Some cities, such as Chicago, know that the glory days of the industrial era are over, but most Midwestern cities hold on to the past and are cool, if not hostile, to the needs of the future.

The global age will belong to the spry and imaginative. In this new era, down-home verities don't work anymore. The Midwest needs to get smart, fast. It also needs to get together, to act as a region. But one barrier looms higher than any other. It's the political barrier, the balkanization of the Midwest into a hive of squabbling states that would rather fight than cooperate. It is to this political roadblock that we now turn.

CHAPTER 13

The Blue and the Red

Globalization presents the Midwest with regional problems and regional opportunities. These problems and opportunities are virtually the same in every state. Yet no Midwestern state even considers cooperating with its neighbors to meet this challenge.

Every expert I talked with found this ridiculous. "All the states have blinkers on," Ted Crosbie lamented in Iowa. "They're fighting over the same table scraps. Everybody's thinking state by state. Nobody's thinking regional."

In the global era, states are simply too weak and too divided to provide for the welfare of their citizens. This has nothing to do with ideology: Republican and Democratic state governments flounder equally. In the Midwest, nothing displays this weakness like water—specifically, the water in the Great Lakes.

Apart from the land itself, Great Lakes water is the Midwest's richest resource. The lakes hold no less than 18 percent of all the fresh surface water on earth. This water gives the Midwest a huge comparative advantage: in the future, any investor whose business requires lots of fresh water will have only one place to go. We live in an era when more and more Americans, for baffling reasons, choose to live in parched places such as Las Vegas and Phoenix. No one thinks the Great Lakes water can be piped into the arid West: the cost and the technology required are prohibitive. But this water does assure the Midwest a steady supply of the lifeblood of civilizations. Six Midwestern states share the Great Lakes shores and part of the Great Lakes basin—Minnesota, Michigan,

Ohio, Indiana, Illinois, and Wisconsin; so do Pennsylvania and
New York and the Canadian provinces of Ontario and Quebec.

Climate change is already beginning to lower water levels in
some of the lakes and threatens their long-term health. With so
much of their future riding on this health, you'd think these states
would have joined long ago to regulate their use and control any
diversion. In fact, a Council of Great Lakes Governors exists and
does some useful environmental work. But the states themselves
have been squabbling—even suing each other—for a century over
such basic issues as the amount of water that can be diverted from
the lakes and who can use it. Each state has its own needs and its
own political pressures, and these squabbles have kept the states
most responsible for the lakes from framing any policy for their
use. In a crisis, the federal government could dictate this policy—
and the booming arid areas of America have more votes in Washington these days than does the Midwest.

This vulnerability may—or may not—be about to end. In 2005,
the states ended six years of grinding negotiations with an agreement, called the Compact, establishing a legally binding and constitutional framework giving them control over use of the lakes
and setting rules for using the water. But the Compact doesn't
come into force until all the states ratify it. Two years after the
signing, only two states, Minnesota and Illinois, have done so.
With luck and no shift in the political winds, the other states may
ratify it. But both luck and political winds do shift, so ratification
anytime is far from certain.

Geographical and political reality insists that the states deal with
Great Lakes issues. But the states have done a terrible job with the
region's premier economic and ecological resource, which is basically a local issue. There's no reason to think they can cooperate
constructively on anything else, especially the global changes of the
twenty-first century.

The reason is a deep, intractable problem. Midwestern states make
no sense as units of government. Most Midwestern states don't really hang together—politically, economically, or socially. In truth,
these states and their governments are incompetent to deal with

twenty-first-century problems because of their very history, rooted in the eighteenth and nineteenth centuries.

As we saw in chapter 2, six Midwestern states—Ohio, Michigan, Indiana, Illinois, Wisconsin, and part of Minnesota—grew out of the Northwest Territory, which Congress established in 1787. The Northwest Ordinance provided that the districts of the Territory, then largely unsettled, could be divided into states when they got enough people. "Not less than three nor more than five states" could be carved out of the Territory, it said. It even dictated some of the boundaries of these states. Canada and the Ohio River marked the northern and southern borders. The vertical state lines between Illinois, Indiana, and Ohio were laid out pretty much where they are today. The Ordinance left open the possibility that both Indiana and Illinois could stretch all the way to Canada, but said that "if Congress shall hereafter find it expedient," then two other states could be formed. This is how we got Michigan and Wisconsin.

The rules set by this Ordinance influenced the later admission to the Union of the other Midwestern states—Iowa, the rest of Minnesota, Missouri—that were carved out of the Louisiana Purchase. Some state lines followed natural divisions—the Mississippi and Ohio rivers, for instance, or the Great Lakes. Others resulted from political maneuvering within the broad outlines of the Ordinance.

The border between Ohio and Michigan, for instance, was fixed by the opéra bouffe Toledo War of the 1830s. Because of a surveying glitch, both states claimed a 468-square-mile strip that included the area that later became Toledo. Troops were mustered and soldiers marched. Michigan captured nine surveyors, but the only bloodshed came when an Ohioan named Two Stickney stabbed a Michigan sheriff in a brawl. In the end, Ohio got the Toledo Strip. As compensation, Michigan got its Upper Peninsula.

And there the Ohio-Michigan border stays to this day. Given its genesis, it didn't make much sense in 1833, and it makes no sense at all now. What's left of the auto industry sprawls across Michigan and Ohio in one undivided swath. The two states prospered together, and they're suffering together now. If the state line that meant so much to Two Stickney wasn't there, they could even work together. But will they? Not a chance.

Instead, what we have is endemic duplication. Each state has its specialty. Iowa knows corn, Ohio knows materials, Minnesota knows medical devices. But each state now tries to duplicate the other. Working together, the states could play to their strengths. But in the Midwest, state governments are paid *not* to cooperate. No governor ever gets credit for a factory that opens in a neighboring state. No legislator brags about jobs created across the state line, even if some of those jobs go to his constituents.

"Sure, it would make sense to come together to fight off Georgia or South Carolina," a Michigan economic-development official in Lansing told me. "But we're historical economic adversaries in competing for jobs. These big companies seldom say they're going to invest in Michigan or Alabama. Instead, they say they're going to be in the Upper Midwest, so everybody in the Midwest ends up competing."

Officials in each state get elected by voters in that state and paid by taxpayers in that state. They answer to their own governor, and governors like nothing better than to cut ribbons. Nobody in one state owes anything to anyone in the next state, as far as they can see—and none can see farther than the state border. Midwestern states might prosper by cooperating, but no state employee ever got a raise or promotion by thinking about the state next door.

"Say a machining plant opens across the state line in Indiana," the Lansing official said. "That means some jobs for people who live in Michigan. But there's no ribbon-cutting for our politicians, and no tax revenue for our treasury. We get paid to put business in Michigan, not in other states. A plant in Ohio or Indiana is nothing but a near miss."

As with state governments, so with the big state universities. As we saw, these universities, instead of combining their strengths, play to their weaknesses with unneeded duplication and competition.

In their early days, the states really did control commerce within their borders. Then came the technological revolution—railroads and the telegraph—that made commerce national. It took the federal government a half century after this technological transformation, until 1887, to create the Interstate Commerce Commission and pass the laws necessary to regulate this new national economy;

the states fought it well into the twentieth century. Now commerce has escaped national boundaries and has gone global. But in many ways, it's anarchy. Almost no global governance exists. National rules and regulations are becoming meaningless. As for the states—well, their power seeped away decades ago.

State governments, beholden to their voters, may never be able to work together. State universities are different, especially as state support for them dwindles. In fact, these schools may hold the greatest promise for a regional future. In the next chapter, we will look harder at this future, and how far we have to go to get there.

The state lines, decreed in the eighteenth century, were already meaningless by the time they were drawn in the nineteenth century. The reason was immigration—the flow of people who populated the Midwest. The new populace came from different places, and that made all the difference.

Much of the Midwest drew its earliest inhabitants from New England or northern Europe. In the mid and late nineteenth century, these people—British, Germans, Dutch, Scandinavians—settled the northern part of the old Northwest Territory states, plus most of Iowa, Minnesota, and the lands to the west. Chicago and the other big industrial cities drew a more diverse workforce at the same time—Irish, Lithuanians, Italians, Poles, Russians, and other Slavs. In Chicago, these hard-muscled workers set the rough-and-tumble political tone from the start. Elsewhere, the northern Europeans and New Englanders brought a high-minded legacy of good government and social welfare that turned the early days of Midwestern politics into a model of governance.

Millions of Southern blacks moved up into the northern Midwest during and after World War II. More recently, other millions of immigrants, mostly Hispanic, have arrived. Both became voting blocs to be courted, but they have modified the politics of their states without really transforming them.

In the southern reaches along the Ohio River, though, another and different wave of immigrants had arrived in the late eighteenth and early nineteenth centuries and set a different social and political pattern. These were the pioneers, trailblazers of the

Daniel Boone variety, largely Scots-Irish who settled first in Appalachia, then moved west and north across the Ohio to settle in southern Ohio, Indiana, and Illinois. Good soldiers and hunters, they valued independence over community and were more inclined to avoid governments than to build them. Like other Appalachians who moved west into Texas and the Southwest, they were fiercely militaristic, nationalistic, and religious.

In truth, they were more Southern than Midwestern, and the counties they settled keep that flavor to this day. The original settlers were pro-slavery interlopers in a territory that, thanks to the Northwest Ordinance, was officially antislavery: many belonged to the Ku Klux Klan until well after World War II. They were smaller farmers and trappers in states that moved rapidly into big farming and industry. Many still call themselves rednecks, proudly. Today, they have more in common with George Bush's red-state base than with the blue-state cities with whom, by the whim of history, they share a state.

The areas that make up Illinois, Indiana, and Ohio were so divided politically and economically that it may not have made sense to unite them into states. Over time, other factors worked to deepen and harden these divisions.

Each state is divided in its own way. Ohioans, for instance, talk about the split between the "Three C's"—Cincinnati, Columbus, and Cleveland. Cincinnati, the old Queen City of the West, was the big apple of the Northwest Territory while Chicago and St. Louis were still the pipe dreams of boosters. Today, it hugs the Ohio River, welcomes northern Kentucky into its economic embrace, and in attitudes and atmosphere represents the middle states more than the Midwest. Columbus, in the heart of Ohio, has emerged as its biggest city, capital and home of its biggest university, a white-collar success story in a state marked by blue-collar distress. Cleveland, once an industrial powerhouse, has lost its industry and most of its people; it sits, sour and crumbling, on the northern fringe. The three cities have little in common besides the license plates on their cars.

Political power in Ohio has shifted from the once-mighty industrial cities—Cleveland especially, but also Akron, Dayton, and

Toledo—to the heavily Republican suburbs and exurbs around them and to the impoverished Appalachian counties of the south. Ohio is truly a swing state: Bush and Karl Rove mobilized its Republican strongholds to carry the vote, crucially, in the 2004 election; Democrats dominated in 2006. Neither party knows how to make Ohio work as a cohesive whole.

Indiana is three states (maybe four, if you count the steel-mill strip around Gary on the northwestern fringe, which is so much a part of metropolitan Chicago that, unlike most of the state, it sets its clocks to Chicago time).

Southern and northern Indiana split along I-70, which runs through the middle of the state. Northern Indiana, from Indianapolis on north, is Midwestern in atmosphere and economy—flat and open, with big farms, an industry based on automobiles, and a society based on unions. Thanks to northern Indiana, the state still leads the nation in the share of its economy that comes from industry.

Southern Indiana, from Indianapolis on south, is Dixie—hilly, scenic, with small farms and small towns, more akin to Louisville than Chicago. It contains two of the Midwest's gems, Indiana University at Bloomington and the architectural mecca of Columbus, but both are cultivated outposts not typical of their region. Southern Indiana is beginning to draw industrial investment, especially in cars, but mostly for the same reason that the same companies invest in Alabama—no unions.

Indianapolis sits astride I-70 and is a region unto itself—by far Indiana's biggest city, its capital, a center for business, increasingly prosperous in a state that is increasingly impoverished. To the degree that the rest of Indiana regards Indianapolis at all, it is with jealousy. Indianapolis and its eight suburban counties provide 80 percent of Indiana's economic growth.

Illinois, like Indiana, is three states, and for the same reasons. The southern third, again south of I-70, is a satellite of the South—more given to fundamentalist religions, gun racks in pickup trucks, and a deeply conservative Republicanism. Apart from Southern Illinois University at Carbondale, the biggest employer in the region is the prison system.

Most of the rest of the state is called downstate, to differentiate it from Chicago, even though some of it, such as Rockford, is actually north of the city. It is an unfocused place, with its big university in Champaign, its state capital in Springfield, its economic centers in Rockford, Decatur, Peoria, and the Rock Island–Moline complex along the Mississippi. What unites this heterogeneous region is a dislike of the third Illinois, Chicago.

Chicago dominates Illinois—politically and economically. The city's Democratic machine, in a shifting alliance with downstate Democrats or suburban Republicans, controls the legislature. Worse, it does this almost absentmindedly. If the rest of Illinois obsesses about Chicago, Chicago gives the impression—an accurate one, in fact—of never thinking about the rest of Illinois.

This drives non-Chicagoans nuts. The current governor, a Chicago Democrat named Rod Blagojevich, has never moved into the governor's mansion in Springfield; whatever his reason, the rest of Illinois regards this as a deliberate snub. When I was in Peoria recently, the local newspaper, furious over some gubernatorial sin, renamed him "Chicagojevich"—apparently the worst epithet at hand.

While this lower tier of Midwestern states splits along north-south divides, Michigan is riven by an east-west chasm rooted in economics, politics, and religion. Eastern Michigan is the Land of the Auto. It's the home of Detroit and Flint, the cradle of the American auto industry, the northern anchor of a three-state automotive empire. Eastern Michigan invented the assembly line, the modern union, and the American dream. It was the arsenal of democracy in World War II. It is wildly ethnic, Slavic and Greek and Armenian, heavily Catholic, with the most Belgians of any place outside Belgium and America's largest concentration of Arabs. It has America's poorest city, Detroit, and one of its best universities, in Ann Arbor. And it is a Democratic stronghold.

Western Michigan was once heavily forested and so became the center of the American furniture industry. It is Dutch in flavor and religion: the Dutch Reformed Church dominates. It is conservative, staunchly nonunion, and strongly Republican.

Given this divide, you would think that the two halves of Michigan would never agree on anything, and you would be right. Two Michigans, one eastern and one western, might make sense. One Michigan doesn't.

Interestingly, the only part of the state that is growing is the part that, until now, was left behind. The far north has been a scenic but backward region of tiny towns and pretty lakes, making a living out of tourism along the Leelanau Peninsula, Mackinac Island, and the other attractions of its Great Lakes setting. Now northern Michigan, and northern Wisconsin and a few other scenic areas, are the only nonmetro regions in the Midwest, apart from packinghouse towns, that are gaining people—mostly owners of second homes and, especially, retiring baby boomers. These newcomers are a force in the economy and may keep coming in numbers sufficient to make the north what it has never been, a political power in its own right.

Missouri, by contrast, is half-Midwestern, half not. The Missouri River runs west to east across Missouri from Kansas City to St. Louis, dividing the state geographically, psychologically, and politically. If any part of Missouri belongs in the Midwest, it's the north, especially these two major cities. South of the river, the state belongs to the Ozarks, closer to Arkansas than Illinois. Branson, the booming capital of kitsch and country music about ten miles north of the Arkansas border, is the cultural Rome of this region.

Missouri, like so many Midwestern states, has no business being a single state, and its government shows it. Locked away in Jefferson City, a small town in the middle of the state, the Missouri state government is regarded as feckless by anyone who hopes the state will amount to anything.

St. Louis, for instance, never looks to Jefferson City for leadership. Most economic leadership there comes from local businesses, I was told in St. Louis, because "the state government is not a good partner. There's an urban-rural split, and it's very hard to reach any consensus."

When the Greater Kansas City Community Foundation issued a report on the city's future, it pretty much told the state to get out of the way. "Nations and states still matter," it said. "They particularly can do their cities harm. But cities have to take the lead. San Diego did not become San Diego by looking to Sacramento, nor Seattle to Olympia." When the authors talked about Sacramento and Olympia, one felt they really meant Jefferson City.

If so, they must have talked to Dean L. Hubbard. Hubbard is president of Northwest Missouri State, an excellent state school in Maryville. Hubbard's school recently struck a deal with a California company, Ventria Bioscience, to produce proteins from genetically modified rice for use in antidiarrhea medicines. But the state legislature delayed the necessary funding and Ventria pulled out, killing a deal that could have been the core of a bioscience industry in a depressed part of the Midwest that needs every dollar and every job it can get.

What spiked the deal, Hubbard says, was old-fashioned state politics in Jefferson City. According to him, the speaker of the House wanted to divert some state education funds to private schools by freezing money for state schools at 2000 levels. Other politicians blocked this, so the speaker delayed appropriation of any state school financing. The Ventria project became collateral damage.

Missouri voters approved a constitutional amendment permitting human embryonic stem cell research, but state legislators tried to gut the amendment. They've failed so far, but the political uncertainty led the Stowers Institute in Kansas City to suspend a $300 million expansion of its cancer research facilities.

Iowa, Minnesota, and Wisconsin are different. Unlike other Midwestern states, which have been divided all along, these three were once cohesive units, held together by trusted institutions that set their agenda and mediated their politics.

Iowa once took its lead from the *Des Moines Register*, when that paper was locally owned and expertly edited. The state listened to WHO radio in Des Moines and rooted for the Hawkeyes at the University of Iowa. Iowans believed they belonged to one big statewide family that rose and fell together.

The Wisconsin Idea, a high-minded platform of civic involvement, was virtually invented by the University of Wisconsin and led by reformist politicians such as the La Follettes. The University of Minnesota performed the same role in Minnesota, when that state was united behind a politics of social welfare created by its legendary Democratic Farmer Labor Party but endorsed by Republicans who came from the same progressive culture.

In all three states, this unity has vanished. Iowa has still not moved to the extreme politics of many states. But there is a breakdown in interests between its metro and nonmetro regions—basically, a split between the prosperous areas around Des Moines and Cedar Rapids, and the other, more rural parts of the state. The Des Moines area and the towns in the Cedar Rapids–Iowa City corridor prosper in the global economy: anyone within a sixty-minute drive of these cities can share in this prosperity. In the rest of the state, population shrinks, small towns die, factories close, and resentment—of the cities, of the universities, of globalization itself—grows.

"The conventional wisdom says that it should be urban versus rural," says Philip Wise, a Democratic state representative from Keokuk, an old Mississippi River town that is a long way from the global action. "That's wrong. It's metro versus nonmetro. Where I come from, I've never lost a vote running against Des Moines."

The *Register*, now owned by the Gannett chain, has abandoned most of Iowa, focusing instead on the region around Des Moines. Readers in the major cities can get the *New York Times* and thus plug themselves into the global conversation. In the small towns that dot the rest of the state, citizens get some news from television, which gives stock-market updates but doesn't even try to cover the broader economy, local or global. Iowans, dealing with different facts, can be forgiven for seeking different solutions.

Despite this, Iowa remains perhaps the most balanced Midwest state, with the most effective state government. The state's two senators are the conservative Republican Charles Grassley and the liberal Democrat Tom Harkin. The legislature is split fifty-fifty between Republicans and Democrats, which means the two sides must work together to avoid gridlock. Tom Vilsack, until recently the governor, worked skillfully enough with the two sides to get the legislature to pass bills that raised teachers' salaries, improved water testing, promoted early-childhood education, and financed the Iowa Values Fund, which aims to create jobs in life sciences, information services, and advanced manufacturing.

Two aspects of globalization, economics and immigration, are dividing politics in Minnesota. The Twin Cities region of Minneapolis and St. Paul accounts for no less than 63.8 percent of the state's economy and 75 percent of its personal income. A few other cities, such as Rochester, do well. The rest of the state, mostly rural and remote, shrivels. Seeing no benefit from globalization, voters there see no reason to vote for the policies—support for education, especially higher education, and the promotion of biosciences—that might help their state prosper in a globalized world.

Immigration has had a sharp and unexpected impact in Minnesota, which has always seen itself as a tolerant and open-minded state. The early wave of refugees—Hmong, Somali, Sudanese— brought to the Twin Cities by church groups has been joined by a new wave of Hispanics drawn by jobs, in the cities and in small meatpacking towns. As we saw in the chapter on immigration, these twin waves have produced a backlash, a white flight from the cities to the suburbs, at least partially driven by the desire of urban whites to flee these new, darker neighbors. Once in the suburbs, these exurbanites have joined with the bitter rural residents to form an anti-tax, anti-Minneapolis, anti-immigrant bloc that has transformed Minnesota politics.

Minnesota, once as reliably Democratic as Massachusetts, is now a swing state. The old Democratic Farmer Labor alliance lies in tatters. Farmers and labor no longer make common cause. Farmers vote Republican, labor Democratic. Abortion is a big issue driving rural Catholic Minnesotans to the right. The current governor, Tim Pawlenty, is a Republican and an engaging populist best known for his advocacy of controls on immigrants— precisely the people that Minnesota most needs if its economy is to thrive.

Immigration, in fact, is the issue that best shows the inability of states to deal with the challenges of globalization. All across the Midwest, individual towns, meatpacking towns such as Storm

Lake and Beardstown, try to handle this new reality intelligently. But when state governments deal with immigration, fear and hatred rule. Pawlenty's attempts to limit undocumented immigrants, or the Iowa legislature's silly resolution proclaiming English to be the state's official language, aren't much help to towns where schools struggle to educate students whose families speak no English at all.

Wisconsin's main economic area, around Milwaukee, has virtually seceded. Every civic leader I talked with in Milwaukee said the city feels closer to Chicago than to its own state. Milwaukee, in fact, is the northern outpost of a great tristate economic area sweeping south through Chicago and into northern Indiana. Thirty-five percent of Wisconsin's economic output comes from Milwaukee and the area forty miles south to the Illinois border. Once an independent economic power of its own, Milwaukee now belongs to Greater Chicago, which means it no longer belongs to Wisconsin.

"What Chicago does has more impact on us than what the state government does," Tim Sheehy, president of the Milwaukee Metropolitan Association of Commerce, told me. "We're definitely tied to the Chicago economy. When we sell Milwaukee, we sell Chicago—the airport, the quick train trip."

As Sheehy says, "You could take Milwaukee out of Wisconsin and there's not much left there." This isn't quite true: Madison ranks as a global city in its own right. But in fact an important part of Wisconsin belongs to the Chicago economic region, and another important part, in the northwest, belongs to the Minneapolis–St. Paul region. That doesn't leave much of Wisconsin to think and act together as a state.

One reason Midwestern states are fragmented is that they were almost planned that way. Each contains a surplus of little fiefdoms called counties—a lot of counties. Iowa has 99 counties, Indiana 92, Illinois 102, Missouri no less than 114. This made sense in the nineteenth century, when all transportation was by horse and buggy over semipassable country roads. Each county was laid out so a farmer in its farthest reaches could travel to the county seat, do business, and get home the same day. Legend has it that the real reason was to enable an unmarried couple to ride to the county seat, get a marriage license, and get home before nightfall, forestalling any twilight hanky-panky among the hedgerows.

The Midwest also has so many counties because the Northwest Ordinance decreed it. The Ordinance did more than outlaw slavery in the region, promote schools, and guarantee freedom of religion and other rights; it also enshrined the Jeffersonian ideal of local government. Representatives were to be elected from the counties or the even smaller townships. This reflected the idealism of the day but only complicates matters now.

In those days, each county had real control over the political and economic life within its borders. Towns competed vigorously to be the county seat because it got the courthouse, the government jobs, and most of the legal business. It also got the railroad station, the hospital, the biggest stores, and the county's leading newspaper. Each county sent its own representative to the state legislature. One hundred years ago, these counties had clout.

No more. Today, any farmer can drive his pickup across any county in thirty minutes. In many Midwestern counties, population is down to a few thousand, and shrinking. Two thirds of Iowa's ninety-nine counties have been losing people for decades. Many Midwestern counties have lost their railroads, and some are losing their hospitals. Daily newspapers go weekly, and small-town Midwesterners think nothing of driving forty or fifty miles, across two or three county lines, to the nearest real city to do their shopping.

About all that is left are the courthouse and the bureaucracy it provides—for judges, recorders, clerks, sheriffs. Architecturally, the courthouse still counts. Most of these county seats are built around a central square, with the splendid nineteenth-century courthouse in the middle and a veterans' memorial on the grounds. These courthouses are to the small county seats of the Midwest what cathedrals are to the country towns of Europe—their architectural hearts, soaring symbols of self-government, pride, and sturdy individuality. It makes no more sense to tear them down, now that counties have lost their meaning, than it does to tear down the cathedrals, just because Europe has gone secular. But it also makes no sense for the balkanized counties of the Midwest to retain their individual governments, their overlapping and competing jurisdictions, their redundant bureaucracies. Most counties and county seats even have their own economic development offices, competing fiercely with neighboring towns, even though a new factory anywhere in the neighborhood would mean real jobs for its neighbors just down the interstate.

By all means, keep the courthouses, but turn them into museums, which is what they really are.

The tiniest fragments of this political mosaic, even tinier than counties, are townships, which are geographical areas about six miles across, or such governmental units as school districts, park districts, sanitary districts. Most of them have the authority to levy taxes or regulate businesses. It sounds democratic. Actually, it's a mess. The Chicago region has 1,200 separate units of government, including 6 counties, 272 towns and cities, 113 townships, 306 school districts, and hundreds of other special districts, most with taxing powers. Naturally, they agree on nothing except the need to keep as much power as they can.

"These tiny boxes don't have the size or the ability to compete globally," the Minnesota political scientist Myron Orfield said. "All they can do is to try to steal a store or a strip mall from the town or township next door."

If anybody paid serious attention to these political lines, nothing would get done. But where things do get done, it's because these lines are ignored. St. Louis's economic reach extends across the Mississippi River into Illinois. Chicago is a tristate economic area stretching from Milwaukee into northern Indiana and spanning fifteen counties, none of whom have much to say about the businesses that drive this process. Minneapolis reaches into Wisconsin, Cincinnati into Kentucky, Detroit into Canada. In other words, business and investment go where they want to go, and if some counties and townships collect some taxes along the way, they have little power to speed things up or slow them down. In the real world, they're irrelevant.

There is another reason why state governments are botching the economic needs of their states. Some 150 to 200 years ago, state capitals were picked not for economic reasons but for geographic ones. Many of them remain in this isolated irrelevance today, far from the real action of the territories they are meant to govern.

In the Midwest, as in many other states, the capital lies as close to the center of the state as possible. This made sense in the nineteenth century, for the same reason that county seats lie in the center of counties: travel was hard and governments wanted to put themselves close to as many citizens as possible. This is why Springfield is the capital of Illinois, Columbus of Ohio, Des Moines of Iowa, Jefferson City of Missouri. (It's also why Albany is the capital of New York and Sacramento of California.) Lansing and Madison may be somewhat south of the middle of Michigan and Wisconsin, but they stood solidly in the center of the nineteenth-century settlements in those states.

The location of these capitals may have made geographic sense, but they made no economic sense at all. In the nineteenth century, the major business and industrial centers of the states—Chicago, Detroit, St. Louis, Cleveland, Cincinnati, Evansville, Kansas City, Milwaukee—lay near the source of their wealth, which was water. Lakes and rivers made these cities the early centers of commerce. But these lakes and rivers defined the borders of the states, not the center.

Over the years, some capitals, such as Des Moines and Indianapolis, have come to dominate their states economically as well as politically. A couple, like Madison and Columbus, also contain their state's major university. Only one Midwestern urban area—Minneapolis–St. Paul—combines economic power, the major university, and the state capital. The other capitals are like Springfield, far from the economic and intellectual action. In this era of globalization, with overnight shipping and instant communications, this shouldn't make any difference. In fact, it does. Global cities such as Chicago depend on face-to-face contact, and isolated state capitals live out of earshot of this conversation. The winds of globalization are transforming state economies and generating new thinking about state futures, but the news takes a long time to get to the statehouses and legislatures.

The result is that states seem to go out of their way to make things worse. The Brookings Institution has documented the many ways in which state governments, through short-sighted policies, have damaged their biggest cities. States set the boundaries of urban jurisdictions and decide whether or how they can merge. They tell cities who they can tax and how, whether this helps the cities or not. State governments help finance local infrastructure and dictate, from miles away, how that money is spent. State priorities on education and workforce programs leave city residents incompetent to deal with the global job market. Highway funds go to rural areas, not to cities that need them more: job creation money goes to wealthy areas, not to the core of battered cities.

The last fifty years have transformed the urban landscape. Federal highway policy revolutionized commuting. Old industrial cities became emptier, and poorer; new suburbs sprawled, and drew the wealthy and the middle class. Industry came and went. Through all this, state laws written a century ago shackled the efforts of cities to deal with these changes. Today, as the landscape changes again, they still do.

The fragmentation of metropolitan regions into hundreds and thousands of tiny taxing districts can't be changed without state approval. School funding, based on property taxes, means that schools in rich suburbs can spend twice as much or more per pupil than inner-city schools. Most states decree that gas taxes go to highway maintenance, starving mass transit. In Ohio, rural counties get more money for highways than do cities, which have more roads and more traffic. Funding for low-income housing goes mostly to inner cities, guaranteeing that these neighborhoods will remain low-income. In Michigan, state funding for job creation goes mostly to more-affluent areas. Chicago's schools only began to improve when Mayor Daley persuaded the state government to give the city—not the state—control over the school system.

"At best," Brookings says, "these communities have been treated with benign neglect, with state programs and investments focused more on managing their decline than on restoring and sustaining their economic and fiscal health. At worst, state policies and investments have actually worked against them, encouraging growth in new communities at the expense of cities and their residents."

Brookings solution: new enlightened state policies aimed at revitalizing older cities. It isn't going to happen. Midwestern states are too fragmented and their governments too controlled by rural and suburban areas to see any common cause in supporting cities. As we saw in Minnesota, mostly white suburban and rural areas are less likely, not more, to take seriously the problems of cities and their multi-hued residents. The argument is made that cities can act as the economic locomotive of their states: a strong, vigorous city can generate vitality that energizes an entire region. In fact, globalization is beginning to isolate cities from their hinterlands: the hinterlands see this trend and are disinclined to do anything to speed it up.

State governments and the people who support them are too far removed from the real needs of the future economy. Any policy that depends on state leadership is doomed to failure.

It is tempting to blame the Midwest's failures on its residents: to imagine that those most affected the small farmers, the rural dwellers, the factory workers, the residents of clapped-out, old industrial towns—don't understand what globalization has done to them, so cannot press for the policies that might solve their problems. In fact, they see clearly what globalization has done and want no part of it. They identify globalization with cities and universities, with traders in Chicago and editorial writers in Des Moines, with Chinese engineers in Ann Arbor and yuppie bankers in Columbus. They perceive that most of these people—globalization's winners— have never spent thirty seconds worrying about globalization's losers. If a global future means better universities or freer trade or scientific infrastructure, at the expense of their old secure way of life, they want to stop this world and get off.

Across the Midwest, the 2006 elections saw a swing toward Democratic candidates that was widely interpreted as a cry of pain, a populist protest against globalization, by these rural and industrial victims. Certainly, the war in Iraq and the dwindling popularity of the Bush administration contributed to the swing toward the Democrats here, as in the rest of the nation. But from Ohio and Indiana through Iowa and Missouri, it was the closing factories and vanishing farms that most seemed to translate into votes against globalization and the Republican Party, which is most closely identified with it.

Geographically and economically, Midwesterners are the people that Larry Summers calls "the anxious global middle." Before, the conventional wisdom held that these people, the ones left behind by globalization, voted "values"—usually summed up as guns, God, and gays—and for Republican candidates who ran on these values, even as they promoted globalization. If they are finally revolting, it means that they may finally have had enough and are voting their pocketbooks, against outsourcing and free trade, tax cuts for the wealthy, deregulation, and the unprecedented concentration of wealth at the top.

Tom Frank's best-selling book *What's the Matter with Kansas?* popularized the thesis that poor people who voted Republican were voting against their own economic self-interest and were, in effect, the victims of a giant con. Some Midwestern experts think this thesis still holds, despite the 2006 election. Certainly, Frank's book came up time and again in conversations with Midwestern political analysts such as Tom Beaumont, a political reporter at the *Des Moines Register*, who said, "When I read Tom Frank, in my mind I substituted the names of Iowa towns for the Kansas towns in his book."

My own reporting indicates that Tom Frank was right, but that Republicans cannot take these "values" voters for granted. Globalization cuts both ways. People who have lost almost everything else economically do hold on to the few things they have left, which boils down to "values": religion, or the sanctity of traditional marriage, or the American flag, or the right to carry a gun, or a suspicion of foreigners that comes naturally in places that are a thousand miles away from any other country. But they also are beginning to wonder if the economic deck is stacked against them.

"Some get caught up in the Christian right, or in the values thing," Ted Johnson, the UAW local president in Newton, Iowa, said. "There's nothing like seeing a fifty-dollar Chevy with a Bush-Cheney bumper sticker."

In Greenville, Michigan, there was no sign that the Electrolux closing created many Democrats among the workers who lost their jobs. "They just have no political sense at all," said John Kreucher, the AFL-CIO official who had come to town to help the Electrolux workers sign up for retraining and other benefits. "Mostly, they vote Republican, for moral reasons, because of abortion or guns, not their paycheck. If you try to persuade them different, they just think you're making fun of them. Basically, I think Tom Frank is right on the button."

Maybe so, but Democratic candidates in the 2006 election campaigned largely on the economy and, to a lesser degree, on the war in Iraq, and the results indicated this paid off. The rural areas and small industrial cities of the Midwest, hit hard by globalization, are responding to candidates who can explain what's happening, if not offer solutions. The same towns and cities have supplied more than their share of the Americans fighting in Iraq: many young men and women in these places enlist because it's the best job going. Anti-war candidates had to phrase their campaigns carefully. People in these towns and cities support the troops, who are their children. To criticize the war is to suggest that these children are dying in a vain crusade. Once inside the polling booth, however, many voters no doubt turned away from the administration and the party that launched this crusade.

Whatever the cause of the 2006 swing toward the Democrats, there is no reason to think that it has redrawn the Midwest's basic political geography, which reflects a sharp urban-rural split in voting patterns. In all Midwestern states, even swing states like Iowa or Wisconsin, post-election maps show vast seas of rural red, surrounding a few blue islands—Chicago, Milwaukee, Iowa City, Cleveland, and other big cities or college towns.

City dwellers vote solidly Democrat, rural dwellers vote solidly Republican. The farther away an American lives from a city, the more likely he or she is to vote Republican. (One political theory holds that population density is a sure predictor of voting behavior: the farther away a person lives from his nearest neighbor, the more likely he or she is to be Republican. This hypothesis explains the conservative dominance in the Great Plains and the glitzier exurbs.) This is the urban-rural split on the hoof. Distance lends distaste, and dictates votes.

This was brought home to me by the sheer rage against cities, liberals, and the government in a commentary that an Iowan named David Kruse posted on his Web site, the CommStock Report, after the 2000 election. Kruse lives in Royal, a tiny town in conservative northwest Iowa. He is an agricultural commentator and market analyst whose articles are generally respected. In this case, he said, eloquently, what many of his neighbors were thinking:

"Frankly, I believe that ethics mean more in rural America than they do in urban America. I don't tell urban communities how they should live. What I see, however, are arrogant, liberal, urban elitists epitomized by the *Des Moines Register* that think they are smarter, more sophisticated, and better than those of us living in rural America. They think they know how much nitrogen we should put on our corn. They think Washington and Des Moines know best and we poor dumb folks out here need their guidance and education. They think everything outside the city limits is a city park and that they should administer it. . . .

"They are the ones with the strong economy. The economy in which computer chips are worth more than corn. The ones where they pay $1.19 for a plastic bottle of spring water, $30,000 for an automobile, and complain about the cost of a gallon of gasoline. Urban America is spoiled rotten. Their values change with each passing fad. Big city folks decide what's politically correct and then belittle us when we don't passionately embrace their causes. Rural America rejected their arrogance in this election. Rural America expects leaders and people to display character and integrity. Urban America expects to forgive leaders and people for their lack of character and integrity. We hold our leaders to a higher standard of conduct than they do. The honesty, the integrity, work ethic, and productivity of workers in rural areas far exceed those in states that voted for Bush than states that voted for Gore."

A lifetime of bottled-up rural resentment exploded in this tirade. I talked with Kruse six years after he wrote it, and he had cooled down. In fact, he said he voted for Bush in 2000 on the basis of character and against him in 2004 on the basis of performance. "But the attitudes [expressed in his article] still exist around here," he said. "People still feel this way. Attitudes have hardened, if anything. Bush's core base here is hardened. Fundamentalists are at the core of this base, and there's a lot of religion around here."

Globalization is part of it, too, he said. "There's a feeling of losing out, but it goes deeper. Traditional farming and the organizational structure of farming are changing. It's a more business-organized structure," and rural areas are having a hard time accepting it. (Kruse, interestingly, is almost an avatar of agricultural globalization. He is president and CEO of Brazil Iowa Farms, LLC, which has invested $23 million in twenty-two thousand acres of cotton and soybean fields in the western part of Bahia state in Brazil. His son Matthew lives in Brazil and runs the operation there.)

This urban-rural split is not unique in the Midwest—not at all. Globalization is dividing cities from countrysides all over the world. We see this in China, where Shanghai booms as villages starve, and in India, where all the action is in cities like Mumbai and Bangalore, and in Europe, where London and Paris thrive while the old factory and mining towns shrivel, and in Russia with its obscene gap between Moscow and the vodka-sodden villages, even in Africa, where Lagos and Nairobi, noisome as they are, become irresistible magnets for young wannabes. It's true in other

American regions, too, in New England and, especially, in the dry-ing, dying reaches of the Great Plains.

All this happens for reasons we know well—that globalization re-duces income from commodities such as food and rewards those who live nearest universities, who have the most access to broad-band, who have ideas that can be bounced off other people with other ideas.

These political tensions rooted in globalization add up to divi-sions, between people and classes and regions, that make states ever more incompetent to cope with the global problems that their citizens face. If the global future is up to the states, it's not going to happen. The challenges are too great for any one state to meet, but no state or its government is even considering cooperating with its neighbors, to merge their weaknesses into strength. As we've seen, each state is split within itself, too divided, politically and socially, to summon the unified will. Beyond that, even if Midwestern states wanted to invest in the future, they're too strapped paying for the past and present to afford it.

We've seen how states are cutting funding for education, espe-cially for the major universities where the Midwest's twenty-first-century economy will be created. And we've seen why—that state governments are under pressure to prop up automaking and other dying industries, that prisons have been the biggest job-spinners in many depressed areas and states are spending more money on prisoners than students, that governors and legislators have to pay for the upkeep and retraining of globalization's los-ers before they can think about creating its winners. A few tax increases would ease this pressure, but, as we know, Americans have become allergic to paying for the civilization in which their children will live.

Perhaps all this will change. Perhaps rural areas will recover and the urban-rural split will heal. Perhaps globalization will stop cre-ating winners and losers and start benefiting everyone equally. Per-haps voters will start voting for their true economic interests. Perhaps state governments will realize that they're competing now with China and India, not with the state next door. Perhaps legislatures will take money from prisons and give it to universities. Perhaps all-white Midwesterners will realize that any future for the region must include Mexicans, Africans, and Asians. Perhaps they will understand that if they really want this future, they must pay for it.

Perhaps all this will happen. Perhaps pigs will fly. But don't bet on it.

There's got to be a better way.

CHAPTER 14

Global Midwest

No real future exists except the future that the Midwest creates for itself. That future must be crafted regionally, by the Midwest acting as a single unit, not as a mélange of hostile states but as one region that shares not only a past but a future.

New England and the South have already learned this. So has California, a region unto itself. So have many regions inside the European Union: as the sway of their national governments wanes, areas such as the Upper Rhine Valley and Catalonia have emerged as centers of power.

When Midwesterners talk now about regions, they usually mean individual urban areas—a city like Chicago and its suburbs. I mean something more—the Midwest as a whole, or subregions big enough to link cities. Most suburbanites, after all, are in the suburbs to get away from the cities and see no common causes. Chicago feels more affinity to Milwaukee than to its own suburbs, such as Winnetka or Schaumberg. People in Winnetka may work in Chicago, but want nothing more to do with it. People in Milwaukee want to be like Chicago.

In a globalizing world, national governments pretend to be in control, but they aren't. Cities and states that used to look to Washington look now in vain: declining aid to states and futile federal attempts to repair American education—all show that national capitals no longer run their countries. The Europeans learned this long ago: that's one reason for the European Union. Americans are learning this just now.

Washington cannot solve the Midwestern dilemma, but states are just as helpless. The federal system of states is not about to be repealed. But neither is globalization. If the Midwest is going to cope with globalization, it has to shake off the dead hand of nineteenth-century state-based politics and create a Midwestern future.

The states themselves won't disappear. Nor should they. They stand enshrined in the Constitution as a crucial source of diffused power, symbols of a nation as big as a continent, too big to be run from one city on the Eastern seaboard. States can fix roads, run prisons, administer aid, oversee parks. So long as the federal system lasts, governors and senators will be elected by voters within their states and will answer to them. Like the federal government, state government has its uses and is not about to go away.

But increasingly, both federal and state governments find themselves ignored when real business is done. Global corporations do global commerce. Communications and products flow unimpeded across borders. Nonprofit and nongovernmental organizations span the globe, striking alliances with NGOs in other countries. Hungry workers flood into richer countries, whether those countries want them or not. There is no global government, but, increasingly, governance goes global: trade, accounting laws, antitrust regulations, standards, and many of the other rules that govern how the world works are set at international levels, not national ones.

If governments don't recognize these changes, voters do. The midterm election in 2006 brought to Congress a new group of Midwestern populists who want to protect manufacturing jobs, preserve the family farm, save small towns, keep companies from moving out, keep our young people from moving away.

Well, so do we all. But in reality, the jobs are gone, the farm is sold, the town is on life support, the companies have left. For every Chicago or Warsaw, dozens of towns and cities are sliding downhill. For every thriving suburb, hundreds of tiny farm towns won't exist fifty years from now. For every Medtronics or Eli Lilly, thousands of rusting factories, icons of the industrial era, are obsolete in the global era. Cargill and ADM are Midwestern corporations that rule the global market, while their policies and packing plants deform the Midwestern landscape. The great companies—Ford, General Motors, Delphi—that created the Midwestern economy sink into incompetence and bankruptcy, pulling that economy down with them. Unions that once harnessed idealism to power and created a nirvana of economic decency live on, much shrunken, tied to the middle of the last century. Politics is ruled by state-based structures that haven't made much sense since the nineteenth century. States choke on the immigrants who could revive their economies. Universities graduate physicists and bioscientists who will leave the Midwest for jobs elsewhere, while millions of children leave high schools without the knowledge or skills they need to cope with the global economy in which they will spend their lives. The universities themselves struggle to free themselves from the grip of the states that created them.

None of this is pretty, and none of it is new. The transformation of the Midwest economy has been going on for a half century. But globalization brings these trends to full speed. A region that had lost its competitive edge to other American regions now finds itself competing with the whole wide world.

Certainly, the impact of globalization can be tempered. A sane farm policy—insurance programs instead of direct payments, support for conservation and rural communities, more support for research and less for individual farmers—could slow the march toward consolidation and encourage both small farms and the environment. New trade agreements and tax laws can help keep jobs here, or at least help the victims of outsourcing cope with their future. Some rural areas can be saved through education or access to digital communications.

But these are palliatives, gifts from Washington to keep the Midwest sullen but not rebellious. Basically, they keep things from being even worse but don't make them better.

Besides, national governments, such as the one in Washington, are too clumsy, too limited by frontiers, too *national* to cope with a postnational world. But the smaller building blocks—cities, counties, and states—are too weak and isolated to swing much weight by themselves in an economy that spans the globe. It's a big world out there. Almost no city or state, acting alone, can marshal the forces—financial or intellectual—to compete.

Still, they try. Iowa competes with Minnesota, Ohio competes with Indiana, Muncie competes with Anderson, Galesburg competes with Peoria. But the real competition these days isn't between neighboring states or cities, but between the Midwest and regions in Asia, Europe, and Latin America that know how to cooperate and are doing it to win the global game. Before the Midwest begins to act regionally, it must learn to think regionally.

The first step is to create a Global Midwest Forum, a roundtable for the region's best minds to identify the issues and trends that assail the Midwest and set the agenda for future action. This forum would bring together businesspeople, academics and educators, mayors, scientists, philanthropists, journalists—all leaders with a stake in the Midwest's future and some ideas for what to do about it. Governors and other state leaders can be included, but they cannot take the lead. These state officials answer to voters inside their own states, and their vision stops at the state line. Such a forum would have no power beyond the power to focus the Midwestern mind, to grab the attention of the people with the power to ignite real action.

I know from my conversations across the Midwest that the region is loaded with thoughtful people who see the need for a regional approach. But most of these thinkers do their thinking in isolation. Few are aware that other Midwesterners in other states are thinking the same thoughts and seeing the same solutions: even these advocates of regionalism can't see beyond their state lines. If the key to creativity is a critical mass of creative people bouncing their ideas off each other, then the forum is where this mass could gather. This is where the leaders of Anderson and Newton could meet, to seek the solutions that elude them now. It could enable Peoria to give counsel to Dayton. It could bring together civic leaders in Grand Rapids and Kansas City, both trying to create a health complex from scratch. It could be a table where college presidents from Missouri and Michigan could talk about freeing themselves from their state capitols. It could be a sounding board for businesspeople from Minneapolis, Des Moines, and St. Louis, all now working in isolation on mutual problems.

Richard Florida proposes a "global creativity forum" to "bring political, artistic, business, scientific and other leadership to the table." This forum, he says, will lead to a Global Creativity Commission to take steps toward the policies "required for success in the creative age." The Midwest could learn a lot from forums like this, but first it has to be invited—and has to have something to say.

The Midwest is short on think tanks. The few that exist ignore their own backyards. These worthies write papers on issues, such as transatlantic relations or nonproliferation, where the Midwest has no expertise or comparative advantage; deservedly, they go unread. What the Midwest badly needs is a think tank devoted to Midwestern issues—the role of bioscience in the region's economic future, the retooling of old industrial cities into modern regional centers, cooperation across state lines, new roles for universities, new rail and air patterns meeting the region's economic needs, a regional immigration policy, regional environmental policies, regional research into bio- and nanoscience.

On their own, think tanks don't actually *do* anything, but they create the tools for action. A Midwestern think tank, properly staffed, can bring people together across state lines. It can gather data that now exists only on a state-by-state basis and turn it into a fund of regional information. It can investigate which projects must be done by states, and which can better be done by nongovernmental forces operating over and around the states. It can do joint projects with other regions or—more important for the Midwest—with other institutions in Canada, especially in Ontario. If this thinking leads to action and solutions, then the rest of the nation will be forced to pay attention. Many times in American history, the Midwest has led the way into the future. It's time to do it again.

For a model, the Midwest could look to the Southern Growth Policies Board, a think tank founded in 1971 to do research, issue reports, think about problems, host advisory councils, and spread the news about the Southern economy and how it can grow. The board was set up by thirteen state governments, but the South, because of its history, finds it easier to think as a unified region than the Midwest does. The leadership of the states hasn't kept the board from drawing on business, academia, and the South's other power centers.

For a Midwestern think tank to thrive, it needs financial and in-tellectual firepower. Fortunately, the Midwest has both. If the re-gion is short on think tanks, it is long on foundations—MacArthur, Kauffman, Eli Lilly, Upjohn, McKnight, Joyce, and Danforth, among others. Many already do valuable work in their own neigh-borhoods: the Joyce Foundation, for instance, supports efforts to improve the quality of life in the Great Lakes region; one of its pro-grams, on environmental issues, already crosses state lines. Some foundations, such as The Cleveland Foundation or the Chicago Community Trust, necessarily focus their grants locally, but most others have no such limits. Because they have money, they have clout. When they speak, everyone listens. But mostly, they work in isolation, seldom thinking or spending together on big projects, such as the future of their region.

The Midwest is not only rich, it's smart. As we've seen, it is home to the greatest concentration of brainpower in the world: it has the huge research universities in the Big Ten, plus other titans like the University of Chicago and Washington University, and research labs like Argonne and Fermi. It has medical centers like Mayo and the Cleveland Clinic, topflight liberal arts colleges like Grinnell, Oberlin, Carleton, Lawrence and Knox, plus urban universities like Drake, Butler, Macalester, Wayne State, Creighton, and the University of Illinois at Chicago, plus a rosary of first-rate Catholic universities such as Notre Dame, DePaul, and Marquette.

These schools should be the kindling for an intellectual fire that could light the region. But they exist now as isolated embers. There is a Committee on Institutional Cooperation, or CIC, that exists to promote collaboration among the Big Ten schools and the University of Chicago. In practice, it encourages shared access to libraries and some joint purchasing; beyond that, the CIC, founded fifty years ago and located in Champaign, seems a drowsy place with little real impact on its member schools.

Instead, each college and university, locked within its own state, competes with every other school and duplicates what they do. The Midwest has excellent schools of engineering, business, law, and medicine; it also has second-rate schools of engineering, business, law, and medicine, because each university insists on having these trophy faculties. A rational regional approach would let each university do what it does best. Resources spread across the region could build true centers of educational excellence.

In building a Midwestern future, cooperation on biosciences and on the investment to finance it is a good way to start. In fact, some tentative starts already exist. The Mid-America Healthcare Investors Network is an association of nearly fifty Midwestern-based venture capitalists, with more than $2 billion under management, who seek out bio investments in the Midwest.

The most promising venture is the Midwest Research Universities Network, or MRUN. In fairness, MRUN is impressive more as a potential base of cooperation than for its achievements so far. Run on a shoestring by Allen Dines at the University of Wisconsin, it brings together twenty Midwestern institutions—mostly universities but also medical centers such as Mayo or the Cleveland Clinic—to bring joint proposals to venture capitalists and to leverage the institutions' brainpower to create start-up companies. Dines started MRUN in 2002 after a meeting in Chicago where he realized that most of the Midwestern university officials dealing with technology spin-offs had never even met each other.

MRUN might work because it works around state governments, helping universities in the Midwest that collaborate with universities in Germany or China to realize they can also work with universities in neighboring states. "We're not competing with those states," Dines says. "We're not trying to get people to come here from Michigan. We're trying to get on the radar screens in London or Texas."

Other institutions exist to speak for the Midwest, but most of them speak in a whisper. A Midwest Governors Association keeps an office in suburban Chicago and turns out periodic newsletters that no one reads; even a former governor who once led it told me that he himself never took it seriously. As noted above, the Council of Great Lakes Governors is serious about the ecology of the region's inland seas but doesn't go beyond this narrow mandate.

A new organization, the Great Lakes Manufacturing Council, has been set up in Michigan, just in time to preside over Midwestern manufacturing's funeral. The Great Lakes and St. Lawrence Cities Initiative is a coalition of Great Lakes mayors working to protect the lakes. Several Midwestern states sponsor an Upper Midwest Freight Corridor study dealing with freight traffic, an important subject to the region. In Washington, an office called the Northeast-Midwest Institute does some statistical work and lobbies for the state governments, which pay its rent. Like most of these other organizations, it is useful enough, but doesn't pretend to be a center of new thinking on what the Midwest really needs.

If any institution could focus thinking on the Midwestern economy, it is the Federal Reserve. The Fed and its twelve regional banks house some of the sharpest minds and best statisticians in the country. Unfortunately, the Midwest has a lot more Feds than it needs. Instead of one Federal Reserve Bank for the Midwest, there are five, and they split the region five ways. Each does useful work, but there is little evidence that they even talk with each other, let alone work together.

The Midwestern Feds are in Chicago, Cleveland, St. Louis, Minneapolis, and Kansas City. The South has one, in Atlanta. So does the Southwest, in Dallas, and the West, in San Francisco. The reason for the Midwestern surplus lies in the politicking that surrounded the founding of the Fed in 1913. Midwestern Democrats and populists hated the idea of a central bank so much that President Woodrow Wilson won their support only by scattering branches across the Midwestern landscape: Missouri got two Feds simply because Wilson needed the support of one of its senators, James A. Reed. There's no chance that this fiscal gerrymandering will ever be reversed or that the five outposts will be united in one coherent bank. But this political trading of the early twentieth century, like the drawing of state frontiers in the nineteenth century, echoes down the decades, ensuring that the Midwest today remains much less than the sum of its parts.

It's galling to admit that the best thinking being done about the Midwest finds its sponsorship in Washington, at the Brookings Institution. But at least most of it is being done by Midwesterners, led by Michigan's John Austin (though Austin's Brookings report, called *The Vital Center*, encompasses the Great Lakes region, not the Midwest itself, so includes parts of New York and Pennsylvania).

Austin sums up the region's profits and losses and concludes that it has "one foot planted in a waning industrial era [and] the other in the emerging global economy." He, too, calls for a regional approach toward better education, more research spending, more investment in alternative energy, creation of a Great Lakes venture-capital fund tapping state pension funds and university endowments, cooperation between states to promote health-care reform, and a new transportation policy, including high-speed trains. Among other things, he wants any student from a Great Lakes state to be able to attend any public university in the region at in-state tuition rates. The Great Lakes region should coordinate its branding as America's "North Coast," to promote tourism.

Austin's report brims with good ideas. But he calls for state and federal governments to take the lead. He admires what the Europeans have done by creating the European Union, where national governments cooperate across frontiers on an enormous amount of economic activity, from trade to transport to energy. But the EU, successful as it is, is a special case. The European project has its roots in the two great twentieth-century wars that destroyed the Continent. After World War II, the Europeans, including their governments, shared a historical determination to bury this past and create a postnational arc of peace and prosperity.

The Midwest lives in the decay of decline, not the destruction of war, and cannot draw on the memory of horror to change its history, as the Europeans have. There is no reason to think that state governments or their voters will suddenly see the need for regional cooperation, nor that the federal government will give priority to a region with a stagnant population and declining political power.

Another Michigan thinker, James Duderstadt, has a different idea. Duderstadt wants the CIC schools—the Big Ten universities and the University of Chicago—to take the lead. These schools have been locked inside state lines by habit, history, and funding. But all aspire to be global universities. As state funding dwindles, they are forced to find new roles, both to support themselves and to serve their communities. These communities will exist not in the old industrial world but in a new economy, in which the vital raw materials will no longer be iron and steel but knowledge and education. The new economic cornerstone is not the factory but the university.

These schools, Duderstadt writes, are perfectly placed to "analyze the economic and social challenges presented to the region by the global knowledge economy, develop a vision and strategic plan to secure its future prosperity, and work with others to execute this strategy." More than state governments, they are equipped to answer the key question: "In an increasingly knowledge-driven global economy, what will replace factory-based manufacturing as the economic engine of future prosperity in the industrial Midwest?"

As Duderstadt says, it won't be government. "Both political parties are largely trapped in the past, driven by the desire to protect old sacred cows (e.g., big business, big labor, big government, and wealthy campaign contributors) or by 'value-morality' ideologies (abortion, gay rights, creationism) that are distracting public leaders and public attention from what really matters in a 21st-century global economy. As citizens, we simply must demand that our public leaders stop backing into the future." Duderstadt was writing here about Michigan, but he says his indictment applies to all Midwestern state governments.

Universities, by contrast, have the power, prestige, and contacts to tap people with both ideas and the clout to make things happen. Duderstadt wants a "steering group," similar to the forum suggested above, to bring together business, government, and academic leaders to chart a road map into the future.

As the Midwest moves toward that future, leaving the past behind, "the social disruption is going to be enormous," Duderstadt told me. Hard decisions must be made. State governments, unsupported, can't make them. Someone else must lead.

But where should they lead? Globalization changes everything, in economics and in life. As it transforms the Midwest, nothing will remain the same. So no idea, no area of life, is off-limits for leaders who must deal with this change.

The first task is to tell the truth, that the Midwest's golden era is gone forever. Much of the Midwest is in denial. It will take courageous leadership to speak the truth.

Public investment is scarce and must be spent where it will do the most good. That means that some cities, such as Muncie or Galesburg, will shrink, in population and wealth. Some isolated farm towns should be allowed to die. No place survives once the economic reason for its existence vanishes. There is no point in spending public money to prolong the death rattle of doomed communities.

Often, the wreckage is ecological as well as economic. Many industrial towns and cities are left now with the abandoned hulls of old factories, rusting away on land poisoned by generations of pollution, probably unsellable, certainly of no use to any twenty-first-century investor. Civic boosters talk about cleaning up the sites, or turning them into malls or museums: it probably won't happen. The old steel mills on the southeast side of Chicago are as derelict now as they were the day they closed, twenty years or more ago.

Nothing is sadder than workers who did everything right, who had every reason to expect a job for life, who worked hard and honestly and, in midlife, find themselves on the shelf. If they can be retrained, they certainly should be. But many can't. The government owes them enough money to stay alive, but no more than that. Any focus for the future, in money or other resources, must be on their children.

In this education is key. Midwestern leaders must persuade both voters and parents that an education that once was good enough for an assembly-line job isn't good enough now. In any public budget, schools must take top priority.

Beyond that, the Midwest has to decide what kind of education it wants. As a recent national study suggested, twelve years of high school may be too much. Perhaps many students can go straight to community or vocational colleges after their tenth year in school. Perhaps high schools and community colleges can work together, like the schools in Storm Lake, codesigning high school classes that would carry college credit. Perhaps some students, like the Caterpillar trainees in Peoria, only need to spend one intensive year in a community college to get the math and science skills necessary to cope with a job in the global marketplace. Perhaps some university students should graduate in three years, others in five. Perhaps the major state universities must reject state funding and chart a new course, based on research and more tied to the industries that will support the Midwest in the future. Perhaps smaller universities should abandon research and concentrate on educating the students who will run those industries. Certainly, John Austin's idea—in-state tuition rates for any Midwestern student to any Midwestern university—should be adopted.

Clearly, an educational system created by and for the industrial era must be reimagined for the global era. The Midwest needs to do this reimagining, then guarantee its schools the political support to do the job.

Washington is no answer: as the Midwest's population shrinks, so does its congressional delegation and its clout in the capital. When it comes to federal action, the Midwest must stand in line, behind burgeoning regions such as the South and Southwest. But Washington still ordains national policy in areas of vital interest to the Midwest. This includes agriculture, trade, transport, environment, immigration, education, and many other areas. When these national policies are framed, the Midwest's voice must be heard. Now, there is no Midwestern voice, just a babel of senators and representatives, elected by their own states and districts and speaking for them. At the moment, it doesn't occur to most of them that what's good for the state next door might directly benefit their own voters. Like most Midwesterners, these people have no idea that the problems besetting their own voters are identical to those besetting voters in the next district or the next state.

Immigration is vital, and an immigration policy based on walls and border police hurts the Midwest. The region lives on trade and needs a balanced trade policy: that is, a national policy that neither chokes off trade nor strikes mindless deals that hurt more people than they help. The Midwest, with its wind and corn and switchgrass and coal, holds the nation's energy future: it has a regional stake in national policies to promote that future.

It is time to identify Midwestern policies on these issues and speak with one voice in Washington. A Midwestern forum or think tank could help do this. So could a Midwestern version of the Southern Growth Policies Board. The Chicago Council on Global Affairs (CCGA) has issued task-force reports on such subjects as immigration, agriculture, and the integration of Mexican immigrants into urban societies; more reports are planned.

The Midwest's congressional delegations should be part of any deliberations and should be actively encouraged to work together. A separate Midwest lobbying office in Washington could keep the region's needs on these delegations' agendas.

The Midwest needs to speak with one voice globally as well as nationally. Almost every Midwestern state keeps trade and investment offices in such overseas metropolises as Shanghai, Tokyo, Brussels, and São Paulo. Each state office battles every other state office to get a Japanese factory or European lab on its side of the state line. Each is paid by its state government and wouldn't dream of cooperating with any other state government. The idea that investment anywhere in the Midwest helps everyone in the Midwest is as foreign as the currency these offices spend on rent, business lunches, publicity, and the other expenses of selling their states.

This is mindless duplication. In places like these, where most people aren't quite sure where Wisconsin or Iowa is, the Midwest should sell itself as a single region, not as a fragmented collection of states. Instead of eight small and overworked trade offices, the Midwest should market itself with one big office, backed by the kind of research and resources that a Global Midwest Forum could command.

The stakes here are enormous, particularly regarding China. China has earned billions of dollars selling goods to America, but its investment in this country—especially in the Midwest—has just begun. It owns part of a taconite mine in northern Minnesota, has set up some warehouse and distributions points near Chicago for its imports, and expressed interest in buying Maytag before Whirlpool bought it. All China experts are sure that, one of these days, China will use its billions in dollar reserves for investments that will dwarf the Japanese investment wave in the 1980s. No one knows where this investment will go. California and the West Coast have the built-in advantage of proximity. But if China wants to do manufacturing and processing in the United States, the Midwest has existing factories and experienced workers to do the job. There's irony here: many of these factories have been closed and their workers idled by competition from China. But these assets exist, in a central location with good transport, and the Midwest is hungry for money and jobs, no matter the source. At best, Chinese investment could do what Japanese investment has done—create jobs and vitalize communities. Perhaps it will do what Japanese investment has not—create new jobs where the old jobs were lost, in old manufacturing towns, instead of going to new, mostly nonunion places.

The competition for this Chinese money will be fierce. Once again, the Midwest cannot count on Washington to do this work for it. One big reason is that the national and the regional policies might not be the same. The federal government deals with Europe or Asia on many levels—not only economic, but military, political, and diplomatic. When Beijing scowls at Taiwan, U.S.-Chinese relations suffer. The Midwest has a simpler task. It wants to sell its wares in China and draw Chinese investment to the Midwest. No Midwestern fleet patrols the China Sea, no Midwestern diplomats deal with China over North Korea. Midwesterners, as Americans, hope that Washington knows what it's doing. But in the meantime, they have deals to make and business to do.

The Midwest has a proximity problem. Its big cities and universities are just far enough apart to prevent the kind of regular contact that comes naturally to movers and shakers along the Boston–New York–Washington corridor. Good interstate highways lace the region, and airlines, big and small, serve the major cities. But distance counts, and so does regular contact. Venture capitalists don't want to travel more than an hour or two to visit their investments; in San Francisco this is possible, in Chicago it's hard. Creative people need to have lunch with other creative people: that's how creativity happens.

High-speed rail is the answer. At the moment, Amtrak trains inch across the Midwestern landscape. In Germany and other European countries, people treat trains like buses. Businesspeople in Frankfurt know they can stroll into the train station and, within an hour, catch a train for Berlin, Munich, or Hamburg that will get them there faster than an airplane. The train from Berlin to Frankfurt, a distance of 417 miles, takes only four hours, and they're talking about cutting that to less than three. The Midwest stretches seven hundred miles from Cleveland to Des Moines, six hundred miles from Minneapolis to St. Louis, a region not much bigger than Germany. In an era of gridlocked airport security, trains become an economical and speedy alternative. German-style trains would put Chicago within four hours of Minneapolis, two hours of St. Louis, one and a half hours of Indianapolis. The University of Michigan and the University of Chicago become two hours from each other; so do the University of Wisconsin and Purdue.

High-speed trains are a hard sell in America. Nine Midwestern states have put together a Midwest Regional Rail Initiative to study the problem, but any agreement is not in sight. Amtrak, financially underfunded and politically undersupported, exists as a poor cousin of the airlines, forced to use tracks owned by other railroads that regularly shunt Amtrak's passenger trains aside so their freight trains can go through: no wonder Amtrak trains regularly arrive so late. But the Amtrak service, especially its Acela liners, help hold the Northeast Corridor together, and the Europeans have proved that trains are the solution for short- and medium-distance travel. It's not that Amtrak can't work. It's just that we have to start taking it seriously.

In many ways, digital communications will be the railways of the future. Already, European countries and regions are laying the fiber-optic cable that will carry the communications—the goods of the global age. Many American cities and regions have lagged, but the regions of tomorrow will be linked by this network, which will power global industries—health care, bioscience, finance, high-tech research. Some Midwestern cities like Chicago already have this capacity, and most of the Big Ten universities share a digital network. But only a comprehensive net that links the region's cities and schools will enable them to multiply their economic power.

As a former newspaperman, I worry about how Midwesterners will learn about the globalized world that will determine their future. Once the Midwest boasted excellent newspapers—in Chicago, Minneapolis, Des Moines, Detroit, St. Louis, Madison, Cleveland—committed to telling their readers about their world. Some, such as the *Minneapolis Star-Tribune* and *St. Louis Post-Dispatch*, had their own foreign correspondents; now only the *Chicago Tribune* does. A few, such as the *Milwaukee Journal-Sentinel*, still send reporters on trips to China or Europe to describe how Milwaukee connects to the world. Most don't even do that. Midwestern readers know that something's going on out there that is changing their lives, and they look to their local newspapers to explain it to them.

But newspapers are failing, and it's not just because the world has become so complex and interconnected. Newspaper publishers, panicked by falling circulation, have latched onto a report, issued by the once responsible journalism school at Northwestern University, urging papers to draw readers by stressing local news. There's only so much space in a paper. All over the Midwest, local news, no matter how trivial, is squeezing out the global coverage that readers need to make sense of their world.

I realized how far this had gone when I got a letter from a friend, an editor of the biggest newspaper in his Midwestern state, saying he was focusing on local news because "readers are getting national and international news from other sources. We are rebuilding our news organization into an information center that can feed a multitude of platforms—community magazines, community newspapers, the core newspaper, various web sites—with custom content that can serve communities that advertisers want to reach: communities such as younger mothers who universally don't read newspapers."

This jargon is the background noise to a Midwestern newspaper abandoning its responsibility to its readers. If I were a resident of this editor's city and curious about the world, I couldn't read about it in my local paper. Instead, I'd have to read the *Tribune* or, more likely, the *New York Times* or *Wall Street Journal*. Or I could scour the Web. All carry plenty of global news, but none takes this news and applies it to the particular circumstances of my life and my city. This is what good local papers do. This is what Midwestern newspapers used to do, and do less these days.

Many newspapers are owned by national chains, such as Gannett, with no real ties to their state. In state capitals, Iowans or Minnesotans have access to the *New York Times* or the *Financial Times*. In small towns, Midwesterners read a local paper, full of club news or high school sports, or (more likely) get their news, so-called, from Fox TV.

A good newspaper sets the agenda for its city, or its state, or its nation. If the Midwest is to act as a region, it needs a trusted publication to set the regional agenda. No such Midwestern publication exists. Instead, we seem to be moving toward national newspapers, such as the *New York Times*, while papers like the one edited by my friend concentrate on local news. Europeans, living in smaller and more centralized countries, already have this pattern. But no national American paper—not the *Times*, nor the *Journal*, nor *USA Today*—can see the news from a Midwestern angle, nor tell the Midwest, a special region with special needs and interests, what it needs to know.

The Midwest needs a regional journal, with global coverage and thoughtful analysis, to supplement the parochial local press and to set the regional agenda. Perhaps the *Tribune* or the *Journal-Sentinel* will be that paper. More likely it will be an elite publication, similar to *Le Monde* in France or the *Financial Times* in Britain, reaching decision-makers but few others. Even more likely, it will be a Web site, taking over as newspapers decline.

Many Midwestern institutions and people already act globally. Universities have campuses abroad. Cities have sister states. Midwestern doctors cure diseases in Africa, Midwestern professors teach in China, Midwestern businesspeople do business in Europe.

For these institutions and people, there's nothing strange about globalization. It's part of everyday life.

Similarly, regionalism, on a smaller scale, is no stranger to the Midwest. Much of the industry that built the Midwest grew regionally, easily crossing state lines. The best example was Auto Alley, the hub of America's automobile industry, embracing great swaths of Michigan, Indiana, and Ohio. Today, many Midwestern cities—St. Louis, Kansas City, Minneapolis–St. Paul, Davenport, Omaha—have more to do with the economic region across state lines than they do with the states that make their license plates. Chicago dominates a tristate Illinois-Wisconsin-Indiana region.

This is the future. As the Midwest goes both global and regional, it will be powered by the players—cities, industries, universities—that have common interests and common goals. Scholars already see the United States and its economy dominated by huge "megapolitan" areas combining dense, wealthy creative cities and their suburbs in a new belt of urban living. The Bos-Wash Corridor is one. So is Cascadia, the northwestern region stretching from Portland to Vancouver. So is the Northern California high-tech mecca centered on San Francisco.

And so is the Midwestern megapolis, from Milwaukee and Madison through Chicago, across northern Indiana and southern Michigan into Ohio. If this megapolitan region includes too many dying factories, it also includes the universities where the future will be invented, and the old industry that could be the basis for the bioscience and nanoscience, the chemicals and drugs and new materials, on which this future will be built. This is what the people in Peoria meant when they told me about the Discovery Corridor, a biosciences belt running across three states from St. Louis to Indianapolis.

This means universities talking to universities, cities talking to cities, companies talking to companies. In the global economy, global companies strike alliances across national frontiers with other global companies, competing and cooperating at the same time. In the same way, towns and cities have to reach across state lines to strike alliances, drawing on each other's knowledge and experience. Already, six hundred U.S. cities, tired of waiting for

Washington to recognize the reality of global climate change, have signed a voluntary pledge to reduce greenhouse gas emissions to the standards set by the Kyoto Protocol. Midwestern cities are well represented—Chicago, Indianapolis, Des Moines, Cleveland, and Minneapolis among many others.

This is the final reason why the global Midwest must soar across state lines and over state governments to build its future. This future belongs to the unorthodox, the imaginative, the creative, the fresh thinkers. These creative global citizens overwhelmingly live in the cities, and these cities must be free to create the future.

Globalization really does lead to an urban-rural split. In too many states, the present is anchored to rural areas and small towns that control state governments and state legislatures. More and more, these rural areas and their people are being left behind, cut out of the global conversation, far from the global action, embittered by loss and resentful of the global elite in cities and college towns. To the degree that state governments are controlled by global losers, they'll be crippled in meeting globalization's challenge.

The job of state government in this new world is to get out of the way of this new regional future, while providing some sort of safety net for those left behind. The job of the new dominant cities is to join in new and powerful alliances, to mount a twenty-first-century power base, to leverage their strengths to create a new Midwestern century.

All Americans have a stake in what happens to the Midwest. This book began by noting that the Midwest is the bellwether of America: whatever happens in this country happens first in its heartland. Today, once again, it is the place where the next American future will be created. But the Midwest cannot count on the rest of the country to do this work or even provide much help. Whatever the global future holds for the Midwest, it must be created by the Midwest itself.

Epilogue

I happened to be in my hometown on a Wednesday night in the summer of 2006 when the Boone town band played. The band has played these weekly summer concerts for sixty-five years; as a teenager, I played in them myself. About four hundred people gathered in the pavilion on the edge of the park, a block from the house where I grew up. Many brought their own lawn chairs. The United Methodist Church served ice cream. The band opened with the national anthem, then played a march, a von Suppé overture, two medleys of show tunes, an arrangement of Wagner for French-horn quartet, another march, and closed with "America, the Beautiful"—a program almost identical to the ones we played decades ago. Old oak trees that were big when I was a boy towered overhead. It was a beautiful night and I ran into old friends, which is what happens on occasions like this.

This is pure community and holds real value. If we lose it, we lose something important to the American soul. It may be even more important now that, increasingly, most of the people in Boone weren't born there and don't work or shop there. With so much of life so fragmented, these rites become vital to an increasingly elusive sense of place, of home. High school football games, county fairs, stock-car racing, bring Midwesterners together, even as the one big time-honored communal ritual—Friday nights on Story Street, as stylized as a Latin paseo or promenade—has died out.

The critic Edmund Wilson wrote once about revisiting the scenes of his youth and finding that all the familiar buildings were gone, alive in his memory but erased from the earth. Not so in

Boone. Almost everything is still there, just as I remember it. It is the town itself, its core, its character, that has changed.

The house where I grew up is still there, and so is the wooded ravine beside it. The homes of my friends still stand, and look the same, and so do the high school, and Goeppinger Field where I covered the Friday night football games, and the old *News-Republican* building, and the Holst Hotel building, and the fairgrounds, where we helped the traveling circuses pitch their tents, and old Highway 30, renamed Mamie Eisenhower Avenue, two lanes through the heart of town, and the Citizens National Bank building on Story Street where my father's office occupied the second floor and, indeed, the pavilion in the park where the band played and where we used to sneak in under the stage during revival meetings, to gawk through cracks in the wood as the sinners came down the sawdust trail to be saved.

Other families live in those homes now, of course. The *News-Republican* building is shuttered, and the Holst Hotel itself is long gone. The Citizens National Bank building is still the tallest building in town, seven stories high, but it's U.S. Bank now, part of U.S. Bancorp, with 2,499 branches in twenty-four states. The fairgrounds still get used: the people of Boone turned out there to welcome the town's National Guard contingent, about four hundred men and women, back from Iraq. Mamie Eisenhower Avenue still winds through town, but Highway 30 itself has been moved south of town and widened to four lanes, to speed the people of Boone on their daily commute to Ames or Des Moines.

So much of the Midwest is like this. It looks the same—the small town water towers, the endless fields of corn and soybeans, the hulking factories, the old main streets. But look close and you'll see that the towns are shrinking, the factories are empty, the main streets are half vacant, the fields are farmed now by one family where once a dozen families made their living.

Still, community counts. Boone, so far, has been tenacious enough to cling to this sense of community. It comes together for band concerts and to honor its soldiers. But in too much of the Midwest, these old traditions have died out, because the economy that supported them went away. If there are no jobs, no factories, no schools, then people leave. One day, tradition is gone, and no one knows where it went.

This book has chronicled change in a region that prizes stability. This change is happening—has already happened. More will change. Nothing's coming back. In my heart, I regret this. The Midwest created me, and I liked it just the way it was. But it can't stay the way it was. That's not possible. The Midwest's task now is not to try to reclaim what is lost, but to seize the future.

What happens next is vital not only to the Midwest but to all of America. A healthy nation cannot house a diseased heart.

The first era of Midwestern history is over. The next one has begun. We can make of it what we will.

Acknowledgments

This book owes many debts, none greater than to The Chicago Council on Global Affairs and its president, Marshall Bouton. Marshall encouraged my first explorations of the impact of globalization on the Midwest. Later, he anointed me the first Council Fellow, gave me a writing base, and backed the project, logistically and otherwise. Without the Council's backing, this book would not have happened. My thanks to Marshall and to my other CCGA colleagues, especially Bob Cordes, Juliana Kerr Viohl, and Sharon Houtkamp.

A grant from the Joyce Foundation funded my travels around the Midwest and other research, and I'm immensely grateful to its president, Ellen Alberding, and vice president, Larry Hansen. Special thanks is due to Ernest Mahaffey, good citizen and valued friend, whose gift financed the early reporting of the issues that underlie this book.

Gary Morris, my agent at the David Black Agency, fought to find a publisher for this book who believed in it as strongly as he did. He struck gold with Bloomsbury and Nick Trautwein, the kind of editor every author should have. Nick saw immediately what I wanted to say and labored to help me say it. My thanks to both Gary and Nick, to Nick's colleague Elizabeth Peters, and to Alex Kotlowitz, the distinguished Chicago writer who introduced me to Gary.

Any book of reportage owes much to the generous men and women who shared their time and wisdom with the author. From factory worker to university president, all proved that the Midwest deserves its reputation for hospitality and kindness. Many people who opened their doors to me are cited in the text, but others also deserve my thanks. None, however, merits blame either for the book's errors or its conclusions, which are all mine.

In Chicago and Illinois, I'm grateful especially to Bill Testa, and to Saskia Sassen, J. D. Bindenagel, Bob Rosenberg, Kenneth Johnson, Rick Mattoon, David Oppedahl, Paul Greene, Christi Parsons, David Perry, Tim Jones, David Greising, Greg Burns, Terry Nichols Clark, Dawn Clark Netsch, Roger Luman, Michael Frias, Sylvia Puente, Alejandro Silva, Clare Munana, Julio Flores, Joseph White, Sean Murdoch, David Moberg, Chad Broughton, and Bob Seibert. Special thanks to old friends Pat and Ron Miller for their constant support.

In Michigan, my thanks to Mike Shore, Jim Donaldson, Ron Kitchens, Mike Reagan, Don Burns, Lou Anna Simon, Don Grimes, Mark Murray, Birgit Klohs, and Jenny Shangraw. Mike Huckleberry's hospitality warmed my visit to Greenville, as it has for so many reporters.

In Ohio, thanks go to Richard Stock, Evan Scott, Frank Samuel, Steve Kelley, Ben Sutherly, Stephanie Irwin, John Nolan, Rich Tincher, Chris Kershner, Mark Sniderman and his colleagues at the Cleveland Federal Reserve Bank, Richard Herman, Joe Frolik, and Edward Burghard.

In Minnesota, I was helped by Rob Johnson, Brian Atwood, Ann Markusen, Carl Goldstein, Kathy Fennelly, Carol Byrne, Jennifer Reedy, Art Rolnik, Bob Isaacson, Robert Kirschner, Lee Munnich, Ben Lilliston, Jay McLinden and his Anoka County colleagues, Jennifer Ailes, Sue Halena, Robert Baker, Brian Beeman, the Reverend Tim Johnson, Roseann Inderreiden, Louis Johnston, Ernie Diedrich, Paul Hetland, Sue Slupe, Pete Turok, Roger Giroux, and old friends Marlin and Ann Weimer and Myron Stolte.

In Wisconsin, my thanks to Joel Rogers, Ed Friedman, Aaron Olver, Don Nichols, Allan Klotschke, Dan Broderick, Virginia Carlson, Brian Reilly, Carlos Santiago, my sister and brother-in-law, Mary and Kipp Koester, and, especially, John Schmid.

In Indiana, my guides included David Goodrich, Bobby Fong, John Krauss, Norm Heikens, Martin Jischke, Chris Hurt, Phil Paarlberg, Pat Kiely, Bill Witte, Graham Toft, Dennis Ryerson, Jerry

Conover, Roy Budd, Kevin Smith, Brad Bishop, Joy McCarthy-Sessing, Tracie Davis, and Randy Maxson.

In Nebraska, Richard Piersol introduced me to Ted Kooser. Margie Rine led me to some of Ted's most evocative writing. Omaha economist Ernie Goff was generous with his time and knowledge.

In Missouri, I'm grateful to Bob Coy, Roger Beachy, Rob Rose, Doug Rasmussen, Denny Coleman, Ellen Soeteber, and Robert Holden.

Many Iowans helped, among them Tom West, Paul Lasley, Cornelia Flora, Neil Harl, Rex Honey, William Decker, Dave Swenson, Bill Clark, Bob Fisher, Larry Adams, Dale Carver, Scott Rector, Donovan Olson, Mo Kelley, Robert Eby, Carolyn Cochran, Steve Dust, Dave Kraemer, Elaine Ditsler, Jeff Fetterman, Chuck Crabtree, Steve Siegel, Marlena Bandurski, and Davis Maahs.

A book becomes an obsession and an obsessed writer is hard to live with. My wife, Barbara, supported this project from the start and sustained both it and its author with love, faith, and forbearance. I owe her much, of which the dedication of this book is only a down payment.

Notes

Prologue

1 *there was a bustle*: "Main Street USA," London *Sunday Telegraph* magazine, 1964, exact date missing, 24 et seq.
3 *"I had a friend"*: Interview by author, Lincoln, Nebraska, June 25, 2006.
3 *Story Street is still*: Interview by author with Robert Fisher, June 29, 2006.

Chapter 1: Caught in the Middle

8 *In a recent speech*: Ben S. Bernanke, speech (Federal Reserve Bank's annual economic symposium, Jackson Hole, Wyoming, August 25, 2006), www.federalreserve.gov/boarddocs/speeches/2006/20060825/default.htm.
8 *Geopolitics had a lot*: Richard Freeman, "What Really Ails Europe (and America): The Doubling of the Work Force," *Globalist*, June 3, 2005, www.theglobalist.com/DBWeb/StoryId.aspx?StoryID=4542. Also Clyde Prestowitz, *Three Billion New Capitalists: The Great Shift of Wealth and Power to the East* (New York: Basic Books, 2005).
9 *In my hometown*: Interviews with author, June 2006.
12 *Nandan Nilekani, founder*: *Financial Times*, July 22–23, 2006, W3.
13 *Tom Friedman, the*: Thomas L. Friedman, *The World Is Flat* (New York: Farrar, Straus and Giroux, 2005).

13 *But Friedman's "flat world"*: Richard Florida, "The World Is Spiky," *Atlantic Monthly*, October 2006, 48–51.

14 *Larry Summers, the*: Lawrence Summers, "The Global Middle Cries Out for Reassurance," *Financial Times* (London), October 29, 2006.

15 *The Italian philosopher*: Cited by Koichi Ohara and Hiroshi Matsuda, *International Gramsci Society Newsletter* 12 (February 2002).

Chapter 2: The Midwest and the Globe

18 *The first settlers in*: Cullom Davis, in *Heartland: Comparative Histories of the Midwestern States*, ed. Madison (Bloomington: Indiana University Press, 1990).

19 *This Midwest also shares*: Northwest Ordinance, http://usinfo.state.gov/usa/infousa/facts/democrac/5.htm. A good brief history is available on Wikipedia, http://en.wikipedia.org/wiki/northwest_territory. Also see Peter T. Harstad in Madison (1990), and Andrew R. L. Cayton and Susan E. Gray, *The American Midwest* (Bloomington: Indiana University Press, 2001).

20 *But the fact is*: Andrew R. L. Cayton, "The Anti-Region: Place and Identity in the History of the American Midwest," in Cayton and Gray (2001).

21 *Instead, Midwesterners flaunt*: Madison, *Heartland*.

22 *These small-town values*: Bethany McLean and Peter Elkind, *The Smartest Guys in the Room* (New York: Gotham Books, 2003).

23 *So I went to Nebraska*: Interview with author.

25 *"Instability can be an"*: Richard Sennett, *Financial Times* (London), March 7, 2006.

Chapter 3: From Rust to Bust

27 *"Just imagine"*: Interview with author, February 27, 2006.

28 *Dayton, of course*: An excellent history of Midwestern manufacturing and industrial cities is Jon C. Teaford's *Cities of the Heartland:*

The Rise and Fall of the Industrial Midwest (Bloomington: Indiana University Press, 1994).

28 *Delphi, the successor*: Among the many stories on the Delphi bankruptcy are Nick Bunkley, "47,600 Take Offer of Buyouts at G.M. and Delphi," *New York Times*, June 26, 2006; and Steve Franklin, "Delphi's Plight Signals Auto Industry's Woes," *Chicago Tribune*, October 12, 2005.

29 *These are big*: I am indebted to the *Dayton Daily News* and to reporters John Nolan and Stephanie Irwin for their stories on Delphi and their other help to me.

30 *"It's been death"*: Interview with author, May 1, 2006.

30 *Austin is a University*: John Austin, "Great Lakes Economic Initiative," Draft Framing Paper, February 24, 2006, sponsored by the Brookings Institution. An edited version of this draft was published by Brookings as *The Vital Center*.

31 *Some of this was*: Malcolm Gladwell, "The Risk Pool," *New Yorker*, August 28, 2006.

34 *"In a very short"*: Patrick M. Barkey, *Indiana Business Bulletin*, March 13, 2006, www.bsu.edu/mcobwin/ibb/COMM/web0313.htm.

35 *"Production isn't doomed"*: Interview with author, March 30, 2006.

35 *Barkey's right*: Howard Wial and Alec Friedhoff, "Bearing the Brunt: Manufacturing Job Loss in the Great Lakes Region, 1995–2005," Brookings Institution, July 2006.

35 *"We are the center"*: Interview with author, February 2, 2006.

36 *"Michigan's problem is"*: Telephone interview with author, March 2006.

37 *At Dundee, south*: *Detroit Free Press*, October 13, 2006.

39 *"We've got fifty-seven hundred"*: Interview with author, May 2, 2006.

42 *the University of Dayton"*: Author interviews with Joe Tuss and with Richard Stock, University of Dayton, May 1, 2006.

Chapter 4: Unplugged

44 *For most Americans*: Brian Page and Richard Walker, "From Settlement to Fordism: The Agro-Industrial Revolution in the American Midwest," *Economic Geography* 67, no. 4 (1991).

44 *The industrial era needed*: Austin, "Great Lakes Economic Initiative."

44 *"Many of them"*: Interview with author, April 2006.

45 *Muncie once had*: Data on Muncie from interview with Patrick Barkey and other local experts, 2006; Barkey, "Outlook," *Indiana Business Review*, 2006.

46 *"created the biggest"*: Interview with author, March 30, 2006.

47 *"Things stabilized in"*: Interview with author, March 30, 2006.

47 *"There's a malaise"*: Interview with author. Analyst asked not to be identified by name.

48 *"The trouble was"*: Interview with author, March 30, 2006.

48 *But Anderson once*: Jeremy Peters and Micheline Maynard, "Company Town Relies on G.M. Long After Plants Have Closed," *New York Times*, February 20, 2006; and Ted Evanoff, "The Guide Era Closes in Anderson," *Indianapolis Star*, January 13, 2007.

49 *Now there isn't*: Information on Newton from author interviews June 18–19, 2006, and from *Des Moines Register*, May 10–11, 2006.

50 *"That company decided"*: Interview with author, June 21, 2006.

52 *What we have*: Austin, "Great Lakes Economic Initiative."

53 *Kalamazoo, Michigan, was*: Interview with Ron Kitchens, CEO, Southwest Michigan First, March 1, 2006; Neal E. Boudette, "Kalamazoo, Mich., Pegs Revitalization on a Tuition Plan," *Wall Street Journal*, March 10, 2006; and Michelle Miller-Adams, "A Simple Gift?" *Employment Research* (Upjohn Institute), July 2006.

54 *Greenville certainly looked*: Information on Greenville from author interviews, March 2–3, 2006; stories in the *Greenville Daily News* and the *Grand Rapids Press*; Kathy Barks Hoffman, "Greenville, Families Struggling as Plants Close, Salaries Drop," AP, in *Lansing State Journal*, November 27, 2005; and Greg Burns, "City Left in the Cold as Refrigerator Factory Closes," *Chicago Tribune*, November 6, 2005.

55 *Once, the Electrolux*: Interview with George Bosanic, Greenville, March 2, 2006.

58 *But since that day*: Interview with George Bosanic, October 2006; Julia Bauer, "United Solar Ovonic to Build Second Plant," *Grand Rapids Press*, September 9, 2006.

58 *"People do lose jobs"*: Transcript of president's meeting with young Indian entrepreneurs, www.whitehouse.gov/news/releases/2006/03/20060303-3.html.

59 *Warsaw began with a*: Information on Warsaw from interviews by author, especially with Brad Bishop at Zimmer Corporation, Joy McCarthy-Sessing, Chamber of Commerce, and Randy Maxson, interim executive dean at Warsaw campus of Ivy Tech Community College. Also history of Warsaw at www.warsawcity.net/History/historycity.htm.

Chapter 5: Mega-Farmers

62 *And Melvin Stucke*: Interview with author, May 2, 2006.

65 *William Heffernan, a*: William D. Heffernan, "Biotechnology and Mature Capitalism" (paper presented at the National Agricultural Biotechnology Council, Lincoln, Nebraska, June 6–8, 1999).

65 *As Drake University*: Neil D. Hamilton, "Why Own the Farm When You Can Own the Farmers?: Contract Production and Intellectual Property Protection of Grain Crops," *Nebraska Law Review* 73, no. 48 (1994).

66 *There were 3 million*: USDA, "Food and Agricultural Policy," 2001. Other good sources on both national and Midwestern trends include "Why Worry About the Agriculture of the Middle?" a white paper prepared for the www.agofthemiddle.org Web site; Russell L. Lamb, "The New Farm Economy," *Regulation*, Winter 2003–4; and "Turning Over the Soil," a series in the *Des Moines Register*, beginning July 17, 2005.

67 *There are reasons*: USDA, "Food and Agricultural Policy," 2001. Also Economic Research Service, USDA, "Farm and Commodity Policy: Government Payments and the Farm Sector," 2006, www.ers.usda.gov/Briefing/FarmPolicy/gov-pay.htm; and Chicago Council

on Global Affairs, "Modernizing America's Food and Farm Policy," 2006.

68   *As the* Des Moines Register: Anne Fitzgerald, "The 'Big' Debate: Is Consolidation Good for Farming and Iowa?" *Des Moines Register*, July 24, 2005.

68   *Missouri's Heffernan*: Most of the data on consolidation comes from Heffernan and his colleague, Mary Hendrickson, at their Web site, www.foodcircles.missouri.edu/consol.htm. Their informative papers include "Consolidation in the Food and Agriculture System," 1999; "The Global Food System: A Research Agenda: Concentration of Agricultural Markets," 2005; and "Consolidation in Goods Retailing and Dairy," 2001.

69   *Cargill is an economy*: Corporate brochure, 2001, cited in Sophia Murphy, "Concentrated Market Power and Agricultural Trade," Institute for Trade and Agricultural Policy, August 2006.

70   *Eventually, much of this*: See Heffernan and Hendrickson.

71   *Smaller operators raise*: Economic Research Service, USDA, "Hogs: Background," www.ers.usda.gov/Briefings/Hogs/Background.htm; "Modern Day Hog Farms," University of North Carolina, www.uncd.edu/courses/rometech/public/content/survival/Wesley_Lindsey/Modhog.htm; and "Factory Hog Farms Stirring Controversy," Wisconsin Stewardship Network, www.wsn.org/factory farm/hogart,html.

71   *As Roger McEowen*: Interview with author, June 28, 2006.

72   *"These big farms"*: Interview with author, June 27, 2006.

75   *In* Nature's Metropolis: New York: Norton & Co., 1991.

77   *In this landscape*: Interview with author, November 30, 2005.

78   *"The first few years"*: Interview with author, October 5, 2006.

Chapter 6: From Hometown to Slum

82   *So, in a different way*: History and background on Eldon and *American Gothic* are from these Web sites: www.arts.ufl.edu/art/rt_room/wood/gothic.html; www.state.ia.us/iowahistory/sites/gothic_house/gothic_house_history.html; and www.npr.org/programs/morning/features/patc/americangothic/index.html. Also from author

interviews with residents of Eldon, June 18, 2006, and with Steve
Siegel, Wapello County supervisor, June 19, 2006.

85   *Iowa politicians say*: All information on these towns gathered during author visits.

87   *A reporter on*: Author interview, September 1992.

89   *Between 1960 and 1980*: U.S. Bureau of the Census, *Chicago Tri-
bune*, October 7, 1992; www.committeeof82.org; and Rural Policy
Research Institute, "Demographic and Economic Profile, Iowa,"
May 2006.

90   *The Center for the*: Weiler (March 2004), and Weiler and Jason
Henderson, "Beyond Cows and Corn: Rural America in the 21st
Century," *Main Street Economist*, October 2004.

91   *In other words*: Speech to Chicago Council on Global Affairs,
Chicago, February 15, 2006.

91   *As a matter of fact*: Interview with author, June 29, 2006.

92   *The rural pathology*: "Obesity: America's Economic Epidemic,"
Main Street Economist (Federal Reserve Bank of Kansas City),
2006.

93   *So new businesses don't*: Lois Wright Morton et al., in "Solving the
Problems of Iowa Food Deserts," *Rural Sociology* 70, no. 1
(2005), and in "Rural Food Insecurity and Health," in *Critical
Issues in Rural Health* (Ames: Blackwell Publishing, 2004). Also
telephone interview with author.

94   *The latest survey*: Pew Internet and American Life Project, "Home
Broadband Adoption in Rural America," February 26, 2006.

94   *But as Edwin Parker*: "Closing the Digital Divide in Rural America," *International Journal on Knowledge Infrastructure Development, Management and Regulation* 24, no. 4 (May 2000).

95   *"There's got to be"*: Interview with author, June 25, 2006.

97   *Almost every Midwestern*: "States Employ New Strategies to Diversify and Strengthen Region's Rural Economy," *Firstline* (Midwestern Office of the Council of State Governments) 12, no. 9
(October 2005).

97   *Some thinkers advocate*: Lee Munnich et al., "Rural Knowledge
Clusters: Innovation and Vitality in America's Rural Communities," Humphrey Institute of Public Affairs, University of Minnesota, prepared for USDA Fund for Rural America, September

2003. Also Munnich speech to Chicago Council on Global Affairs, Chicago, February 14, 2007.

Chapter 7: The New Midwesterners

101   *The Mexicans started*: Almost all information on Beardstown came from author interviews there, May 24–27, 2006. Useful background information has also appeared in S. Lynne Walker, Copley News Service, "Beardstown: Reflection of a Changing America," *Springfield (Il) State Journal-Register*, November 9–12, 2003; Lisa Kernek, "Growing Pains," *Illinois Issues Online*, September 2001; and in various issues of the *Cass County Star-Gazette* (Beardstown).

103   *Midwestern states know it*: Stephen G. Bloom, "Immigration Comes to the Small-Town Midwest," *Wilson Quarterly*, Summer 2006.

112   Almost all Storm Lake information is from author interviews there, June 22–25, 2006. Other useful sources included Mark A. Grey, "Meatpacking and the Migration of Refugee and Immigrant Labor to Storm Lake, Iowa," Northern Iowa University, March 31, 2006; the Web site of Representative Steve King, www.house .gov/steveking; stories in the *Storm Lake Times*, especially Art Cullen, "A World Away, but So Close," October 22, 2005; and an author interview with Grey, June 30, 2006.

120   *The state government*: Mark A. Grey, "State and Local Immigration Policy in Iowa," in *Immigration's New Frontiers*, ed. Anrig and Wang (New York: Century Foundation, 2007); also, Grey, "Meatpacking and the Migration of Refugee and Immigrant Labor to Storm Lake, Iowa," http://migration.ucdavis.edu or through mark .grey@uni.edu. Also Grey interview with author, June 30, 2006.

Chapter 8: New Blood for Cities

123   *Chicago, too, has*: U.S. Bureau of the Census, www.census.gov; Ron Grossman, "Global City, Global People," in *Global Chicago*,

ed. Charles Madigan (Urbana: University of Illinois Press, 2004); and Richard C. Longworth, "Urban Diversity" (unpublished paper for Eurodiv Project, European Union, Milan, 2005).

124 *Cleveland, on the other*: U.S. Bureau of the Census. Also, Robert L. Smith, "Can Immigrants Save the Region," *Cleveland Plain Dealer*, July 13, 2003. Interviews by author with Ronn Richard, president of The Cleveland Foundation, and Richard Herman, founder, Go Global Cleveland, May 4, 2006.

125 *"Immigration laws are"*: Speech to Chicago Council on Global Affairs, May 16, 2006.

127 *Now they're coming*: Grossman, "Global City"; and Longworth, "Urban Diversity."

128 *This new European*: Timothy Ready and Allert Brown-Gort, "The State of Latino Chicago: This Is Home Now," Institute for Latino Studies, Notre Dame University, 2005; and "A Shared Future: The Economic Engagement of Greater Chicago and Its Mexican Community," Chicago Council on Global Affairs task force, 2006.

129 *Rob Paral, Chicago's*: Speech to Chicago Council on Global Affairs, May 16, 2006.

129 *The problem is*: Ibid.

130 *Amazingly, some of this*: "A Shared Future," 2006.

131 *Successful cities attract*: Richard J. Daley Forum, University of Illinois at Chicago, April 4, 2006.

131 *By that standard*: Federation for American Immigration Reform, www.fairus.org. FAIR favors more restrictive immigration legislation, especially on undocumented immigration. Its Web site uses Census Bureau data on many cities and is both accurate and comprehensive.

132 *Minnesota corporations, like*: Cited in Madison, *Heartland*, which contains much of this history.

133 *"It's been difficult"*: Interview with author, 2005.

134 *The pollster Stan*: Greenberg et al., for the Minnesota Community Project, "The Changing Shape of Minnesota: Reinvigorating Community and Government in the New Minnesota," December 14, 2004.

136 *The surprising thing*: Katherine Fennelly, University of Minnesota, author interview.

136 *A third, and*: See Katherine Fennelly, "Prejudice Toward Immigrants in the Midwest," in *New Faces in New Places*, ed. Douglas S. Massey (New York: Russell Sage Foundation, 2005).

137 *David Goodhart, the*: "Too Diverse?" February 2004, and "Diversity Divide," April 2004, both in *Prospect*, www.prospect-magazine.co.uk.

139 *David Card, an*: David Card, "Is the New Immigration Really So Bad?" Department of Economics, University of California–Berkeley, January 2005. See also Roger Lowenstein, "The Immigration Equation," *New York Times Magazine*, July 9, 2006, an excellent review of the debate.

139 *The evidence is*: Ready and Brown-Gort, "State of Latino Chicago."

141 *American banks are*: Ibid.

Chapter 9: Global Chicago and Other Cities

144 *The city had peaked*: Richard C. Longworth, "Chicago: City on the Brink," *Chicago Tribune*, May 10–14, 1981.

145 *"If you have to be"*: Nelson Algren, *Chicago: City on the Make* (Chicago: University of Chicago Press, 2001, latest edition); and Thomas Geoghegan, "Chicago, Pride of the Rust Belt," *New Republic*, March 25, 1985. The Chicago literature is rich. Some good sources include Donald L. Miller, *City of the Century* (New York: Simon & Schuster, 1996); Charles Madigan, ed., *Global Chicago* (Urbana: University of Illinois Press, 2004); Charles Bowden and Lew Kreinberg, *Street Signs Chicago* (Chicago: Chicago Review Press, 1981); Terry Nichols Clark, ed., "Trees and Real Violins: Building Post-Industrial Chicago" (working paper, University of Chicago).

145 *"this magical, beautiful city"*: Bernard-Henri Levy, *American Vertigo* (New York: Random House, 2006).

145 *In the eighties*: *Economist*, March 18, 2006.

146 *In most listings*: For instance, see J. V. Beaverstock et al., "A Roster of World Cities," Loughborough University, Globalization and World Cities Study Group and Network, www.lboro.ac.uk/gawc/rb/rb5.html.

146 *"Globalization takes place"*: P. J. Taylor, "Leading World Cities: Empirical Evaluations of Urban Nodes in Multiple Networks," *Urban Studies* 42, no. 9 (2005).

147 *In their youth*: Jon C. Teaford, *Cities of the Heartland* (Bloomington: Indiana University Press, 1994). This is the best book on Midwestern cities, and I have relied on it for much of the history in this chapter.

149 *Chicago, Lord knows*: Joseph Cortright, Impresa Consulting, "The Young and Restless in a Knowledge Economy," for CEOs for Cities, December 2005.

150 *What is a global*: The best thinking and writing on global cities is by Saskia Sassen, mostly in her book *The Global City*, 2nd ed. (Princeton: Princeton University Press, 2001). See also her chapter "A Global City," in *Global Chicago*, ed. Madigan, and her article "The Deep Economic History of Place: It Matters," *Urban Age* 1 (Summer 2005), for the Cities Program at the London School of Economics, www.urban-age.net.

153 *Chicago has a place*: For instance, Beaverstock et al., "Roster of World Cities."

153 *These cities form*: Witold Rybczynski, "Cities and Globalization," *Zell/Lurie Real Estate Center Review*, Spring 2004.

155 *Between 1986, and*: Data from the Federal Reserve Bank of Chicago.

157 *Virtually all of*: See Teaford, *Cities of the Heartland*; and Daniel Nelson, *Farm and Factory* (Bloomington: Indiana University Press, 1995).

157 *So far, many*: Edward Glaeser et al., "Urban Growth and Housing Supply," Harvard Institute of Economic Research, Discussion Paper Number 2062, February 2005. Also John Gertner, "Home Economics," *New York Times Magazine*, March 5, 2006.

159 *Cleveland, by contrast*: Diane Suchetka, "Poverty Jumps in Suburbs of Cleveland," *Cleveland Plain-Dealer*, December 7, 2006.

160 *What happened?*: Interview with author, May 4, 2006.

160 *Back in the 1980s*: Guhan Venkatu, "Cleveland (on the) Rocks," *Economic Commentary* (Federal Reserve Bank of Cleveland), February 1, 2006.

160 *In all my travels*: Edward W. (Ned) Hill, Cleveland State University, telephone interview with author, May 18, 2006.

161 *And it's a funny*: Alan Berube and Elizabeth Kneebone, "Two Steps Back," Brookings Institution, December 2006.

161 *In talking about*: Richard Florida, *The Flight of the Creative Class* (New York: Harper Business, 2005). Also, *The Rise of the Creative Class* (New York: Basic Books, 2002).

163 *That density*: Outlined at www.coolcities.com, and in "The 'Cool Cities' Program! Request for Proposals," Michigan State Housing Development Authority, April 2004.

163 *Florida has even*: See Florida, *Flight of the Creative Class* and *Rise of the Creative Class*.

165 *Like creative people*: "Percent of People 25 Years and Over Who Have Completed a Bachelor's Degree," U.S. Census Bureau, American Community Survey, August 25, 2004.

166 *Harvard's Edward Glaeser*: Edward l. Glaeser and Christopher Berry, "Why Are Smart Places Getting Smarter?" Policy Brief-2006-2, John F. Kennedy School of Government, Harvard University, March 2006.

Chapter 10: Left Behind

168 *The industrial age*: Good histories and background on this migration and its aftermath are in Nicholas Lemann, *The Promised Land: The Great Migration and How It Changed America* (New York: Vintage Books, 1992); The Chicago Tribune, *The American Millstone: An Examination of the Nation's Permanent Underclass* (Chicago: McGraw-Hill/Contemporary, 1986); and William Julius Wilson, *The Declining Significance of Race: Blacks and Changing American Institutions* (Chicago: University of Chicago Press, 1980). My own reporting since 1976 in Northern cities, especially Chicago, supplements this literature.

170 *Of Chicago's fifteen*: "Still Separate, Unequal: Race, Place, Policy and the State of Black Chicago," Chicago Urban League report, June 21, 2005.

170 *Forty-six percent*: Consortium on Chicago School Research, University of Chicago, "Graduation and Dropout Trends in Chicago: A Look at Cohorts of Students from 1991 to 2004," January 2005; and "From High School to the Future: A First Look at Chicago Public School Graduates' College Enrollment, College Preparation and Graduation from Four-Year Colleges," April 2006.

170 *Economic distress spans*: U.S. Census Bureau figures, available through city profiles on Wikipedia.

171 *But no one is*: Interview with author, September 22, 2006.

171 *In Cleveland, Ronn*: Interview with author, May 4, 2006.

171 *Peoria, Illinois, is*: Interview with author, May 24, 2006.

173 *There was a nostalgic*: Josh Noel, "Activists Look Back but Plan for Future," *Chicago Tribune*, July 24, 2006.

173 *"The history of racism"*: Telephone interview with author, May 18, 2006.

174 *Senator Barack Obama*: Barack Obama, *The Audacity of Hope* (New York: Crown, 2006).

Chapter 11: Flunking Out

177 *The poll, sponsored*: "What Is the Culture of Education in Michigan?" poll conducted by EPIC/MRA, April 1–21, 2005.

177 *"There's a big"*: Telephone interview with author, April 2006.

177 *"We're doomed"*: Nolan Finley, *Detroit News*, May 1, 2005.

177 *In more measured*: Jennifer Granholm, *Detroit News*, May 1, 2005.

179 *(States differ on*: Northeast-Midwest Institute, "Educational Attainment of Persons 25 Years of Age or Older," 2000.

180 *The failure of*: "The Nation's Report Card: Science 2005: Trial Urban District Assessment of Grades 4 and 8," National Center for Education Statistics, U.S. Department of Education.

180 *A report by the*: "Public Education and Black Male Students," Schott Foundation for Public Education, 2004.

181 *Perhaps Chicago can*: See Cortright, "Young and Restless." Also Robert Weissbourd and Riccardo Bodini, "Grads and Fads: The

Dynamics of Human Capital Location," prepared for Chicago's
Global Future Study Group, Chicago Council on Global Affairs.

181 *"We're sleepwalking"*: At Chicago Council on Global Affairs
meeting, June 14, 2006.

182 *In my Iowa*: Interview with author, June 28, 2006.

182 *Faced with this*: "Tough Choice or Tough Times," report issued by
The New Commission on the Skills of the American Workforce,
Washington, December 14, 2006.

183 *Now, even that*: Data from Office of Financial Aid, University of
Michigan, academic year 2006–7; and "State Prison Expendi-
tures," report by Office of Justice programs, U.S. Department of
Justice.

183 *(Michigan, like other*: "Skilling Heads to Dorm-Style Prison," As-
sociated Press, in *Chicago Tribune*, December 12, 2006.

184 *As the* Economist: "The Brains Business: A Survey of Higher Education," *Economist*, September 10, 2005.

185 *James Duderstadt*: Duderstadt, "The Great Lakes Region and the
Knowledge Economy: A Roadmap to the Future" (presented to
Higher Education at a Crossroad at the Federal Reserve Bank of
Chicago, November 2, 2006).

186 *Other Midwestern states*: "State General Fund Spending for the
Board of Regents and Regents Institutions," Legislative Services
Agency, Fiscal Services Division, State of Iowa, provided by Elaine
Ditsler, Iowa Policy Project.

187 *These universities can't*: At Chicago Council on Global Affairs
program, June 13, 2006.

187 *The smaller colleges*: See Greg Burns, "Can SIU Stay in the
Game?" *Chicago Tribune*, December 3, 2006.

187 *As Duderstadt says*: See "The Brains Business," *Economist*.

189 Katharine C. Lyall, see Katharine C. Lyall and Kathleen R. Sell,
"The De Facto Privatization of American Public Higher Education," in *Change*, January/February 2006.

190 *In Newton*: Author interviews with Doug Frazer at Newton
DMACC, June 20, 2006; and with Chuck Crabtree, Indian Hills
Community College, June 19, 2006.

190 *In Warsaw*: Author interview with Randy Maxson, Ivy Tech,
March 31, 2006.

191 *Most community college*: Telephone interview with Carol D'Amico, Executive Vice President, Ivy Tech, May 2006.

192 *I was impressed*: Interview with author, May 24, 2006. Also John Stuart Erwin, "Caterpillar Inc.'s Think Big Program at Illinois Central College," in "Sustaining Financial Support for Community Colleges," ed. Katsinas and Palmer, *New Directions for Community Colleges* 132 (Winter 2005). Also "Caterpillar Dealer Service Technician Training Program Description," Illinois Central College, 2005.

194 *Phoenix isn't alone*: Michelle Howard-Vital, "The Appeal of For-Profit Institutions," *Change*, January/February 2006. Also University of Phoenix Web site at www.phoenix.edu, and http://en .wikipedia.org/wiki/University_of_Phoenix.

195 *This may be*: Norman Draper, "Those with Thick Accents Need Not Apply?" *Minneapolis Star-Tribune*, March 13, 2006. Also telephone message from Jennipher Ailes, aide to Heidgerken, and Freeport Chamber of Commerce.

195 *If universities know*: Jodi S. Cohen, "U of I Reverses Course on Out-of-State Enrollment," *Chicago Tribune*, May 15, 2006.

196 *Alan S. Blinder*: Blinder, "Offshoring: The Next Industrial Revolution?" *Foreign Affairs*, March/April 2006.

Chapter 12: Betting the Farm

198 *More than one*: Norm Alster, "New Distillation Method Fuels Interest in Ethanol," *New York Times*, March 26, 2006.

200 *Certainly, Cargill and*: Author interviews at Eddyville, June 19, 2006, with John Johnston, Eddyville mayor; Jeff Fetterman, Cargill plant manager; Steve Siegel, Wapello County supervisor; and Chuck Crabtree, Indian Hills Community College.

202 *But this isn't all*: Ethanol economics is complex. I'm grateful for the tutelage and patience of such experts as Roger McEowen, Dave Swenson, and Paul Lasley at Iowa State University, Wally Tyner at Purdue, and Robert Thompson at the University of Illinois, in interviews and briefings in early 2006. Tyner, Otto Doering, and Chris Hurt at Purdue have issued valuable and clear

reports on ethanol in a series of articles entitled "BioEnergy" on the Purdue Web site.

206 *There is an awful*: James R. Frank, director of Biotechnology and Biodefense Applications at Argonne National Laboratory, in a presentation at the Federal Reserve Bank of Chicago, September 8, 2005.

207 *"Look," he said*: Interview with author, May 5, 2006.

208 *A recent Battelle*: "Growing the Nation's Bioscience Sector: State Bioscience Initiatives 2006," prepared for BIO expo by Battelle Technology Partnership Practice and SSTI, April 2006.

208 *Cortright concedes that*: See Joseph Cortright and Heike Meyer, in "Signs of Life: The Growth of Biotechnology Centers in the U.S.," published by The Brookings Institution, Washington, June 2002.

210 *Across the region*: Walter Plosila, "State/Regional Partnerships in the Biosciences," Battelle, May 3, 2006. Also author interview with Frank Samuel, science adviser to Ohio governor, in Columbus, May 3, 2006, and with Ted Crosbie, science adviser to Iowa governor, in Ankeny, May 21, 2006.

210 *In an office park*: Interview with author, May 21, 2006.

211 *I talked with*: This executive asked not to be quoted by name.

212 *In Kansas City*: Data on Stowers Institute for Medical Research from Web site, www.stowers-institute.org.

212 *In Grand Rapids*: Matthew Miller, "MSU to Build New Med School," *Lansing State Journal*, November 17, 2005. Also data from The Right Place Inc., Grand Rapids, especially "West Michigan Medical Millennium," 2005, and telephone interview with Right Place president Birgit M. Klohs, March 2006.

213 *I spent an*: Interview with author, July 2005.

213 *In 2000, St. Louis*: "St. Louis Battelle Strategy," commissioned by St. Louis Regional Chamber and Growth Association and Danforth Center.

214 *Peoria is an interesting*: Several Peoria leaders helped me. Among them were Dr. Peter Johnsen, then director of the National Center for Agricultural Utilization Research, USDA; Jim McConoughey, president, Heartland Partnership; Roger Luman, managing director, Turner Center for Entrepreneurship, Bradley University; and Dave Koehler, director, Peoria Area Labor Management Council.

218   *Mostly, though, there is*: Author interview with Daniel J. Broderick, managing director, Mason Wells, Milwaukee, September 21, 2006.

Chapter 13: The Blue and the Red

221   *Apart from the land*: Peter Annin, *The Great Lakes Water Wars* (Washington, DC: Island Press, 2006) is an excellent source both for the history of the lakes and their exploitation and the current politics surrounding their future use.

223   *As we saw*: The text of the Northwest Ordinance is at http:// usinfo.state.gov/usa/infousa/facts/democrac/5.htm or at www.yale.edu/lawweb/avalon/nworder.htm.

223   *The border between*: Two Stickney seems to have been the youngest son of a Major Stickney, who named his sons One and Two. Conflicting versions of the Toledo War are available at www.michigan.gov and at www.publications.ohiohistory.org.

224   *"Sure, it would"*: Author interview with James L. Donaldson, vice president, business development, Michigan Economic Development Corporation, February 27, 2006.

227   *Indianapolis sits astride*: Briefing at Central Indiana Corporate Partnership Inc., November 8, 2004.

228   *This drives non-Chicagoans*: Editorial, *Peoria Journal Star*, May 25, 2006.

229   *St. Louis, for instance*: Briefing at St. Louis Regional Chamber and Growth Association, September 2004.

229   *When the Greater*: "Time to Get It Right: A Strategy for Higher Education in Kansas City," issued by Greater Kansas City Community Foundation, 2005.

230   *What spiked the*: Alexei Barrionuevo, "Biotech Plan in Missouri Suffers Setback," *New York Times*, January 6, 2006; and telephone interview by author with Dean L. Hubbard, April 2006.

231   *"The conventional wisdom"*: Telephone interview with author, February 2006.

231   *Despite this, Iowa*: Author interview with Tom Beaumont, political writer, *Des Moines Register*, June 21, 2006.

232   *Two aspects of globalization*: "The Role of Metro Areas in the U.S. Economy," prepared for the U.S. Conference of Mayors by Global Insight, Lexington, Massachusetts, January 13, 2006.

233   *"What Chicago does"*: Interview with author, September 21, 2006.

235   *The tiniest fragments*: "The Metropolis Plan: Choices for the Chicago Region," issued by Metropolis 2020, March 2003.

235   *"These tiny boxes"*: At Chicago and the LAKESNET Great Lakes Regional Bi-National Conference, Chicago, February 9, 2007.

238   "*Restoring Prosperity*: The State Role in Revitalizing America's Older Industrial Cities," by The Brookings Institution, Washington, 2007.

239   *Across the Midwest*: For instance, see Robin Toner and Kate Zernike, "Incoming Democrats Put Populism Before Ideology," *New York Times*, November 12, 2006.

239   *Geographically and economically*: See chapter 1, Summers, "Global Middle Cries Out."

239   *Tom Frank's best-selling book*: Beaumont, author interview, June 21, 2006.

240   *"Some get caught up"*: Author interview, June 20, 2006.

240   *"They just have"*: Author interview, March 3, 2006.

241   *post-election maps show*: Bill Bishop, "The Schism in U.S. Politics Begins at Home," *Austin American-Statesman*, April 4, 2004, and September 18, 2004. Also maps from *American-Statesman* provided by Bishop. Also Dave Leip's "Atlas of U.S. Presidential Elections," www.uselectionatlas.org.

241   *"Frankly, I believe"*: David Kruse, *CommStock Report*, November 8, 2000, www.thecommstockreport.com/BestOf/Ruralvs.Urban .htm; also telephone interview with author, August 6, 2006.

242   *(Kruse, interestingly*: "Brazil No Longer a 'Sleeping Giant,'" on *Market to Market*, Iowa Public Television, February 25, 2005.

Chapter 14: Global Midwest

249   *For a model*: See www.southern.org for background.

250   *These schools should*: See www.cici.uiuc.edu/AboutCIC/shtml.

251 *The Mid-America*: See Network Web site, www.mhin.info.

251 *The most promising*: Author interview with Allen Dines, Madison, Wisconsin, June 16, 2006.

251 *Other institutions exist*: See www.midwestgovernors.org and www.cglg.org.

251 *A new organization*: See www.greatlakesmanufacturingcouncil .org, www.nemw.org (for Northeast-Midwest Institute and for background on the Great Lakes and St. Lawrence Cities Initiative), and www.uppermidwestfreight.org.

252 *The Midwestern Feds*: See http://en.wikipedia.org/wiki/Federal _Reserve for a concise history of the politicking.

252 *It's galling to*: *The Vital Center*, from Brookings Institution Metropolitan Policy Program, 2006.

255 *Beyond that, the*: "Tough Choices or Tough Times," report issued by The New Commission on the Skills of the American Workforce, Washington, December 14, 2006.

257 *It is time*: See CCGA reports *Keeping the Promise: Immigration Proposals from the Heartland*, 2004; *Modernizing America's Food and Farm Policy*, 2006; and *A Shared Future: The Economic Engagement of Greater Chicago and Its Mexican Community*, 2006.

257 *The stakes here*: "Five Foreign Investment Tips for the U.S. and China," issued by Carlson School of Management, University of Minnesota, October 2005.

Bibliography

Many books have been written about places in the Midwest but few about the Midwest as a region. Most of them, including a stupendous new encyclopedia, *The American Midwest*, were published by the Indiana University Press, which deserves praise for its efforts to define and describe the Midwest and its history.

I found these books and reports helpful in thinking about the Midwest and globalization:

Algren, Nelson. *Chicago: City on the Make.* Chicago: University of Chicago Press, 1951.

Anderson, Sarah, and John Cavanagh. *Field Guide to the Global Economy.* New York: New Press, 2000.

Annin, Peter. *The Great Lakes Water Wars.* Washington, DC: Island Press, 2006.

Beaverstock, J. V., R. G. Smith, and P. J. Taylor. "A Roster of World Cities." Research paper, Loughborough University, 1999.

Bloom, Stephen G. *Postville: A Clash of Cultures in Heartland America.* New York: Harcourt, 2000.

Bowden, Charles, and Lew Kreinberg. *Street Signs Chicago: Neighborhood and Other Illusions of Big-City Life.* Chicago: Chicago Review Press, 1981.

Brookings Institution, Metropolitan Policy Program. *The Vital Center: A Federal-State Compact to Renew the Great Lakes Region.* Washington, DC: The Brookings Institution, 2006.

Cayton, Andrew R. L., and Susan E. Gray, eds. *The American Midwest:*

Essays on Regional History. Bloomington: Indiana University Press, 2001.

Cayton, Andrew R. L., and Peter S. Onuf. *The Midwest and the Nation: Rethinking the History of an American Region*. Bloomington: Indiana University Press, 1990.

Chicago Council on Global Affairs, Task Force Series. *Keeping the Promise: Immigration Proposals from the Heartland*. Chicago: CCGA, 2004.

———. *Modernizing America's Food and Farm Policy: Vision for a New Direction*. Chicago: CCGA, 2006.

———. *A Shared Future: The Economic Engagement of Greater Chicago and Its Mexican Community*. Chicago: CCGA, 2006.

Cronon, William. *Nature's Metropolis: Chicago and the Great West*. New York: Norton, 1991.

Davidson, Osha Gray. *Broken Heartland: The Rise of America's Rural Ghetto*. Iowa City: University of Iowa Press, 1996.

Duderstadt, James J. *A Roadmap to Michigan's Future: Meeting the Challenge of a Global Knowledge-Driven Economy*. Ann Arbor: Millennium Project, University of Michigan, 2005.

Florida, Richard. *The Flight of the Creative Class: The New Global Competition for Talent*. New York: HarperBusiness, 2005.

Frank, Thomas. *What's the Matter with Kansas? How Conservatives Won the Heart of America*. New York: Metropolitan Books, 2004.

Friedman, Thomas L. *The World Is Flat: A Brief History of the Twenty-first Century*. New York: Farrar, Straus and Giroux, 2005.

Garreau, Joel. *The Nine Nations of North America*. New York: Avon Books, 1981.

Held, David, and Mathias Koenig-Archibugi, eds. *Taming Globalization: Frontiers of Governance*. Cambridge: Polity Press, 2003.

Held, David, and Anthony McGrew. *Globalization/Anti-Globalization*. Cambridge: Polity Press, 2002.

Hudson, John C. *Making the Corn Belt: A Geographical History of Middle-Western Agriculture*. Bloomington: Indiana University Press, 1994.

Kaplan, Robert D. *An Empire Wilderness: Travels into America's Future*. New York: Vintage Books, 1998.

Kooser, Ted. *Lights on a Ground of Darkness*. Lincoln: University of Nebraska Press, 2005.

———. *Local Wonders: Seasons in the Bohemian Alps*. Lincoln: University of Nebraska Press, 2002.

Kotlowitz, Alex. *Never a City So Real*. New York: Crown Journeys, 2004.

Koval, John P., et al., eds. *The New Chicago*. Philadelphia: Temple University Press, 2006.

Lieven, Anatol. *America Right or Wrong: An Anatomy of American Nationalism*. New York: Oxford University Press, 2004.

Longworth, Richard C. *Global Squeeze: The Coming Crisis for First-World Nations*. Lincolnwood, IL: Contemporary Books, 1999.

Lorinc, John. *The New City: How the Crisis in Canada's Urban Centres Is Reshaping the Nation*. Toronto: Penguin Canada, 2006.

Madigan, Charles, ed. *Global Chicago*. Champaign: University of Illinois Press, 2004.

Madison, James H., ed. *Heartland: Comparative Histories of the Midwestern States*. Bloomington: Indiana University Press, 1990.

Miller, Donald L. *City of the Century: The Epic of Chicago and the Making of America*. New York: Simon & Schuster, 1996.

Nelson, Daniel. *Farm and Factory: Workers in the Midwest, 1880–1990*. Bloomington: Indiana University Press, 1995.

Norris, Kathleen. *Dakota: A Spiritual Geography*. New York: Houghton Mifflin, 1993.

Prestowitz, Clyde. *Three Billion New Capitalists: The Great Shift of Wealth and Power to the East*. New York: Basic Books, 2005.

Roberts, Sam. *Who We Are Now: The Changing Face of America in the Twenty-first Century*. New York: Henry Holt, 2004.

Sassen, Saskia. *The Global City*. 2nd ed. Princeton: Princeton University Press, 2001.

———. *Globalization and Its Discontents: Essays on the New Mobility of People and Money*. New York: New Press, 1998.

———. *Losing Control? Sovereignty in an Age of Globalization*. New York: Columbia University Press, 1996.

Scot, Barbara J. *Prairie Reunion*. New York: Farrar, Straus and Giroux, 1995.

Shortridge, James R. *The Middle West: Its Meaning in American Culture*. Lawrence: University Press of Kansas, 1989.

Sisson, Richard, with Christian Zacher and Andrew Cayton, eds. *The American Midwest: An Interpretive Encyclopedia.* Bloomington: Indiana University Press, 2007.

Teaford, Jon C. *Cities of the Heartland: The Rise and Fall of the Industrial Midwest.* Bloomington: Indiana University Press, 1993.

Uchitelle, Louis. *The Disposable Americans: Layoffs and Their Consequences.* New York: Knopf, 2006.

Walzer, Norman, ed. *The American Midwest: Managing Change in Rural Transition.* Armonk, NY: M. E. Sharpe, 2003.

Index

A Note on the Author

Now a fellow at The Chicago Council on Global Affairs, Richard Longworth was an award-winning foreign correspondent and senior writer at the *Chicago Tribune*. He was twice a Pulitzer Prize finalist. Longworth lives in Chicago.